FROM ALIEN TO THE MATRIX

READING SCIENCE FICTION FILM

ROZ KAVENEY

I.B. TAURIS

LONDON · NEW YORK

Published in 2005 by I.B.Tauris & Co Ltd
6 Salem Road, London W2 4BU
175 Fifth Avenue, New York NY 10010
www.ibtauris.com

In the United States of America and in Canada distributed by
Palgrave Macmillan, a division of St Martin's Press
175 Fifth Avenue, New York NY 10010

ISBN 1 85043 805 6 Hardback
EAN 978 1 85043 805 2 Hardback

ISBN 1 85043 806 4 Paperback
EAN 978 1 85043 806 9 Paperback

A full CIP record for this book is available from the British Library
A full CIP record for this book is available from the Library of Congress

Library of Congress catalog card: available

Typeset in Adobe Garamond by Steve Tribe, Andover
Printed and bound in Great Britain by MPG Books Ltd, Bodmin

Contents

Acknowledgements

My thanks are due to all the friends with whom I watched and discussed these films. Adi Tantimedh has been a constant sounding board for ideas and a source of useful insights, as have Tanja Kinkel, Oliver Morton, Nancy Hynes, Charles Shaar Murray, Anna Chen and Neil Norman. Kim Newman and John Clute are responsible both in person and through their invaluable reference books for many facts that are correct here and for none that I got wrong. Nick Lowe acted as one of my main sounding boards for the theoretical positions sketched briefly in the introduction.

As always, my thanks to Paule.

In memory of Joseph Hugo Kaveney, 1915–2004

1. Waking into Dream

Competence Cascades, Thick Texts and the Universalization of the Geek Aesthetic

'Waking into Dream' was always the working title for this collection of writings on science fiction film; like many working titles, it has served as a useful seed around which my ideas have crystallized in the two years I have taken to work on the book. I knew, when I started, that a part of my emphasis would be the way that certain works of art, among them science fiction films, have the capacity to act as triggers for the creative and critical imagination.

As I worked on the films I ended up selecting – there are many other important films I have not written about in this volume, and omission is not to be taken as a covert critical judgement – I found myself thinking about film-making, and particularly scriptwriting, as a process; this is not a book about creative constraints in SF film-making, but it is a book which at least occasionally considers them. Similarly, it is not a book about how changes in viewing technology have affected our sense of what the authentic version of a film is – but this too is a subject that gets at least passing consideration.

What that title has come to mean for me is this. We watch these films in order to enjoy them, but also to think about them afterwards, and come back to watching them with an enjoyment deepened and made more complex by that thought. This means, in turn, that the pleasures of the best of these films are not merely those of surprise and exhilaration, but are also that different exhilaration which comes from going around the track a second time and a third. One of the factors which helped determine the selection of films under discussion here is that many of them date from a period recent enough that it was known to those involved that they would be viewed repeatedly both in cinemas and through home-entertainment media – the rise of first the VHS tape and then the DVD has meant that it is now possible for most of us to know films more intensely than has been the case at any previous date.

These are not only science fiction films, they are films whose production and consumption has been crucially affected by the growth of technology. The Internet has meant that it is sometimes possible to choose to know a film's script in considerable detail before seeing it. The presence on many DVDs of a commentary track means that it is possible for any viewer to listen to a canonical version of the director's, and sometimes the principal actors' and technicians', intentions and sense of their own failures and successes. (Some of the most remarkable examples of this have taken place outside SF film – the DVD of Baz Luhrman's *Moulin Rouge* (2001), for example, enables the viewer to re-edit certain elaborate musical sequences like the tango performed to Sting's 'Roxanne' by including all the camera angles from which they were shot.)

This period, the last quarter of the twentieth century, has been one in which the technologies of science fiction, horror and fantasy film-making underwent serious changes. Other film genres were affected by these technological shifts, but far less crucially – David Fincher uses radical make-up and modelling work in *Seven* (1997), serious CGI in *Fight Club* (2000), but this is unusual. Much of this has been due to what I call competence cascades, that is to say, the process whereby a rare set of professional skills is admired and imitated by an amateur following and the professional and amateur worlds influence each other in a process of continuous feedback and change of roles until the professional skills are far more advanced and far less rare.

To take but one example: there have always been professional make-up artists fascinated by the grotesque and monstrous. The actor Lon Chaney built an entire film career from designing monster make-ups for himself and playing roles in those get-ups; other make-up artists produced, for example, the elaborate make-up worn by Boris Karloff in Universal Pictures' *Frankenstein* (1931). Various of those make-ups – the Frankenstein monster or Lon Chaney's *Phantom of the Opera* (1925), for example – became clichés both through movie spin-offery and through the growth of a fan culture dedicated to appreciating, and duplicating, them.

The magazine *Famous Monsters of Filmland* ran from 1958 to 1984 and included regular features in which amateur make-up artists showed their work, and occasional competitions to pick the best of such amateur make-up jobs – the prizes often including a chance to meet the winner's heroes, the professional monster make-up people; the magazine *Fangoria*, which started in 1979, included photo features of how make-ups were achieved. The costuming strand of science fiction and horror fan conventions contributed to the creation of a body of expertise; the artwork of science fiction magazines and comic books helped create a visual vocabulary from which make-up artists could derive ideas for new creatures.

It is not necessarily the case that most, or even many, make-up artists working in this field were ever active in the fandom, but the anecdotal evidence is that some at least of the current professionals in the field grew up fascinated by both actual films and the make-ups crucial to them and by the associated material. What the fandom will have helped do was validate the career choice at all pre-professional stages. What is clear is that, where once these skills were rare, now they are common enough that, during his filming of *The Lord of the Rings* (2001–2003), Peter Jackson could run something like an industrial production line of people producing monster make-ups in large quantities for each day's shooting. It is also clear that ever more elaborate make-ups are becoming easier to do – the technology has improved – and even marginally less unendurable for the actors who have to work with them.

Similarly, the development of computer graphics as a way of creating special effects that would previously, if possible at all, have involved fiddly stop-motion work with detailed models has been a process in which the distinction between talented amateur, semi-professional out-worker and highly paid professional has often been blurred. A fascination with 'how did they do that?' is always likely to become 'I could do that better.' The television space opera series *Babylon 5* was made possible by the availability of ambitious young Californian semi-professionals who regarded its massive set piece battles as a showcase for their talents; the same is true of some of the young New Zealanders who worked on *The Lord of the Rings*. The more people there are around who have a new skill, the more that skill will spread and be defined.

Among such skills, in a way, is the ability to negotiate the complicated Big Dumb Narrative Object of the corpus of SF and fantasy genre writing, picking and choosing narrative tropes and developed ideas and making from them something that either is new, or appears to be with enough verisimilitude to count as such. (I created the term 'Big Dumb Object' to describe plots, common in the 1970s, in which the protagonists found a location so vast and complex that the entire book was taken up with their traversing it. Typical examples of this are Arthur C. Clarke's *Rama* and Larry Niven's *Ringworld*, both of which demanded whole series devoted to their exploration – more recent examples like Ian Macdonald's *Chaga* have actually been referred to textually as Big Dumb Objects, which is flattering. Nick Lowe has usefully suggested that genres like SF and fantasy are themselves Big Dumb Narrative Objects, that part of the pleasure of them is learning to move around them with more than a tourist's sense of location.)

An inability to cope with this material will at times leave even significant critics floundering when they have to try. Reviewing, favourably, Brian Singer's second *X-Men* film, the late Alexander Walker found himself entirely unable to parse the early scene in which the hobgoblin-like Nightcrawler teleports rapidly around the Oval Office. Nightcrawler's abilities, visually presented in that scene, are exhibited at various points throughout the plot – Walker nonetheless found himself unable to describe the relevant scenes accurately. In an era in which there are significant SF films, SF is one of the things that a film critic has to know about.

Historically one of the determining aspects of any genre is the presence of stylistic or narrative tropes; another is the process whereby writers consciously echo earlier use of those tropes. Sometimes that echo is a purely ludic gambit, a way of including the expert reader or viewer in a conspiracy of informed smugness; sometimes, as with the locked-room mystery once fashionable in the detective story, it is a way in which the author can display virtuoso skill; sometimes, and particularly in SF (which has important roots in the polemic mode of utopian fiction), it is a way of taking issue with the political and social assumptions implicit in an earlier use of the material. Randell Garrett's 1958 novelette of interplanetary shipwreck, *The Queen Bee*, involved male colonists lobotomizing a murderess to make her over into a brood-mare; the heroine of Joanna Russ's 1977 novel *We Who Are About To* kills most of her fellow castaways out of a mixture of kindness and preservation of her own autonomy.

Originality in genre work is only some of the time a matter of the completely new plot or idea; it is as often a question of the inventive spin put on a stock matter. It is accordingly sometimes beside the point to consider particular embodiments as in any sense plagiarisms one of another; films from the various sub-genres within SF film, say, should be judged according to the grace notes, if any, specific to a particular incarnation of the Menacing Intruder, rather than by trying to establish a clear line of intellectual primacy between the Terminator, the Predator, the Species and so on. Indeed, I would argue that the extent to which particular screenwriters, directors and so on are comfortable inhabitants of the SF corpus is one of the positive aspects of their work because it means that when they reinvent the wheel, they know that that is what they are doing. James Cameron is the obvious example here, which is why, perhaps, this collection gives so much consideration to his work.

There are huge sub-universes that bud off from genres – possibly the biggest of all Big Dumb Narrative Objects is the corpus of continuity attached to

Marvel Comics. Marvel Comics has accumulated well over half a century's worth of biography of its scores of superhero and super-villain characters, often attaching to those radically different alternate presents, aborted futures and past incarnations. Marvel Comics continuity is a megatext comparable in scale to that of the mythologies of the Ancient Classical European world, say – yet, in its essence and in its obsessive concerns, it is a subset of the rather smaller megatext of all the SF and fantasy genres on which it has always drawn. Accordingly, a film like Ang Lee's *Hulk* (2003) needs to be understood not only in terms of the extended continuity of that particular comic book title, but in terms of the other concerns – nano-technology, bio-engineering, giant mutant poodles – that are tropes imported from the broader SF world.

This process of understanding whence ideas have been drawn and transformed into a particular script – as of understanding how the look of a particular film derives in part from the technical accomplishment and creative innovation of its designers, make-up crew, CGI technicians as well as from the personal vision of a director or producer – is what makes all films, but most especially SF films, thick texts.

What, then, is a thick text? The precondition of reading or recognizing a thick text is that we accept that all texts are not only a product of the creative process but contain all the stages of that process within them like scars or vestigial organs.

The film we first see in the cinema may be further revised to the final form of an extended director's cut; our knowledge of it may be transformed when viewing it on DVD by the presence of deleted scenes – and we may not necessarily agree with the decision to delete them, even where we understand what the arguments in favour of that deletion were.

We have to learn again that all works of art are to some extent provisional – in that they are abandoned rather than ever completed, and in that they are always one particular stage in a notional process which may be picked up again two decades later. (Ridley Scott's 2003 re-edit of *Alien* is a case in point here.) We have to learn that all works of art are contingent – the existence of David Fincher's *Alien³* is a consequence of the decision, at a fairly late stage, to abandon Vincent Ward's rather different version. We have to learn that any particular version of a work of art is likely to be a palimpsest through the surface of which earlier versions may up-crop – the harvesting machines crucial to the original denouement of Joss Whedon's script for *Alien Resurrection* are unexplainedly present on screen in shots of the hold of the pirate ship, The Betty. We have to learn that all works of art are in some measure collective – either because the nature of the specific art (cinema, dance, opera, theatre) involves collaboration, or because they draw on, are inspired by and argue with earlier work. We have to learn that most works of art are compromises – compromises with imperfectly developed visions, with imperfect technique, with the demands of patrons, studios, the Church or the State. To read a film, a novel, a great choral work in the light of these awarenesses is to see it as a thick text.

Reading a film as a thick text encourages us to see it in its context, both chronologically in terms of its being influenced by other films, or influencing later ones, or re-imagined by critics or even its original makers in the light of that influence and its consequences. It enables us to create a criticism which includes a sense of the particular thick text as an object positioned in the broader space of the generic megatext of which it is a part. It makes it possible to include in our sense of it its particular role in the development of the cascade of particular technical competences that were needful to its conception and making.

It is also to regard obsessiveness about reading and understanding as in no way a bad thing, and to regard almost any sort of knowledge as potentially relevant. In the late 1960s, I met briefly a geologist obsessed with the works of J.R.R. Tolkien to the extent that he had made up an entire rationalization of the underlying continental drift implied by the standard map of Middle-earth, and was inclined to mock him gently for it.

These days, I would reflect that Tolkien had a pantheist's obsession with landscape, and that his imagined landscapes drew on observation, and that a geologist's obsession might tell us something useful about how solid that observation was. I would further reflect that a sense of landscape is something that Tolkien shared with, say, Hardy, however less adequately, and wonder what my geologist friend could tell me usefully about Hardy's observation of the world, nor assume that a love of Tolkien precluded a love of Hardy. I would respect a sense of text that tried to read in the light of knowledge; I would, in other words, valorize what we may proudly call the geek aesthetic.

It is not, in the world of broadsheet journalism, fashionable to care too deeply about anything, whether it be socialism or a piece of popular culture, as much as the expression of individual ego and the mockery of others. One of the problems with much writing about popular culture is that it comes from writers whose careers are likely to develop in the direction of writing columns rather than reviews, whose reviews are try-outs for the better-paid column that might be a part of their future. Inevitably, it is hard for such reviewers to avoid the sort of smartass self-promotion which darkens counsel – and to write about popular culture we need to make discriminations as fine as those which apply to the cultural artefacts recognized as high art.

What is mocked as geek culture – television shows, comics, cult films – is art that people not only love, but think about and through. One of the standard assumptions about the consumption of popular culture is that it is necessarily consumed passively – evil moguls feed the masses material that dulls their senses and discriminations; this overestimates the power of, say, Rupert Murdoch to harness absolutely everything to his dark purposes. The Murdoch empire itself includes not only politically reactionary media like *The Sun* in Great Britain and Fox News on American television, but quietly subversive material like Matt Groening's *The Simpsons*. One of the contradictions of late capitalism is that its obsession with market forces stops it stifling work that puts a quasi-oppositional case to the values and political causes it seeks to patronize.

A feature of the geek aesthetic is that popular culture is consumed in an active way – sitting through films and television shows can be the start of appreciating them, not simply an end in itself. A quick check of the Internet via search engines demonstrates how universal such an aesthetic is becoming.

The geek aesthetic is also about hobbyism – I have mentioned the role of this in the development of CGI. Many important contemporary movie-makers started out as fans and an intensive grounding in SF and comics is an important part of the creative personality of key scriptwriters and creators like Kevin Smith, Joss Whedon and Bryan Singer. (The first two of these made breakthroughs into comics scripting after they were well known for their work in films and television – deep love for the form and what it can do that film cannot is the determining factor here.) The existence of large creative fan-cultures centred around fan-fiction, including slash fiction (the exploration in fan-fiction of actual or alleged homoerotic subtext in the canonical work) and vids (the editing of clips from shows or films as videos for a rock or pop track) may well indicate where some future significant creators will come from. And as high-grade computing power spreads and more ways of manipulating digitized material arise, it can be confidentially predicted that fan hobbyism will find ways of growing closer towards professional skills in the most unlikely areas – re-cutting classic films with different digitized actors in the principal roles is a killer application that exists only in people's dreams, as yet.

And popular film and television and comics can be the focus through which a large audience gets a sense of the tragic and the ecstatic. There is a view expressed for example by Richard Jenkyns in his *Prospect* review of my *Reading the Vampire Slayer* that popular culture inevitably debases serious themes on the rare occasions that it touches on them. There are two points to be made here. One is that later generations may reassess what is and is not high culture – Jane Austen's defence of the novel in a period where it was regarded by many as a trivial form is a case in point. The other is that to believe this is a piece of pessimism that goes alongside a deeply elitist view of how society functions. (Rudyard Kipling's short story 'The Janeites' both demonstrates how geeky the appreciation of high culture can become and indicates how a shared obsessive fondness for text can be a useful piece of social glue.)

A recent *Guardian* article on the popularity of Peter Jackson's three films of Tolkien's novel argued that 'we are all nerds (or geeks) now.' What this introduction would argue is that this is not a bad thing – passionate reading of every aspect of the texts of popular culture is one of the cultural strengths of our time, a way of expanding the canon that includes rather than excludes, a way of democratizing critical sensibility. In a time where helplessness is a common feeling, this sense of active involvement with cultural commodities is a positive good.

2. Director as Parodist

Paul Verhoeven's **Starship Troopers**

There is no particular reason why SF films should need to be adapted from written SF, save for the fact that some particular SF novels have a large audience of devotees as well as strong plots, charismatic characters and inventive settings. What is interesting is that almost all adaptations of SF novels as film have been radically unfaithful, both overall and in detail – directors and scriptwriters have been keen to latch on to that devotion but less keen to stick with what was good about the books or stories in the first place.

This is probably less often bad faith than a failure to respect and understand their source material – as a general rule, there is no point in adapting any novel, SF or otherwise, for a film unless you have some real sense of how it works. Neil LaBute's film of A.S. Byatt's prizewinning literary novel *Possession* (2002), for example, is based on a fundamental misreading of the book as being centrally about the two love affairs at the core of its plot rather than being about the cleverness of all four protagonists, the author and the assumed reader; it is a book about being smart and it was a fundamental miscalculation to turn it into a dumb love story. Most science fiction is about intelligence, one way or another, and the sheer dumbness of the films SF novels get turned into is often an insult to what made them good in the first place.

Paul Verhoeven's film *Starship Troopers* is not so much an adaptation of Robert A. Heinlein's 1959 novel as a polemic against it. Large parts of the novel find their way into the film – the whipping post as an element of military discipline, the future society in which citizenship is only earned by military service, the lectures about why this is right and proper, the playboyish hero hardened by combat, the insectile aliens with whom humanity has no especial interest in sharing the galaxy. Yet the general feel of the film is alien to Heinlein and is based on fundamental misunderstanding by Verhoeven of what Heinlein was all about, on a mapping of European fascism on to a very different kind of American militarism and authoritarianism.

This misunderstanding further involves Verhoeven in some complex bad faith – this is a film which purports to denounce militarism and fascism and genocide and ends up imaginatively caught up in them. As so often in Verhoeven's films, he aestheticizes the things of which he claims to disapprove – *Showgirls* (1995), for example, lectures us on the tawdriness of lap-dancing and goes to considerable lengths to show us as much of it as possible. Before *Starship Troopers* has ended, we have grown very tired of, for one example, intelligence officers with a taste for torture striding around rooms with large symbols paved into the floor and wearing high-peaked caps and leather trench-coats. No one ever said Verhoeven was subtle.

Heinlein's novel is, let us be clear, one of his most problematic. It can never be assumed that any of his novels is wholly or simply an exposition of views that he actually held, but *Starship Troopers* comes perhaps closer than some others. It seems likely, for example, that he would have endorsed much of what is said in the book's many history lessons about what was wrong with the late twentieth century – soft treatment of juvenile delinquents and so on. Heinlein believed both in an ethic of service and in military service as an expression of that ethic – all the more so because during the Second World War genuinely poor health and technological war work had kept him out of combat. The chapter headings to *Starship Troopers* include quotations from Jefferson and Paine, as well as from the Bible and the Koran – Heinlein specifically identifies aspects of his future world with Revolutionary America and the Israel of the Judges. All of this is problematic and much of it objectionable – but it represents something a deal more interesting than a recycled European fascism.

Heinlein found himself, as a writer, living in a subculture – the professional and fan world of science fiction – where values he abhorred were common if not dominant; a few years later, SF writers who, like Heinlein, supported and SF writers who condemned the Vietnam war both placed ads in a major SF magazine, and the balance of big names was broadly on the opposition side. His organization of blood donor drives at SF conventions was, almost certainly, an attempt to promulgate the ethic of service in a non-controversial way. Heinlein was an intelligent man who believed in consensus and persuasion as well as confrontation – but he was not above teasing his assumed readership and, as he would have seen it, confronting their prejudices against a military career. It is ironic that the novel in which he did this should have become the basis for a deeply anti-militarist film – as well as for one of SF's most inspired parodies, Harry Harrison's novel *Bill the Galactic Hero*.

Part of what makes this possible is that, even in a novel as simplistic as *Starship Troopers*, Heinlein's views were complicated – he was not a conservative and was far more consistently a libertarian on social issues than many so-called libertarians who regard him as one of their heroes. Inasmuch as *Starship Troopers* is a right-wing novel, it is an odd mixture of libertarianism and communitarianism rather than anything that can legitimately be called fascist, save in the specific that this is a society created by veterans.

His very next novel, *Stranger in a Strange Land*, made clear a level of sexual tolerance and religious scepticism that place him firmly outside the grain of American conservatism, as does the prevalence in his work of the Heinlein woman, the frontier toughie with sharp tongue and brain. (The introduction by Verhoeven of women into Heinlein's space marines is one of the places where the adaptation is truer, in a sense, to Heinlein's overall ethos than the original had been.) It is generally held by those who knew him that his views on sexual behaviour were libertine, however strait-laced his actual behaviour.

Verhoeven and his scriptwriter Edward Naumeier seem at times to understand Heinlein's point of view. One of the few points at which the script directly quotes the book is this:

Rasczak   You. Tell me the moral difference, if any, between the citizen and the civilian?

Johnny   The difference lies in the field of civic virtue. A citizen accepts personal responsibility for the safety of the body politic, of which he is a member, defending it, if need be, with his life. The civilian does not.

More often, they engage with Heinlein via cheap shots like the propagandistic frame narrative, the SS-like uniforms worn by the Intelligence Corps and the steady metamorphosis of Neil Patrick Harris as Carl into an inhuman thug who sacrifices troops in large numbers merely to ascertain the presence of a Brain Bug on an otherwise tactically worthless planet.

Heinlein's novel is in large part about his protagonist Johnny's search for a father in a patriarchal world, a search which is eventually resolved by his reconciliation with his own father in the last segment of the book. Each of the mentor figures – the schoolteacher Dubois, the training sergeant Zim, the various commanding officers under whom Johnny serves, his instructors at Officer's Training School – is in some sense a father figure; they are all part of an adult world to which he aspires. The fact that Zim and Dubois, and Dubois and the recruiting officer Weiss, are old friends makes explicit a more general sense that all of these figures are aspects of the same thing. Inasmuch as it echoes this theme, Verhoeven and Naumeier's amalgamation of the roles of Dubois and Rasczak is an intelligent abridgement.

Generally, however, the role of coincidence in their film is constantly to bring together a small group of contemporaries who are emotionally entangled with each other – as if interstellar war were a giant singles bar. At the end, the surviving trio coo that every time they are in the same place, great things happen; the war will be resolved in Earth's favour because these three have managed, in spite of the deaths of their families and friends, to continue to care for each other.

When Johnny leaves home for the Mobile Infantry, he quarrels badly with his parents; his father sees him as having been unduly influenced by the first of Johnny's replacement fathers, Dubois. On his way to Officer's Training School, Johnny meets his father, who is about to join the unit he has just left – the death of Johnny's mother has caused his father to reconsider his position on the military. At the crucial point when Johnny graduates from being an ordinary soldier to being a potential officer, he and his father meet in a position of equality – his father has accepted that Johnny's preferred father figures were right about the nature of the universe and that he was wrong. By simply killing off Johnny's father along with his mother, Verhoeven and Naumeier at a stroke remove the book's most central theme from their movie.

Not least because he originally planned the book as one of his highly successful novels for young adults, Heinlein had to avoid even the faintest smack of homoeroticism in his portrait of the intense comradeship of front-line troops. There is nothing intrinsically homoerotic about such comradeship, of course, but the history of novels which describe it, particularly when written by men who have not experienced it, is, from Stephen Crane's *The Red Badge of Courage* onwards, one which often slips into eroticism as a default mode. The adoption of family romance as the appropriate alternative mode is an intelligent selection on his part because it enables him to give Johnny's growth and development emotional intensity without risking what would have been largely unacceptable in the SF of the time.

Starship Troopers is, unlike almost all his other novels, including those for young adults, a novel which leaves out female characters. Johnny's unnamed mother, along with his equally unnamed father, pleads with him to withdraw his recruitment into the armed forces and then, as in the film, is killed in the Bugs' destruction of Buenos Aires; in the film, his father dies there as well. The book's main named female character is Carmen, who, as in the film, joins the navy as a pilot; later in the book, she and Johnny have dinner while on leave. It is specifically mentioned that she, and other female pilots, shave their heads – Johnny comments on how attractive this is; needless to say, this is not taken up in the film. In various combat scenes, Captain Deladrier's gender is mentioned almost in passing when praising her piloting skills. And that is that.

However, this is not to say that roles gendered as female are entirely absent from the book. In an interesting passage, Heinlein explicitly so genders the role of a male sergeant in holding together troops whose commanding officer has died heroically saving them:

> Have you ever seen a widow with stern character keep her family together by behaving as if the head of the family had simply stepped out and would return at any moment? That's what Jelly did. He was just a touch more strict with us than ever and if he ever had to say: 'The Lieutenant wouldn't like that,' it was almost more than a man could take.

At the end of the novel, Johnny has become a commanding officer and we see him prepare his troops for the final assault on the Bugs' home world; we also learn, almost casually, that his father is now his sergeant. Johnny's struggle has been solved by becoming his own father, and having his father become metonymically his wife…

If this reading of *Starship Troopers* seems fanciful, it needs to be pointed out that, at almost exactly the same time, Heinlein produced the time paradox short story 'All You Zombies' in which, via hermaphroditism and time travel, the protagonist is all of the following: the orphan girl seduced and abandoned, the child stolen from her, the seducer who impregnated her and the recruiting officer who persuades him to join a corps of time travellers. His next novel was to be *Stranger in a Strange Land*, that equally odd study in messiah-hood, martyrdom and sexual experimentation. Heinlein does not easily map onto any model of what a right-wing militarist should be like – he was an intelligent writer good at trying ideas on for size, particularly in the sexual arena. (His utter contempt for the Religious Right was a theme in his fiction from the 1940s onwards – indeed his *Future History* series includes a period when the USA is taken over by the theocratic followers of an evangelist.)

Other aspects of Heinlein's military universe are clearly in some sense teases of his audience – the widespread use of flogging as a military punishment in his armed forces is represented as a ritual of bonding as much as one of punishment. When Johnny, for a comparatively minor error in training, is sentenced to be flogged, he experiences it as a very painful reminder not to make the same mistake again, one which leaves him feeling connected to the institution of discipline. Heinlein is very careful to make the entire procedure as antiseptic as possible – there is no eroticization here.

The same cannot be said of the film's treatment of Johnny's flogging. In the first case, it is a punishment for a far more serious error, one which has led to the death of one fellow trainee and the departure from the army of another, both of them under Johnny's command as an NCO. Secondly, it almost leads to Johnny's ignominious departure from the armed forces – his resignation is about to take effect when the Bug raid on Buenos Aires changes everything. Thirdly, and almost inevitably, Verhoeven cannot resist allowing his pretty boy hero, Caspar van Dien, to be flogged in the most fetching of poses, flexing his muscles like beefcake and expressing torment by wrinkling his brow. He disapproves of Heinlein's flogging scene, but eroticizes it and makes it hugely more central to the film than it is to the book.

More generally, and reprehensibly, Verhoeven and Naumeier introduce a petty sadism into this world – children are shown being hardened by stamping on harmless insects as surrogates for the enemy Bugs. In a final shot of Carl's researches into the captured Brain Bug he is merely poking it with sharp pointed probes to no obvious effect except torture. The audience is encouraged to share in Carl's sadism – upon its capture, he reads the mind of the Brain Bug and announces 'It's afraid' to the cheers of the on-screen multitude.

The hardening of Carl is merely the most extreme example of the film's general approach to military training. What for Heinlein is Johnny's growth towards responsibility is for Verhoeven simply his gradual transformation into someone who kills and gets other people killed. Heinlein's Johnny is selected for officer training and only goes back to combat after an extensive period; Verhoeven's Johnny merely inherits battlefield command by being the senior NCO when Rasczak is killed and has this more or less automatically ratified because his platoon is needed for another mission immediately. Heinlein means every word of his book's endless and sometimes tiresome lectures about military and civic virtue; Verhoeven and Naumeier can only view them cynically as top-dressing for a society based on military might.

During the capture of the Brain Bug, Heinlein's Johnny is out of action because a roof falls on him; Verhoeven's Johnny hares off to rescue Zander and Carmen in profound dereliction of his orders. (In Naumeier's script, the issue that he has disobeyed orders is at least dealt with by having Carl take responsibility for giving him telepathic orders – in the finished film, Carl mentions having given him her whereabouts, but the issue of disobedience is forgotten altogether.) During the rescue, the black soldier Sugar is incapacitatingly wounded and stays behind to kill the largest number possible of Bugs with a tactical nuclear device; it is to be hoped that Verhoeven produced this particular racist cliché as a piece of sarcasm, but even then it is pretty much unacceptable.

It can be argued that one of the most radical changes made to the book by the film – the replacement of the semi-automated exoskeletons in which Heinlein's Johnny and his comrades fight with equipment rather less advanced and armour distinctly less protective than much in use in the present day – was a decision made on the grounds of cost. Whether produced through CGI or animatronics, representation of Heinlein's armour would have been very expensive – in a film that had to rely on massive amounts of CGI for its Bugs, it would have meant that most of the combat sequences became in essence no more than animations.

The Bugs in the novel are shown as more or less plausible variations on the same species – there are warriors, workers, brains and queens but they are neither radically morphologically distinct from each other nor especially large. When, in the book, Zim captures a Brain Bug, it is of a size that he can use it as a shield. The Bugs of the film are not designed to resemble each other in any way – the warriors are mantises with ragged fractal limbs, or giant beetles that shoot flame, while the Brain Bugs are enormous larvae so huge that they have to be tugged by a squad of humans or Bugs. It makes no sense that the creatures we are shown belong to the same species, nor that they have grown so large on a planet whose gravity human beings experience as Earth-normal.

At the film's most impressive moments, of course, we do not necessarily think of this. The CGI work, while already starting to show its age, has some moments of real impressiveness – as when Rasczak's platoon find a fort full of dead soldiers, occupy it and then watch Bugs in vast numbers stream down from the hills. This is genuinely terrifying. The combination of CGI and blue screen work in parts of the film is also effective – the sequence where Johnny uses his sports skills to mount and kill one of the flame-throwing beetles is particularly exciting. There are times when Verhoeven forgets to be cynical and political, and just enjoy the action film side of what he is making for its own sake, and those are the parts of the film that work.

Verhoeven takes considerable glee in showing us the hideous rendings and maimings that his giant insects can effect on a largely unprotected human body. Zander has his brain sucked out of his skull; the secondary heroine

Dizzy Flores is impaled; Rasczak is cut in two. (As is Captain Deladier, though by a closing bulkhead rather than a Bug.[1] To have two mentor characters cut in half, without any symbolic purpose, looks uncommonly like carelessness.) Minor characters have limbs melted off them, or are fed to flying Bugs' nested offspring. Regularly, characters caught off guard are thrown into the air and dismembered. There is almost none of this in the book; those characters that die, like the male character who shares a name but nothing else with Dizzy Flores, are wounded through holes in their armour.

Heinlein deliberately and mendaciously sanitizes death in combat in order to maintain the argument for its nobility, but Verhoeven goes considerably too far in the direction of glorying in mutilation and degradation for their own sake. This is not so much a matter of 'Few die well who die in battle' or the pathos of Wilfred Owen's poetry as of endlessly and obsessively rubbing our noses in the transformation of the beautiful young into threshed offal.

One of the film's many radical inconsistencies has to do with the loss of limbs – Rasczak has an artificial arm of the most obvious and robotic kind, as does the recruiting sergeant who swears Johnny in, and yet, when Johnny is seriously wounded, he is shown regrowing the damaged parts in a tank. Heinlein's recruiting sergeant is seriously maimed, but only at work and to deter recruits – he has cosmetically adequate artificial limbs the rest of the time.

The film makes intelligent use of one of the book's structural tricks. The book starts with Johnny in action and lets us learn his world from watching him perform as a Mobile Infantryman before going back to show us how he got there. The film copies this, with the additional trick that at the end of the sequence we see the soldier we subsequently learn to be Johnny, killed or left for dead; where Heinlein simply hooks us, Verhoeven and Naumeier go one better by creating suspense – we cannot be entirely sure that Johnny, our protagonist, survives past the point at which the extensive flashback which follows catches up with the real time of the film's opening. The intelligence with which they manage this, of course, throws into sharp relief their choice of easy answers in adapting the leisurely flow of a novel to the fiercer pace of a blockbuster movie.

This is particularly true because of one of the major changes they introduce to Heinlein's structure – the film has several focuses of interest and two main viewpoint characters. Carmen Ibanez is almost as important and her almost effortless success as a young pilot is given a significant amount of screen time.

---

[1] In Naumeier's script, she merely got a crushed leg – and then had her brain sucked out. It is also worth noting that her name drops a letter in the transfer from book to script – for no obvious reason.

Verhoeven picks up from the brief high school and recruitment scenes of the novel in order to introduce us to the central group of flirty Dizzy, brainy Carl, Carmen and sports star Johnny at high school as well as Zander, who plays in an opposing school's team.

All of this group except for Dizzy (Dina Meyer) are played by actors with a background in soap operas – *Melrose Place, Beverly Hills 90210*; Verhoeven cast all of them as pretty airheads and that, pretty much, is what he shows them as being. We are told that Carmen and Zander have to be gifted at maths in order to be good pilots, but we see little sign of this intelligence; Carl's psychic abilities are at least plumbed into the plot via his mental control of his pet ferret and his ESP card testing of Johnny. Johnny in particular is shown as inattentive in class and primarily concerned with the sports field – his athleticism gets used in one memorable sequence and is forgotten about thereafter.

In Heinlein, Johnny signs up out of loyalty to Carl, but never mentions him afterwards, and to impress Carmen whom he likes but hardly knows; in the film, they are dating and he is worried about her interest in Zander, who has already signed up and been accepted for pilot training. His anxiety that he is being traded in for a smarter model runs through the film – Zander becomes Carmen's mentor in pilot training and her regular flight partner as well as her lover – while the early high school scenes also establish the unrequited feelings of Dizzy for Johnny, which again is a plot point throughout the film.

Both Dizzy and Zander get the sort of ironic punitive death you would expect from a slasher movie. The day after she finally has sex with Johnny, Dizzy is killed by being impaled on a Bug arm and expires in his arms saying 'It's all right 'cause I got to have you' in a rescue boat piloted by Carmen; Zander's intelligence – the thing which has made him Johnny's successful sexual rival – gets his brain literally sucked out of his skull by the Brain Bug. Verhoeven knows the patterns he is playing with – Dizzy and Zander die so that Carmen and Johnny can be together – and then sarcastically refuses them: there is no implication that their relationship comes to anything and our last sight of both of them, as of Carl, is as warriors pursuing their chosen careers. Dizzy and Zander die for successfully pursuing love – Johnny and Carmen may rescue each other, but they will never be together. Their true love is the war.

The retributive element in the deaths of Dizzy and Zander makes something of a nonsense of the film's earlier attempts to present a cheerful egalitarian eroticism – unisex shower scenes[1] and so on, and Dizzy's participation in a lot

---

[1] In the commentary to the DVD, Verhoeven talks of how he jollied his cast into this scene by agreeing to take his clothes off as well.

of blokish bonding with Johnny and his friend Ace. The element of bad faith in this has partly to do with the way that sexual egalitarianism means Dizzy acting like a guy and partly with the way that their bonding always feels like courtship. James Cameron's *Aliens* presents a fairly similar mixed-sex military unit and manages to avoid both Verhoeven's utopian presentation of gender relations in such a unit as unproblematic and the cheesy soft-porn aspects of the camera-work.

Heinlein's Johnny is specifically non-Caucasian – though this is referred to casually and at a late stage when he mentions that his family are Tagalog speakers. We are never told in what city Johnny goes to high school – it could be anywhere at all in the world with the sole exception of Buenos Aires, since his mother is visiting that city when it is destroyed. By shifting its location specifically to that city, Verhoeven ups the ante for all of his central characters since it is their home that the Bugs destroy in their first attack on Earth, but he weakens Heinlein's point that the Federation has unified humanity as never before:

Don't they talk Standard English where you come from?

Oh, certainly. For business and school and so forth. We just talk the old speech around home a little. Traditions. You know.

Heinlein never tells us where Johnny's home city is – though it is presumably Manila, since the old speech referred to is Tagalog – because there is a very real sense in which it does not matter. Under threat, there is only one race, the human race.

Verhoeven replaces Heinlein's idealistic sense of human unification with a fairly strong implication of cultural imperialism – if his characters all speak English, it is because American culture has absorbed everything else rather than because English is a convenient lingua franca. Heinlein's high school is there as a bully platform for Rasczak to lay down the ground rules of the society the book inhabits; Verhoeven's high school is an extended quotation from American movies and popular culture. By casting a lot of pretty young people with a background in soap opera, Verhoeven implicitly says that the lowest common denominator of contemporary American culture has replaced everything else that there once was in the world.

The mechanism whereby this has happened is less clear than in Heinlein, where it is reasonably clear that the Federation is what replaced our world order after war and collapse – the reason why military service is the specific model of community service that buys citizenship is that it was veterans who re-established order from chaos. All we know in Verhoeven's film is that the military is firmly in control, without any sense of this having had historical roots. The society Heinlein shows us is at least the pragmatic product of specific contingency without any particular claim to be just or fair.

Heinlein's novel is simply the story of how Johnny Rico grew up and became a soldier – presumably he is called Johnny either because of the wide folksong literature in which that is the young soldier's name or as a riposte to Dalton Trumbo's pacifist tract *Johnny Got His Gun*. Verhoeven's film alternates the story of Johnny, Carmen and their friends with propaganda material in some of which they are being used as recruitment fodder.

Verhoeven used a somewhat similar device in *Robocop*, where the narrative is interspersed with chunks of media-surfing from which we assemble a picture of Robocop's world. Here there is no sense of the random or the arbitrary to the background material – we are being fed it from the Federation's computer net and at every point we are offered an interactive menu with the slogan 'Would you like to know more?' Since the movie is not interactive, and we have no influence on which bits of information we are being fed, this becomes a distinctly unsubtle way of telling us that we have no control and are being fed a line. If Verhoeven means to be telling us something about how media operate in our own world, the point is very laboured.

It is possible to argue that the film's heavy dependence on stock tropes of the army film is justified by the fact that it is presented as the heavy-handed propaganda of an authoritarian state. There are scenes of violent inter-service rivalry – at one point Johnny and Zander's mutual jealousy over Carmen nearly boils over into an Army/Navy brawl – and any moment of stillness or celebration is certain to be balanced by a dire emergency. There is the big shore-leave scene, where Johnny, Ace and Dizzy get matching tattoos, and the long wait for the landing craft to dock. I have already mentioned the noble self-sacrificing death of Sugar. All of these tropes are ironic, so that's all right then. Sometimes, though, crass is just crass.

Because of the decision to frame its narrative with these broadcasts and announcements, the film has to be much clearer about the origin and progress of the war than the novel bothers to be. Sometimes this is effective – there is a strong implication that Earth has deliberately provoked the war with the Bugs by having colonists settle debatable territory – and sometimes it effectively creates mood – the mournful martial music that underscores the aftermath of the abortive raid on the Bugs' home world and the slow sombre pacing of Earth's new Chief of Staff as she takes her place at a rostrum.

Unfortunately, it is precisely in this supposedly objective frame narrative that the film-makers reveal their crass inability to deal with scientific concepts of the most basic kind. I have mentioned the problems of the Bugs' biology already – add to this the existence of giant Bugs that can shoot streams of plasma capable of destroying a large starship in high orbit, and then say inverse square law to yourself under your breath. Somehow the Bugs manage to declare war by aiming an asteroid at Buenos Aires across light years so that it arrives just at the right strategic moment – quite a trick since it, unlike the Earth spaceships, is travelling at sub-light speeds and would have to have been aimed before either humans or presumably the Bugs evolved. This could have been fixed with a line of gobbledegook, but no one bothered – some acknowledgement of the need for plausibility is a minimum SF rule.

Every landscape we see the Bugs inhabit, including their home world, is entirely barren – which enables a generalized reference to Foreign Legion movies, particularly once the platoon is besieged in a fort full of corpses, but begs the question of what the Bugs actually eat when there are no human soldiers for their dinner. (This, it has to be said in fairness, is a besetting sin of SF movies, *Pitch Black* for example, and to a lesser extent of SF books.)

What else is there to say in the film's defence? One or two of the secondary performances have real charm. Dina Meyer's bad girl Dizzy is so much more engaging than Denise Richard's teeth-and-hair portrayal of Carmen that, as so often in films that play with this particular binary, the audience cannot understand the protagonist's preference. Jake Busey lends an angular charm to the role of Ace, particularly in the scene where he serenades Dizzy and Johnny with his electric violin and a very louche grin indeed. Clancy Brown does his usual scary-modulating-to-likeable turn as Zim and Michael Ironside has the right degree of scowling authority to be credible both as Rasczak the schoolteacher and the commander.

Overall, though, Verhoeven's dislike for the book gets in the way of his understanding it; this is an adaptation which suffers from the misapprehension that it is smarter than an original which it in fact significantly dumbs down. The vacuousness of its leads means that there is no possibility of subtext in their performances – any irony has to come from the director and he ladles it on like gravy. The film relies far too heavily on its special effects and most especially on its CGI work – there is no particular sense of escalation from action sequence to sequence except in the sheer quantity of animated giant insects on screen or the number of starships being destroyed at a time. Various of the CGI sequences – the crash-landing of Zander and Carmen's escape pod, for example – simply look cheap and tacky. The architecture and interior design is, presumably by scornful intention, an unholy alliance of fascist monumentalism and LA kitsch, which becomes hard to look at quite quickly. You may not have to love a book to film it, but it helps if you do not positively hate it.

3. Comedy 1

Galaxy Quest

If there is one thing more difficult than producing a good SF film, it is producing a good SF comedy – it means juggling three balls rather than two – and yet such things do exist. *Galaxy Quest* is a well-plotted, well-paced, character-driven movie with a firm sense of how SF has handled various themes and ideas. It is not especially surprising that it won the Hugo, the World SF Convention's Best of the Year award; it would almost have been more surprising if it had not.

It goes almost without saying that *Galaxy Quest* is a parodic handling of the original *Star Trek* television series and of some aspects of the subsequent careers of that show's cast. The ship from the fictional show, the Protector, closely resembles the original Enterprise both in its shape and in its internal design and decor. Most of the technology in the film – ray-guns, transporter beams, enigmatic machines that function primarily as plot devices – is sufficiently close to *Star Trek* to enable specific parody – like dilithium crystals, the beryllium spheres which power the Protector prove on a regular basis unable to take the strain of combat.

The characters make constant reference to the tropes of television SF. When they meet a group of small child-like, nauseatingly cute aliens on a desert planet, Guy, significantly not one of the regular cast, takes it for granted that the aliens will probably turn into monsters at a moment's notice.

Guy   Of course they're cute NOW. But in a second they're
               going to turn MEAN and UGLY somehow and then
               there are going to be a million MORE of them! …
               Jesus, didn't ANY of you watch the show!?

The egoism of Jason Nesmith (Tim Allen), who plays Captain Taggart, is equivalent to that regularly imputed by fans to William Shatner, and cast members make jokes about his habit of going through ordeals which leave him shirtless. Alexander Dane (Alan Rickman) plays an alien, Dr Lazarus, roughly cognate with Mr Spock – though his endless moans about his lost career as a serious Shakespearian actor have rather more to do with *Star Trek: The Next Generation*'s Patrick Stewart. Like Spock, Lazarus is a devotee of an alien philosophy – he acquires a disciple who tries touchingly to live by it.

Gwen DeMarco (Sigourney Weaver) regularly complains that her character, Tawny Madison, never gets to do anything except repeat what the captain or the computer says:

Gwen de Marco   At least you had a PART. You had a character
                  people loved! My TV Guide interview was six
                  paragraphs about this body suit. About my
                  legs. How did I perfect my trademark
                  sidesaddle pose? Nobody ever bothered to ask
                  what I DO on the ship…

Fred   You were the, uh… Wait I'll think of it…

Gwen de Marco   I repeated the computer. 'It's getting hotter,
                  Commander!' 'The ship is disintegrating,
                  Commander!' Nothing I did EVER affected
                  the plot, not ONCE! Nothing I did was ever
                  taken seriously!

Much the same was true of Lieutenant Uhura (Michelle Nichols). Later on, however, she loses her temper with Tommy when he says how irritating he finds it:

Gwen DeMarco   I have ONE job on this lousy ship. It's stupid,
                  but I'm going to DO it. GOT IT?

There are jokes about the possible fate of the surname-less actor Guy, who played a doomed crewman in one episode, comes along for the ride and realizes that he may be yet again the anonymous crewman slated for death by the inexorable forces of story – until, that is, he has it pointed out to him that his obsessive fear of this makes him the plucky comic relief. (When the film ends in a trailer for a revived show, he joins the permanent cast – and gets a surname.)

Galaxy Quest would not be remotely so good a film if parody were the whole point. Nesmith is a joke about the egocentricity of actors in general as much as of any particular actor, but he grows and changes and becomes a hero of sorts in the end. Far more than any other big-budget SFX comedy, such as the two films thus far of the *Men in Black* franchise (1997, 2002), *Galaxy Quest* is a movie with a heart which even ends up making a sort of moral point. A surprising number of its jokes are variations on a few central themes – they are funny both as gags and as SF conceits, and are worked through in terms not only of story logic but also of what might almost be called the philosophical logic of the film.

To summarize briefly, a group of washed-up actors, cast members in the long-ago SF television show 'Galaxy Quest', have come to despise it, its fans and each other – they particularly dislike Nesmith, an egomaniac who played Captain Taggart in the show – and are yet dependent on it and each other, because most of their incomes come from personal appearances at conventions and shop openings. Nesmith is approached by the Thermians, aliens whom he mistakes for just another group of fans in costume – their home, the Klaatu Nebula, is a joke about the benevolent alien visitor Klaatu in the classic anti-war SF film *The Day the Earth Stood Still* (1951) and the film's most famous line of dialogue: 'Klaatu Baradu Nikto'. The reference is not merely a gratuitous piece of fannishness, but drops a hint as to the Thermians' essentially pacific nature.

The Thermians have picked up broadcasts of the show, mistaken them for historical records and rebuilt their entire culture and technology around it – and have made the imagined technology work in practice. Pretending to be the man the aliens think Nesmith is in the crisis of a war with a ruthless alien warlord, Sarris, brings disaster close, as does the first attempt by the rest of the cast/crew to cope when they join Nesmith.

Captured by Sarris, who wants the mysterious Omega 13 device for himself, Nesmith eventually confesses the truth to preserve Gwen DeMarco from torture. Sarris leaves the humans and Thermians to die. The truth is not enough, though; it is acting in accordance with their heroic roles after acknowledging that they are actors which saves the day. The show has given them expert knowledge of story tropes, an example, if you choose to think of it as such, of a competence cascade – Nesmith and Dane trick their executioners by pretending to fight for example. This expert knowledge enables Nesmith and the others to outwit Sarris and destroy his ship. Sarris escapes in disguise and kills them all – Nesmith uses the Omega 13 to turn back time a crucial few seconds and defeat Sarris yet again.

Earlier, Nesmith has snubbed and ridiculed a group of obsessive fans who ask him to resolve technical problems with the Protector's working. At the climax he has to ask them apologetically to talk him and Gwen through the Protector's internal maze of ducts and booby traps in order to abort its self-destruct mechanism – the fans have, like the Thermians, made sense of the show's hints and have elaborate schematics of its workings on their computers. It is also the fans who have guessed correctly the function of the Omega 13.

In one of many nice moments of characterization, when contacted by Nesmith, the young fan Brandon starts apologizing for Nesmith's rudeness to him and saying that of course he knows that the Protector is an imaginary ship in a show – told by Nesmith that it is in fact real, Brandon instantly retracts with a gibber of excitement:

> Brandon   I understand completely that It's just a TV show. There is no ship, there is no Beryllium Sphere, no digital conveyor... I mean, obviously it's all just a -

> Nesmith   It's real, Brandon. All of it, It's real.

> Brandon   (*no hesitation*) I knew it!... I KNEW it!...

This plot brings together two tropes – one specifically identified with the SF genre, the other far broader in its origins – and demonstrates the potential kinship between them. In both instances, aspiration to an ideal by those originally comically unworthy of it produces a close resemblance to the ideal after that aspiration has been persisted in through a serious testing that includes a moment of truth-telling.

The idea of aliens who imitate or appropriate an aspect of human culture was popular in the 1940s and 1950s and had, and has, its dark side, deriving in part from racist attitudes about other cultures that adopt western mores and allegedly get them wrong. This was, after all, an accusation often levelled at the Japanese in the years that culminated in the Second World War and its racist propaganda; it was also a part of the stock of anti-Semitic propaganda from Wagner's 'The Jew in Music' onwards. In SF, it was one of several ideas about human/alien interaction associated with authors who clustered around *Astounding Science Fiction* and its editor John W. Campbell. For Campbell, a man of strong views, it was necessary that alien species always be portrayed as intrinsically less gifted than Earth-derived humanity.

Writers like Christopher Anvil regularly wrote stories for Campbell, in which bureaucratic alien invaders were humiliated and defeated by human insurgents; such aliens never quite understand the culture of the (usually WASP) humans whose territory they occupy, are usually incapable of understanding human jokes and are seen as being as pathetic as they are threatening. Standardly in Anvil and often in such other authors as Eric Frank Russell – most obviously in the novella *Next of Kin* – such aliens are portrayed through analogy with the former German, or the current Soviet, enemy, but in the comic clod-hopper version of propaganda caricature rather than the silkily sinister one.

The classic statement of the idea of alien imitation of humanity, though, was a sequence of stories which Campbell did not publish even though they were a collaboration between two of his regular contributors. The 'Hoka' stories which Poul Anderson and Gordon Dickson wrote throughout their long careers portray a species of teddy-bear like aliens – rather like George Lucas' Ewoks in *The Return of the Jedi* – who are almost entirely without cynicism or any sense of the barriers between truth and fiction. In various stories, Hoka adopt the roles of Sherlock Holmes and Bonny Prince Charlie, and form a space-opera like *Star Patrol* which helps their human ally defeat reptilian invaders.

There is still a vein of condescension in all of this, but the Hoka stories are genuinely funny and warm-hearted by comparison with much of the work of the Campbell school. Anderson was enough of an admirer of Kipling that any idea of human superiority was always going to be qualified in his work by a sense that all things pass. In his work, as opposed to that of most of the Campbell group, the theme of cultural appropriation works in both directions; the mediaeval Englishmen of his *The High Crusade* take over a decadent galactic civilization without having much idea of how advanced technology works precisely because its alien masters make the mistake of thinking that primitive equals stupid or intellectually unsophisticated.

In *Galaxy Quest*, the alien Thermians comically overestimate Earth in general and the cast of 'Galaxy Quest' in particular; their genocidal enemy Sarris proves, in his egocentric cynicism, equally wrong-headed in his assumption that actors from a low-technology world can be no threat to him. The Thermians parallel the Hoka in their seeming entire inability to understand the concept of fiction – they have only learned about lies through regular treachery by the appalling Sarris. After Sarris' defeat, they assume that every bit of the truth told their captain at the climax by Nesmith was itself a deceit aimed at Sarris – they laugh at the brilliance of Nesmith's claim that the original Protector was a tiny model.

One of the reasons why the Thermians are comic is that their actions and ideas are predictable; part of the film's charm is that much of that predictability operates in hindsight. When for example they are asked about other 'historical records' they have picked up from Earth television, they refer to *Gilligan's Island* and say in tones of hushed sorrow 'Those poor people'. Orphaned by Sarris' genocidal war against their people, the Thermians not only believe that the castaways in the show are real, but empathize with them. There is a very funny joke here, but it is a bittersweet one.

The other trope is that of the good actor, who never forgets that that is what he is, and is a better actor for it, yet is nonetheless subsumed by his role; it is by accepting his own human fallibility and flaws that the humbug can earn becoming a genuine hero. This is a specifically modern idea arrived at in opposition to much of western thought.

In *The Republic*, Plato advocated the suppression of dramatic poetry on the grounds that those who read, watched or performed well-portrayed villainy would be more prone to corruption. The Roman Empire and its successor states and the Christian Churches were historically almost equally suspicious of actors, who were seen as vagabonds incapable of virtue because they were caught up in a career of pretence. Actors were denied both civil rights and the sacraments in France as late as the career of Molière; the theatre was banned in Britain during the enforced Puritanism of the Commonwealth.

At the same time, both State and Church were caught up in a paradox about performance – enforcing orthodox observance was always more important than 'carving windows into men's souls'. The performance of virtue might lead to virtuous attitudes – Hamlet recommends to his mother in the closet scene that she 'assume a virtue if you have it not'. On the one hand, there was the standard Christian denunciation of hypocrisy and on the other legislation which penalized non-attendance at state churches by religious dissenters.

The growing respectability of actors in the eighteenth and early nineteenth centuries was closely linked to a heroic style of acting; the men and women who performed the great roles of Shakespeare were increasingly seen as being in some sense participants in the virtue they represented. The idea arose that the actor might have insights into true nobility; one has only to look at the ways in which actors like Kean, Kemble and Mrs Siddons were painted by portrait painters to see this.

A key idea of the 1890s was that acting and pretence has its own truth – that masks are true faces because chosen and artificed. Max Beerbohm's *The Happy Hypocrite* has a roué transform himself with a flexible mask of sanctity in order to seduce a virtuous woman and be transformed by the mask into the good man he never especially aspired to be.

The comparatively slim amount of science fiction which deals with theatre and actors is entirely caught up with this complex of ideas; most notably, Robert A. Heinlein's shiftless, untrustworthy actor hero, the Great Lorenzo, in *Double Star*, replaces, after an assassination, the charismatic saintly politician he originally agreed to impersonate for a short time. In Walter M. Miller's *The Darfsteller*, the ability to enter fully into a character proves to be the one aspect of acting that cannot be replaced by robotics; in an echo of his greatest part, Miller's hero dies rather than give up his ideals.

Actors and actor-speak are handled parodically at various points in *Galaxy Quest*. When Nesmith is pursued by a rock monster, he asks Dane for advice:

Dane   Well you have to figure out what it wants… What's its motivation?

Nesmith   It's a DAMN ROCK MONSTER!!! It doesn't HAVE motivation!

Dane   That's your problem. You were never serious about the craft… (*closing his eyes*) 'I'm a rock… I just want to be a rock… Still. Peaceful. Tranquil.' … 'Oh, but what's this? Something's making noise… No, not noise, no… MOVEMENT. VIBRATIONS. Make the vibrations stop, they go straight into me like a knife!… I must CRUSH the thing that makes the vibrations…'

Nesmith   Am I crazy, or do you actually have something there?

Dane rebukes Nesmith for lack of commitment to method acting and uses it to come up with a tactic that momentarily works.

The contempt Dane feels for Nesmith originally is based on his lack of professionalism – he shows up late for engagements – and yet there is a vestige of an old camaraderie left between them: when Dane himself threatens to walk out of their convention booking, it is Nesmith who reminds him, rather than the other way around, that the show must go on.

Nesmith   You will go out there.

Dane   I won't and nothing you say-

Nesmith   'The show must go on.'

At the film's climax, when they pretend to quarrel and fight in order to distract Sarris' executioners, it is in terms of their faults as actors that they abuse each other – hamminess, scene-stealing – in a routine that works in practice because they have performed it before, in a specific and numbered episode of the show, and because the accusations they make against each other's acting are faults they both regard as moral failings.

It is when Nesmith comes to respect himself as an actor, to use routines and plot tropes he knows from the show intelligently, that he becomes heroic. At one of the film's climaxes, as he moves to attack Sarris' ship head-on in a game of space-chicken, Sarris mocks him for being an actor, and Nesmith says, 'You don't have to be a good actor to recognize a bad one.' At the crunch, he does not call Sarris a genocidal butcher, or a treacherous bully; he criticizes him in terms of the one thing he knows and knows well.

Both Nesmith and Dane have a catchphrase whose essential truth they come to appreciate. Nesmith, in his role of Taggart, constantly says 'Never give up, never surrender' – as, in the course of the film, he comes to be the hero he always pretended to be, this becomes a defining characteristic rather than merely a piece of braggadocio. He humiliates himself in front of Sarris to save Gwen and the Thermian leader Mathasar; he tricks his executioners; he stops the Protector from auto-destructing; he uses a minefield to destroy Sarris' ship; he uses the Omega 13 device when all seems lost. His defining characteristic becomes just this – he never does give up.

Dane has become entirely sick and tired of his own catchphrase, 'By Grabthar's Hammer, you shall be avenged.' He threatens to refuse to say it; he glowers at the convention's screen when a clip of him saying it is shown; he becomes testy with fans, made up with a replica of his finny-headed skull, who utter the line. When his Thermian disciple and admirer Quellek says it, he becomes most vexed. Yet when Quellek is shot down in front of him by one of Sarris' thugs, and dies telling him that he has always looked on him as a father, Dane, quietly, and without any of his usual Shakespearian histrionics, says the line over the dying alien youth and means it with all his heart.

(Significantly, one of the pieces of intelligent stylization which goes on throughout the film is that, during this sequence, when Dane becomes far more totally Lazarus than he usually is, his make-up becomes impeccable. We cannot see the join where his prosthetic skull-piece joins his head – yet a little while later, when the battle with Sarris' forces is over, it looks tacky again.)

One of the running jokes of the film is that the human Dane is perceived, faulty make-up and all, as alien by the far more alien Thermians – their human forms are, we are occasionally reminded, disguises adopted to be more like the crew of the Protector and they are in fact giant octopoids. They feed him the appropriate diet of live bugs in a dubious consommé and, in one of the deleted scenes present on the DVD, Quellek shows him his quarters, which include a spiked bed and an entirely incomprehensible toilet. Quellek, a keen devotee of the Mak'tar, the quasi-religious mental disciplines that are one of Lazarus' defining characteristics, boasts of having learned the appropriate ones to manage the bed and still to be having trouble with the toilet.

To recap this point, we have a scene here in which an alien pretending to be human aspires to the religious and sanitary arrangements of an alien of a different species who is in fact a human actor – and moreover, Quellek's comic aspirations make him a fine and noble being, whose death we experience as genuinely tragic. Of the three Thermians we come to know well as characters, Quellek is never disillusioned about the humans, Mathasar rationalizes his disillusion away – and Laliari seems to understand most of the truth from the beginning and not to care.

One of the most touching things in the film is the relationship between the almost silent Laliari and the laid-back Fred Kwan, the cast's reliable voice of pragmatism – they follow Nesmith into space when Fred reminds them that they might actually get paid for the gig – and the fictional crew's engineer, the legendary Tech-Sergeant Chen. At the point when he is not sure that he can use the ship's teleportation device to save Nesmith from the rock monster – a first attempt at retrieving a pig creature that was also attacking Nesmith having resulted in its eversion and explosion – it is the longing glances of Laliari that inspire him to succeed.

On her first appearance, Laliari's silence is explained as being the result of her communicator not working. Pressed by Nesmith to talk, she emits a series of high-pitched moans and squeaks. Subsequently, and clearly just to establish that she can speak, she has a few business-like lines and is involved in getting the crew of the Protector into space – the sudden revelation that they have been talking to a projected hologram of her is one of their first clues that these are not, in fact, fans and that Nesmith is telling the truth. Thereafter, she hardly ever speaks except with those eloquent longing glances – this is a moderately funny joke about the role of female characters in space opera.

There is a touching lubriciousness to their relationship rare in printed and media SF. Fred arrives on the Thermians' space station minutes later than the others and so never sees the Thermians as octopoids – when he and Laliari start to make out, Guy is at first anxious to undeceive him, then shocked when Laliari starts caressing Fred with her extra limbs and Fred really does not care. What might have been a slightly coarse joke about aliens in disguise – see the equivalent joke about the Martian pretending to be a hooker and seducing Martin Short's Presidential aide in *Mars Attacks* – becomes something far sweeter and more subversive – and of course remains entirely in keeping with the film's running discussion of the relationship between pretence and truth. Fred has the sense to see that Laliari is the seductive sweet female of his dreams whether she is a pretty girl or a giant octopus – he is, as I remarked above, a pragmatist. As well as an old hippy who spends the entire film apparently stoned out of his mind – Tony Shaloub is exquisite in this role.

Laliari comes to Earth with him when the other Thermians leave; we last see her as the assistant to Fred in the trailer for the new TV series. She has taken the self-effacing human name Jane Doe and is playing herself, apparently still and perpetually silent. The handling of this minor character is at once charming and subversive.

The film's other love affair plays a neat game of ambiguity between the fiction of the show and the reality of the actors' lives. It is clear from the questioning of the fans at the convention at the beginning of the film that it is a matter of controversy among them whether the show was to be interpreted as implying romance between the characters Captain Taggart and Lieutenant Madison:

Girl	Miss Demarco? … In episode 15, 'Mist of Delos 5?', I got the feeling you and the Commander kind of had a thing in the swamp when you were stranded together. Did you?
Gwen	The Commander and I NEVER had a thing.
Nesmith (O.S.)	That's her story.

It is clear from the chemistry between them that there was, at some point in the past, a relationship between Nesmith and Gwen DeMarco and that he behaved badly:

Gwen DeMarco	Self control? That's funny coming from the guy that slept with every Moon Princess and Terrakian slave girl on the show! …
Nesmith	Did it ever occur to you that if you had been a little more supportive you could have held on to me?
Gwen DeMarco	I could have held on to YOU! …

In the course of the film, they kiss when they think they are going to die; at its end, they perform a highly theatrical tango-dip embrace in front of the fans that may or may not be a renewal of their relationship.

Significantly, one of the few areas of fandom and its attitude to shows not explored in *Galaxy Quest* is slash, that branch of fan fiction which is predicated around the assumption that there is, on screen, an implied relationship, or at least unresolved sexual tension, between characters of the same sex. The obvious pairing in *Galaxy Quest* would be between Taggart and Lazarus – Laredo being far too young in the days of the show and Chen far too laid back – just as, in *Star Trek*, the ur-slash relationship was that assumed between Kirk and Spock. (The term 'slash' derives from the standard description of such fiction as Kirk/Spock or K/S with the punctuation mark coming to be short hand for the sexual relationships in such slash standards as Buffy/Willow or Angel/Wesley.)

The film is sufficiently knowing about fandom in every other respect that this has to have been a deliberate artistic decision, presumably taken because of Hollywood's reluctance to go anywhere near male homosexuality as a theme and the film's need to get nothing more restrictive than the PG rating it had. Alan Rickman plays Dane as faintly camp – in rather the same way that he plays the angel Metatron in Kevin Smith's *Dogma* – but the only even slightly flirtatious line he speaks to Nesmith, when he refers, after Nesmith has been rescued from the rock monster, to the fact Nesmith has managed to get his shirt off again, is one that could be justified absolutely as a reference to the regular shirtlessness of William Shatner's Kirk.

Obviously, *Star Trek* is not the only SF film or television referenced in *Galaxy Quest*, though it is the most obvious and most prevalent. Gwen DeMarco's character Tawny Madison can be seen as a strong reference by refusal to Sigourney Weaver's other major SF film character – Ripley in the *Alien* movies – as much as directly to Uhura in *Star Trek*. Where Ripley is buff and androgynous, Madison is pneumatically female; where Ripley is wilful and critical of authority, Madison is almost entirely limited in her role to parroting Taggart and the computer. Casting Weaver, with her past as Ripley, in the role of an Uhura equivalent is itself a fairly funny inter-textual joke.

The film makes a clear distinction between the angry unhappy Gwen DeMarco and the perpetually grinning Tawny Madison – as she and Nesmith clamber through the bowels of the Protector, Gwen DeMarco criticizes the writing of the episode which put booby-trap pistons in the ducts: 'The writer of this episode should die.' (It is not clear whether it is a joke or a happy accident that on the soundtrack Gwen says 'Screw that' about entering the tunnel, whereas her lips and online versions of the script say 'Fuck that'; this might be a joke about the compromises needed to get a 12 rating or might simply be that compromise.) Gwen is, attractively, not a good sport.

Yet, interestingly, in a scene deleted from the film's commercial release and present on the DVD, DeMarco makes use of the Tawny Madison persona when, just before she and Nesmith press the button that will save the Protector, they are confronted by two of Sarris' thugs who have chased them through the ducts. She flirts with them and flashes her cleavage at them and manoeuvres them into a position where, speaking to the computer as Tawny always does, she can have it drop a wall on them and crush them to death.

The sexual politics of this moment are complex and problematic, which is perhaps why it was cut as much as because it lengthens a suspenseful sequence – it relates very directly to the themes of persona and truth I have painted as obsessive in this movie. It is, of course, also very precisely something as entirely ruthless as anything Ripley would do, while not even slightly her style. Neil Gaiman has suggested that the tendency of the deleted scenes is to open out the focus of the film's depiction of redemption from Nesmith, who needs it most, to the other actors.

Galaxy Quest is a film with surprisingly few loose ends; almost everything that happens has a pay-off. Brandon and his friends pester Nesmith about the Protector's schematics, which leads to his losing his temper; ashamed of this unprofessionalism, he gets drunk and is hung over when the Thermians collect him in the morning. He is too tired and sleepy to notice his first journey into space and assumes that the first confrontation with Sarris is just a piece of fannish theatrics. On Nesmith's way to persuade the others to go visit the Thermians with him Brandon tries to talk to him again and they collide, exchanging Nesmith's actual interstellar communicator for Brandon's toy one – this means that later on Nesmith has a way of talking to Brandon when he needs to know how to get around the ship. It is perhaps a criticism of the plotting of other films that *Galaxy Quest* is one in which everything adds up.

Many of the details, as well as the overall themes, of the plotting are specifically parodic. The youth of Laredo at the time of the original show is a joke about the obnoxious Wesley Crusher in *Star Trek: The Next Generation*. His less than entire competence at taking the Protector out of dock is a neat reminder that, in fact, he has never done this before – yet, since the entire piloting system is based on his hand movements in the show, all he has to do to become a hotshot pilot is to watch and imitate his own old performances.

Kwan is so totally the same person as Tech-Sergeant Chen that the two entirely blend – his occasional laid-back doper remarks about the state of the engines:

Fred   Hi guys. Listen, they're telling me that the generators
            won't take it, the ship's breaking apart and all that. Just
            FYI.

are a wicked comment at the hysterics of his *Star Trek* equivalent, Scotty, but
he is hardly different when being himself:

Brandon   Mr. Kwan? In episode nineteen, when the reactor fused,
            you used an element from Leopold Six to fix the
            quantum rockets. What was that called?

Fred   Bivrakium.

Brandon   The blue sheath it was encased in – ?

Fred   A bi-thermal krevlite housing.

(*Brandon makes a note, thanks him and exits with his group*)

Guy   How do you remember this stuff?

Fred   Oh I make it up. Use lots of 'k's and 'v's.

This casualness includes opening the hatch of a lander on arrival on a new
planet on the assumption that the atmosphere will be breathable:

(*Suddenly the HATCH opens with a loud PHHHHT of air decompression.
Fred has opened it*)

Guy   What are you doing! You don't just open the door! It's
            an alien planet! Is there air!? You don't know, do you!

(*Fred sniffs the air*)

Fred   Seems okay.

It also enables him to fake brilliantly on his arrival on the Protector; asked a
difficult technical question by his Thermian admirers, he makes them find
the solution for themselves by the Socratic method and convinces them even
more totally of his brilliance. He is perhaps at his sweetest and funniest when

he transports the rock monster into the middle of a group of Sarris' thugs and says with a sigh, 'It's the simple things in life you treasure.'

Both of the film's McGuffins – the blue button that will stop the countdown to auto-destruct and, far more importantly, the Omega 13 device – are, quite literally, reset buttons. It perhaps needs explaining that 'reset button' is the usual critical term for one of the default mechanisms of *Star Trek* plotting: something which, at the end of an episode, restores the status quo in its entirety so that nothing is changed and nothing is learned – one of the reasons why *Deep Space Nine* is often critically preferred to the other shows of the *Star Trek* franchise is that, partly because it has a fixed location and a strong story arc, it generally avoids this device.

Galaxy Quest has a plot in which, quite specifically, the characters grow and change – when Nesmith first learns from Brandon the fans' theory about the point of the Omega 13, he realizes that the thirteen seconds of reset it gives are just long enough to redeem a single mistake. (It is a neat touch that the Omega 13 appeared, and was not explained, in the last episode of the show ever filmed – the first half of a two-parter without a conclusion.) In the universe of this film, a reset button is a way of taking moral responsibility rather than a way of avoiding it – it is when they have pressed the blue button and it has seemed not to work (because in the show auto-destruct countdowns always end with only one second to spare), that Nesmith and Gwen DeMarco momentarily regain their lost relationship and embrace passionately.

One of the strengths of this very funny film is that it knows when not to be funny. At a couple of points – Nesmith's first view of a Saturn-like gas giant with rings and many moons and his belated realization that he is in fact in outer space; Nesmith and Gwen DeMarco's sight of the Omega 13 device during their journey through the ducts – we are given full-on sense of wonder moments in which slightly cheesy CGI is presented absolutely unapologetically and the expressions on the actors' faces do most of the work. At these few crucial points, they and we are reminded why we love this stuff.

At the beginning of the film, the presentation of the show 'Galaxy Quest', its cast and its fans is ruthlessly mocking – the show is cheesy, the actors bored and the fans far too caught up in private jokes and obsessive behaviour. Yet, as *Galaxy Quest* progresses, the film questions its own apparent cynicism. The Thermians have no cynicism or doubts, and are noble almost to the point of being too good to go on existing; the obsessed fans know or guess enough about the Protector to save lives; it is when the actors stop feeling sorry for themselves that they start being heroic.

The values of the show are, after all, however cheesy, preferable to the other world-views on offer – Sarris' cult of simplistic cynical brutality or the world-weary self-hatred of the cast. When Nesmith asks to be taken back to Earth after Sarris' defeat, Mathasar is upset – until Nesmith tells him that he is a worthy captain of the Protector:

Nesmith   What's the matter, Mathasar?

Mathasar   We were hoping you could come with us. M-my people have no commander.

Nesmith   Mathasar, I think your people have a great commander.

And yet, this attack on cynicism is not pushed too far – the Thermians go on to be heroic around the galaxy, but the cast just get their show revived. They have saved the day in extraordinary circumstances – the people they have inspired will go on living the heroism they merely perform.

4. The Decline and Fall of the Alien Invasion

One of the crucial differences between SF and fantasy is that it is possible to spot where an SF trope started, to give it a date, and it is possibly true, on the evidence, that it is possible to see where the usefulness of an SF trope ended, for good. Joanna Russ writes about what she calls the wearing out of genre materials and she has a point.

There are certain sorts of fantasy story like the deal with the devil, or certain sorts of detective story like the locked-room murder which get over-used for a while, but find a way of coming back around again, simply because elegant variations on those themes remain possible. It is not clearly the case that the same applies with at least some of the stock themes of science fiction, and of science fiction film; the evidence suggests very strongly that the tale of alien invasion has had its day and will not recur again as the subject of serious SF or SF film.

When H.G. Wells wrote *The War of the Worlds*, it was not a book that people thought of as creating the sub-genre of tales of alien invasion so much as a new and ingenious twist on an existing genre, the tale of military invasion. In the decades of paranoia which led eventually to the First World War, one of the ways in which the concerned middle classes were warned of the menace of German militarism was books like *The Battle of Dorking*, which prophesied failure by the British authorities to learn the lessons of Sadowa and Sedan and the inevitable subjugation of Britain by Germans with somewhat better weapons and vastly better strategy.

I.F. Clarke's *Voices Prophesying War* tells us more than needs outlining here about the whole genre, in which figures as different as Wodehouse, Saki and Erskine Childers all had a role. When Kipling said of the Boer War, 'It will teach us no end of a lesson/ it will do us no end of good,' he was assuming the British Empire to be a good thing which needed such lessons to remain on top. Like most of his contemporaries, he saw Germany as the major threat to a world peace that was identified with the persistence of British hegemony and saw the besetting sin of Germany as being a combination of racial pride, military caste, sexual degeneracy and intellectual arrogance – the stock German hate figure of the years leading up to and including the First World War (see, for example, the wartime novels of John Buchan, *Greenmantle* and *Mr. Standfast*) has duelling scars, silk underwear and eyeglasses.

Wells' Martians were considerably more cold and pitiless in their intellects than anyone's fantasies of the Prussian aristocracy. Critics like John Carey have pointed out just how reprehensible were Wells' views in this period – he was a racist eugenicist who assumed that 'lesser races' had to go to the wall for the greater good. Once we have accepted, however, that he did say and think these things, it needs taking on board also that he was a man of complex sympathies – see for example his later endorsement of the struggle for equality of African Americans – and that the general effect of *The War of the Worlds* is to make us question the massacres of traditional imperialism rather than to accept them as normal.

After all, if Wells' views were simply those he claimed at that time, the destruction of humanity by technologically superior Martians would be at the very least morally neutral. What he shows us, though, is the pity of it, the horror of having one's nest kicked over by some great foot. The imaginative sympathy with victimhood is part of a side of Wells considerably more sympathetic than all the pernicious nonsense about a caste of technocratic samurai that he was coming out with at the same time and for some time to come – contrary to Carey's claims, Wells changed and learned.

Moreover, the Martians' eventual fate – poisoned by Earth viruses and bacilli – is an interesting comment on the survival of the fittest as well as one which reminds us why so many of imperialism's colonies had nicknames like 'The White Man's Grave'. Like the Martians, the servants of imperialism often died, like Conrad's Kurtz, in a fever-dream of horror; one of our last sights of a Martian in *The War of the Worlds* is of a lonely tripod calling mournfully out to its dead mates. The Martians are at the same time types of all-conquering imperialism and types of doomed degeneration – they have allowed natural faculties to atrophy – but they are also, at the last, in part objects of the reader's compassion.

The War of the Worlds is a complex text, open to a number of readings. The George Pal film based on it, *The War of the Worlds* (1953), though, is rather simpler in its feel. Fifties America is smashed by a mighty war machine which happens, in this instance, to come from space, but which clearly stands for the might of Soviet Russia. The bacteria which undo them are clearly meant, as they are most certainly not in Wells, to act as stand-ins for the hand of God. The George Pal film is efficient and not hugely interesting, but, like the novel, it is actually about something. It is also, noticeably, more part of the future war genre than Wells' novel – it is a warning about unpreparedness and its terrible consequences.

The 1950s was a heyday of novels about alien invasion and it is also the decade in which three perfectly decent versions of the theme appeared in movies. Among the novels, Robert Heinlein's *The Puppet Masters*, later to be a distinctly mediocre film, had its victims of alien infiltration controlled by slugs which rode their bodies like ponies, while Eric Frank Russell's *Three to Conquer* had its alien bacilli possess a Venus expedition and be trapped by a telepath with a bad attitude. In both cases, they prove vulnerable to an Earth virus – smallpox in the latter case – but less for imaginative resonance than because this had become the default plot. The great fear of the period was that something, whether a commissar or a Venusian, could make you do what you did not want to do.

Not an invasion film at all, and from the 1960s, John Frankenheimer's *The Manchurian Candidate* (1962, from the novel by Richard Condon) is, both as novel and film, probably the best expression of this great fear and is equally rude about the Communists and the McCarthyite mirror images who turn out to be part of the same conspiracy. It also, in a very 1950s way, combines both of these with violent misogyny and fear of the mother who sits like a spider at the centre of all the webs in which Lawrence Harvey's hapless hero is stuck.

(Even by the late 1950s and early 1960s, the sinister and competent alien invader had been replaced in fiction either by the comic and loutish alien of stories by Christopher Anvil and Eric Frank Russell, whose temporary supremacy was undermined by the pranks of sly human resistance workers – the unmourned BBC sitcom about Occupied France *'Allo, 'Allo* had something of the same flavour – or by aliens so vast and incomprehensible as to hardly count as invaders at all (Tom Disch's 'The Genocides' is a good example here). Neither of these versions of alien invasion ever significantly found their way into movies.)

The classic expressions of this fear of loss of personal integrity and of being controlled by the Other in the 1950s, however, are Jack Finney's novel *The Body Snatchers* and the Don Siegel film *Invasion of the Body Snatchers* (1956) which is based on it, but feels rather different. The difference comes from their preoccupations – Finney was concerned with suburban conformism and Siegel with Communist take-over – but the mechanism whereby the themes are expressed remains constant – alien pods which hatch exact duplicates, and suck the solid reality, of their victims. The Siegel film ends with one of the classic expressions of that period's paranoia; the phrase 'Watch the skies' was already relevant to an age of massive bombers and would become more so when the Russians put Sputnik into orbit.

The later versions of the film – Philip Kaufman's (1978) and Abel Ferrara's (1994) – go, in a sense, back to the novel in that their preoccupation is with conformism; in one of the most original and terrifying scenes in the Kaufman, one of the hero's friends speculates that perhaps it is better to have your identity and memory carried on by a pod person who knows nothing of your existential angst. In the 1970s, at least, it was possible to consider that zombies have it better. There is also, in the Kaufman film, that wonderful silent scream that the pod people give out when they spot an unaltered intruder.

Less well known than either Pal's *War of the Worlds* or Siegel's *Invasion of the Body Snatchers* is the film adapted from the second of the Nigel Kneale *Quatermass* serials for BBC television. Val Guest's *Quatermass 2* (1957), with its aliens living in high-pressure domes and its human quislings, has a peculiarly nightmare quality simply because of its sense that this is what alien invasion would be like – the aliens would find those who consider serving them a convenient way to prosper and the murder of their fellow humans an acceptable way to proceed. It is very much a product of the Second World War, both in this and in its sense of the capacity of ordinary decent people to resist – there is something very liberating in the sight of its jackbooted security guards knocked over like ninepins by a bunch of country-folk with pitchforks and a vague reminiscence of wartime films like Cavalcanti's *Went the Day Well?* Again, the reason why this is a good film is that it is about something and the thing it is about is something that matters – the question of whether Englishness is to be traditional values or the inauthenticity of grey-suited bureaucrats and their masters.

There is a huge gap in the history of invasion movies in the 1970s and 1980s and one of the reasons for this is the existence of two related cycles. The first of these we may as well call the Alien Visitor film in which the alien is benevolent and the only threat is human incomprehension of this fact. The aliens in Steven

Spielberg's *Close Encounters of the Third Kind* (1977) are standard UFO 'grays'[1] with the trickster material left intact but anything unpleasant taken out, so that we have the imposition of strange mental compulsions on the human characters, notably the one played by Richard Dreyfus, but no anal probes, say. All of this cycle take on pretty much unaltered the beliefs of ufologists in aliens that are frailer and better than us, who will save us from our worst selves.

They are redemptive children, in other words, and linked thematically to all the other children in the Spielberg canon – from the boy robot David in *A.I.* (2001) to the children and childish adults in need of child-likeness of *Hook* (1991) and the girl in the red coat in *Schindler's List* (1993), who is one of the two spots of colour in the film but can change nothing around her. (The other coloured image – paradoxically – is the candle flames at the covert Seder, another example of innocence which can, in this film, redeem nothing.)

The eponymous heroes of John Carpenter's *Starman* (1984) and Spielberg's *ET* (1982) are entire innocents, who appear and affect the lives of those to whom they appear for the better and are persecuted by the agencies of the state and go away again. Thomas Jerome Newton in Nicholas Roeg's *The Man Who Fell to Earth* (1976) is another such case; even if his morality ends up considerably more compromised in his dealings with humanity, the emphasis on the pain he goes through to pass makes up for it. They are secular Christ figures who work miracles and undergo persecution; they are also saintly hippies threatened by the straight world – there is a sense in which all of the revisionist alien movies of the 1970s and 1980s are a rerun of the 1960s round of the culture wars in American society.

The other cycle, more complexly at odds with the Alien Invasion film, is the Malevolent Alien Visitor cycle. There is never any question of the aliens in John McTiernan's *Predator* (1987) and its sequel, Stephen Hopkins' *Predator 2* (1990) sticking around long enough to qualify as an invasion; Earth is a place where they come to hunt and that is that. They are in a sense comprehensible, because their interaction with humanity is on the basis of a few very simple motivations – they are hunters and they have a shame culture which regards heroism as admirable even in a prey who makes the hunt costly. And that is that – a tussle with Arnold Schwarzenegger and a few skulls are pretty much what they came for in the first film, and finding among the teeming millions

1. People who claim to have undergone alien encounters describe various sorts of alien, of which the most common are the large-eyed, large-foreheaded, bald, grey-skinned beings known as 'grays'. These are usually described in the literature as benevolent, but are also prone to be the ones responsible for abductions, impregnations and alien probes. The famous faked filmed autopsy of an alien involves a gray.

of a city an adversary – a tough honourable cop – whom they can respect in the second.

Somewhere between the Malevolent Alien Visitor and the full-blown Invasion motif is the single alien which, if allowed to breed, will infest the Earth and humanity by corruption. Because there is no sense of such aliens as a version of society, there is an area of distinction between this and the Body Snatchers motif – these aliens are always monsters, of which the best example is probably John Carpenter's *The Thing* (1982). Films in which they occur make extensive use of SF tropes but are most naturally regarded as horror films because, with one or two exceptions, the plot structures are simply mappable as moving towards the defeat of the interloping evil.

Paradoxically, *The Thing* is at once the key film of this sub-genre and a major exception to many of its expectations. The Thing is a defrosted alien visitor which eats and copies any life form it can which, in the context of the Antarctic bases it infests, means dogs and humans. Its abilities and malevolence exist in every cell of its being – which is why the blood of those it has copied will flee from a hot needle revealing its presence – and in danger it will split into many parts each of which is potentially lethal. In one instance, the head of one of the possessed detaches itself, uses its tongue to pull itself to safety and then sprouts spider legs – 'You have got to be fucking joking' says one of the doomed spectators. The film is a product of one of the first waves of serious special effects and the endless rococo mutations and recombinations of the Thing as it absorbs more victims and finds more ways of being lethal is the aspect of the film which has dated worst – there is nothing as faded as last year's special effect.

This obsession with the grotesque, with sensation at the expense of logic, is what makes *The Thing* a prickly hybrid of SF and horror; it only opts for SF in its grandly bleak ending, where the two human survivors wait for death in the cold, each unsure whether either of them is still human. One of the most disturbing aspects of the plot is this sense of an inability even to trust yourself – the doctor, who is one of the first of the group to understand the implications of their situation and destroys their radio and transport, may already by this point be unconsciously the Thing.

Like Howard Hawks' *The Thing From Another World* (1951), Carpenter's *The Thing* is based on 'Who goes there?', a John W. Campbell short story. The business with the blood and hot wire – alien cells have independent motive for self-preservation – is taken from that story, and is a pretty standard piece of Campbellian problem solving – the difference is that in the Carpenter film, it does not help all that much. On the other hand, the bleak solution – the survivors allow themselves to freeze to death in order to be sure that the monster cannot survive – has a grim logic of which the Campbell of the 1950s, who published Tom Godwin's 'The Cold Equations' would have approved. (In the Godwin story, a young female stowaway is jettisoned by a mercy mission whose success her extra weight jeopardizes.)

What also makes *The Thing* a Campbellian film is the performance in it of Kurt Russell as the single necessary competent man who will ensure the alien's defeat. He is, specifically, not an intellectual and his efforts are counterpointed by those of the camp doctor. He is the man who knows he can trust himself – which ought not to work and ought to be less interesting than an entirely subverted heroism that can never be trusted; Russell, however, brings a rugged minor star's stardom to the mix and we are left swallowing the consoling myth that there are people who can trust themselves.

In *The Thing's* various imitators, of which the two *Species* films, Ronald Donaldson's *Species* (1995) and Peter Medak's *Species 2* (1998) are probably the least unimportant, the money shot is always the one where the apparently human reveals itself as grotesquely other. Natasha Henstridge, as the girl built from an alien construction kit, suddenly turns into a giant cocoon which devours those who go near it, or into something a lot more unprepossessing still. (Like the alien in the *Alien* films, her metamorphosis is designed by the Swiss artist H.R. Giger.) This motif of being devoured is almost always quasi-sexual in feel – jaws open wider than jaws can ever open and pull the victim into a fatal penetration. The *Alien* movies are an influence here rather than a part of the cycle – even the weakest of the quartet is about far more than that. The essential thing about the Malevolent Visitor or Alien Infestation movie is that they are never about anything except sensation and dread.

None of these deals with a full-blown military invasion, though – partly, of course, because even filmed invasions are costly to mount. Of the three important invasion films of the late 1990s and the early twenty-first century, the least repellent is Tim Burton's *Mars Attacks* (1996) because it may not be about anything, but at least has a grisly sense of humour. It is one of those comedies where it does not matter whether any particular joke works or not, because another one will be along in a minute – its CGI aliens are knockabout demons out of cartoons, spiritual kin to *The Simpsons'* bloodthirsty Itchy and Scratchy.

At their best, the cruel jokes are good cruel jokes: an old lady watching the television oblivious while Martians creep up on her with a huge spherical ray-gun only to find themselves annihilated by her country music. Jack Nicholson's glad-handing President alludes to Rodney King's famous press conference speech with its folksy idealistic eloquence, taking the hand of the Martian leader just before that hand separates from the Martian's body and turns into a spiky creature that runs over his body, stabs him in the back and becomes a flagpole announcing Martian victory.

The Martians are evil sexless children – their weapons look like toys and it is significant that the first humans to make effective retaliatory use of them are two boys who have spent far too much time playing arcade shoot-'em-ups. Their pie-tin-like ships are an effective joke about the use of CGI in films – no expense has been spared to make them look as fake as possible, especially in the various sequences when the ships dance around in geometric patterns. Their massacres are always pranks as well – a saucer chops down the Washington monument and then nudges it repeatedly in order to aim it properly at fleeing Boy Scouts.

Most of the human beings are in dysfunctional relationships – Natalie Portman's Taffy cannot stand living in the White House and the effect it has had on her parents, the President and First Lady, yet loves the chance to tell Rod Steiger's general to keep the noise down when he starts ranting outside her bedroom door. The film's eventual hero, Richie, is largely rejected by his redneck family for having long hair and not being a marine like his brother, who dies trying to surrender. Even the salt-of-the-earth black couple played by Jim Brown and Pam Grier are divorced and only reunited in the ruins of Washington at the end.

Part of the movie's occasional charm comes from its touches of innocence – at the end, Richie (Luke Haas) and his grandmother are decorated in the ruins of Washington by the dead president's teenage daughter – as well as its deep cheesiness: the Martians are vulnerable not to bacilli, but to broadcasts of Slim Whitman, singing his version of the 'Indian Love Call', which makes their vast naked brains explode. It would have been rather more logical, given Tom Jones' presence in the film, if his singing had been the Martians' fatal weakness, but perhaps this was not allowed by his management.

One of its strengths is the way its random surreal humour touches some of the time on genuine anxieties of a year or so later – the opening shot of a herd of burning cows is something that no one who was in Britain during the foot and mouth epidemic can watch in quite the same way. It is also odd that much of the time it feels like a parody of Roland Emmerich's *Independence Day*, which was released later in the same year; a substantially final script of 'Mars Attacks' was around for some years before the film was made so there cannot have been any influence. Ultimately, though, it is very minor Tim Burton – that rare thing, an idea of his which sounds better as an idea than it did on the screen.

One of its jokes is peculiarly apposite to the other major invasion films of its period – it picks up on the extent to which they were both going to be about homosexual and other male panics and has one of its grotesque Martians disguised as a silent hooker seduce its way into the White House with the help of Martin Short's concupiscent aide. The reason it fails is that it is distracted from murdering the President and his wife by pausing to blast a pet bird – one of the Martians' weaknesses turns out to be an unreasoning hostility to flying creatures.

This is also a film in which the era's James Bond, Pierce Brosnan, is symbolically and literally castrated by transformation into a bodiless head. There is a warped romanticism to his relationship with Sarah Jessica Parker's fashion reporter Natalie, whose head has been grafted onto the body of her chihuahua – in a bizarre and tasteless, yet touching, moment, their severed heads manage to roll together for a final kiss as the Martian flagship sinks. Earlier, her husband Jason (Michael J. Fox) crawls through the first massacre to die with her only to be annihilated at the last minute and leave her clutching at his severed hand; romanticism is at once punctured and endorsed throughout this sweet and sour film.

The Martians are defeated not by germs and not by military might, but by cheap country music and by the sorts of people who listen to it – the Burton film both endorses and parodies a sort of populism that is uncomplicatedly present in *Independence Day* and Lawrence Kasdan's *Dreamcatcher* (2003). It is, after all, the fancy people whom the Martians especially kill and humiliate – Brosnan's character is a pretentious pipe-smoking English smoothy. All the attempts to communicate with the Martians are exploited by them as occasions for more mayhem. Brosnan argues that the release of a symbolic dove may have provoked the massacre of first contact, but a visit by the Martians to Congress turns into more mass murder.

Yet there is no simple denunciation of pacifism here; Annette Benning's reformed drunk sees the coming of the Martians as hope for the planet and lives to discover otherwise to comic drunken disillusion. Her values are nonetheless quasi-endorsed by the film's ending, as she and Tom Jones bond with animal life at Lake Tahoe and he sings 'It's Not Unusual' – she is a twerp but she is shown as being onto something. Earlier, animals have reacted to the Martians with instant hostility – the head of Natalie's chihuahua is last seen using her body to strangle Martians – and their return as if from a hard winter clearly represents a natural wisdom.

The film's cheerful nihilism extends to the hawks as well as the doves – a belated attempt to annihilate the Martians with nuclear weapons is absorbed by their defences and turned into a whiff of smoke that their leader inhales. Rod Steiger's hawkish general is repeatedly ignored by his President and then miniaturized and stepped on by the Martian leader. Richie's family make a lot of noise about fighting to the death – his parents are busy loading shotguns as he leaves them to rescue his grandmother and boast that the Martians will never get their television – yet their trailer is simply picked up, wrecked and discarded by a vast Martian machine without any ado.

Many of the minor parts – Pam Grier's Washington bus driver, Jim Brown's heavyweight turned casino greeter – are played by iconic figures who survive because their stock roles are of survivors. We know, on the other hand, that other stock figures like Danny De Vito's craven lawyer, Jack Black's marine and Joe Don Baker, his redneck father, will die because that is what such characters played by those actors usually do – there is a joke here about standard expectations, but not a very effective one.

The fact that much of this material crops up again in *Independence Day*, only without having any fun poked at it whatever, is a significant part of the problem with that film – *Independence Day*'s opening with an alien looming sinisterly over the US flag left on the Moon is unintentionally almost as funny as anything in the Burton film. We get the conflict of hawks and doves, the populism, aliens dedicated to pop-eyed malice and an unparodic sentimentality at the film's close. The stock material *Mars Attacks* mocks is here presented utterly without irony.

Jeff Goldblum's computer expert is educated in being less of a fancy pants by his elderly father and by Will Smith's pilot. It is significant that, in both cases, they get their authenticity from performed ethnicity, Jewish or black – the agenda of reactionary films had at least moved on in this respect. Randy Quaid's deranged victim of alien abduction saves the day at the end, and is explicitly a good ol' boy, albeit one with multicultural pretensions.

Will Smith's stripper wife fails to save the life of the President's wife but brings her to him so that she can die in his arms – again, the dying woman's social pretensions are stepped on when she has a moment of unease about the fact that her rescuer used to be a stripper. One of the most profoundly rabble-rousing moments comes when the President himself insists on leading the fighter assault on the nearest alien ship – he renounces the idea of special privilege for himself.

There are some complicated ironies here in retrospect. The populism of this film, and the populism both participated in and mocked by *Mars Attacks*, were part of the cultural phenomena that led to the emergence of George W. Bush as President. Drinking beer and choking on pretzels in front of television sports broadcasts, the millionaire preppy president always portrays himself as a man of the people, claiming that critical journalists are part of 'an elite'. In the crisis of September 11th, he let his sense of duty to the continuance of his office stand in the way of any premature gallantry, and took his time about visiting the New York or Washington sites of atrocity. The President of *Independence Day* is, after all, a fictional character.

As in *Mars Attacks*, but without a shred of irony, the peacemongers are doomed – a group of hippies waving peace signs at the ship which hovers over a New York skyscraper are the first to be annihilated when the countdown ends and the massacre begins. Where Brosnan's smooth expert is at least allowed to put the case for advanced aliens being friendly, there is never any question in *Independence Day* but that anyone who expects benevolence is a fool. It is almost as if massacring peaceniks is a positive act even when performed by aliens.

There are, of course, some very nice touches in *Independence Day* – the aliens are here not to rape or devour but merely to pillage; they are a fleet of star travellers who strip-mine any world they come across and lack all empathy for other intelligent life. Goldblum's realization that the message everyone is trying to decode is not for us – that it is a countdown to a synchronized attack – is a neat reversal of the Search for Extraterrestrial Intelligence (SETI) cliché. It is not, of course, an especially original one – most films about the translation of alien messages have always suggested that those messages were a delusion and a snare, that anything they suggested we build would probably be a dangerous devourer, as in *Species*.

This is explicitly an anti-revisionist film about aliens. Will Smith's bellicose jokes mock the entire idea of communication and friendship as presented in Spielberg's *ET*. A group of hippy liberals who think they are going to be taken up into a mothership in the style of Spielberg's *Close Encounters* are among the first to be vaporized when the aliens attack major landmarks. The aliens are presented as absolutely evil – when one of them manages to communicate via Brent Spiner's dying scientist, its message is of absolute hatred.

Like Wells' and Pal's Martians, they are individually effete – Will Smith manages to capture one by punching it out – and dependent on superior firepower. One of the film's climaxes – the trickery whereby Goldblum and Smith enter the alien mothership in a drone captured as a result of the Roswell crash and trick its computers into accepting a computer virus – is clearly an attempt at an update of the comeuppance of Wells' Martians at the cilia of bacteria. As such, it lacks even the default resonance of the smallpox in Russell's *Three to Conquer*: it is a default, but Emmerich has no idea how to make it work.

The entire witlessness of a climax which depends on the entire unlikeliness of alien computers into which you can straightforwardly tap with your laptop cannot be overstated. The ending of the film makes little sense come to that, since what the human victory has actually done is either to commit pre-emptive genocide or to maroon vast numbers of deeply hostile aliens on earth with no immediate way of leaving it (the crashes of the alien battlecruisers are not presented in a way that implies no survivors). Nor is it made especially clear how the aliens know which monuments to destroy in an attempt to break Earth's spirit: they flame the White House because it makes for a spectacular shot, not because it makes especial sense that they do so.

The film is not concerned with logic or even with the systematic presentation of populist themes so much as with a complex of anxieties around homosexual panic and a homosociality inoculated against eroticism. Both Will Smith and Jeff Goldblum's characters have friends who die as part of their education in doing the right thing; Goldblum's friend, played by Harvey Fierstein, is explicitly gay and something of a sissy, whereas Smith's friend is a fellow pilot who jokes around their relationship as sexually ambiguous. With these friends prophylactically dead, Smith and Goldblum can bond safely with each other and engage in a ritual of victory over the aliens that involves the lighting of huge cigars. Sometimes a cigar is just a cigar, but not, we feel, here.

Randy Quaid's character has been abducted by alien visitors and subjected to indignities which appear to have included the famous anal probe – when he mentions his experiences to his fellow townsfolk whom he is trying to encourage to take the invasion seriously, they mock him with this. His experiences have left him a drunken wreck – clearly, in this version of reality, penetration is the one thing which can entirely destroy a man. At the climax of the film, he destroys the alien battlecruiser that is attacking the Roswell base and is about to unleash its disintegrator weapon by, with a shout of 'Hallo Boys, I'm back!', flying his jet straight into the weapon, which is housed, behind a large mechanical sphincter, in the bottom of the ship. His revenge is to return unwelcome destructive penetration in kind – there is something particularly unwholesome about the way the film's climax combines this motif with standard all-American triumphalism.

There is a pattern in the films of Roland Emmerich of malevolent or threatening homosexuality contrasted with overtly redeemed but actually erotic homosociality. In *Stargate* (1994), we have the menacing alien overlord that unmasks as the disturbingly beautiful and androgynous Jay Davidson – previously known for playing a trans character in Neil Jordan's *The Crying Game* (1992) – contrasted with the pure love between Kurt Russell's officer and a peasant boy whom he adopts as a replacement for his dead son. In *The Patriot* (2000), Jason Isaacs' effete British officer is contrasted with the pure fellowship of the American rebels, at one point echoing, in a tableau of hero in *pietà* pose with dead companion and a flag waved behind them, a notorious scene from the Nazi film, Schenzinger's *Hitlerjunge Quex* (1933). His work hit a major American nerve, but not in a good way.

At the time of writing, the most recent, and spectacularly the worst, of the alien invasion cycle is Lawrence Kasdan's *Dreamcatcher*, adapted by Kasdan and William Goldman from one of Stephen King's weakest novels. King wrote it when recovering from a traffic accident which almost killed him – it is hard to see what Kasdan and Goldman's excuse is, particularly given Goldman's prior record as an adaptor of King. 'The Body' is one of King's best and most personal short stories, and Goldman's script for Rob Reiner's *Stand by Me* (1986) is that rare thing, an adaptation better than a good original. His adaptation of King's *Misery* is hardly inferior.

Dreamcatcher usefully combines almost all the motifs I have discussed above and demonstrates how little mileage any of them any longer have. In the mentally handicapped Duddits, who proves to be a good alien biding his time to ensure the defeat of the bad aliens, we have a classic example of the alien Christ-figure, despised and rejected of men, who is the best self of the four boys who save him from abuse, and to whom he gives psychic powers – telepathy, precognition, direction, an ability to find lost things – which help defeat the other aliens.

The alien invaders are at the same time a force who come in deceiving peace and an infestation, a fungal growth which bursts from the anus of the afflicted as a giant shit-smeared worm with very sharp teeth. They are figures of sexual anxiety – one of the four friends, Beaver, trapped in the area of infestation when out hunting, loses fingers and then most of his face to one of these things, while another of his companions, Pete, is actually castrated. Rarely has the combination of sexual anxiety and alien attack been so entirely combined.

Another of the group, Jones (Damien Lewis), is a clairvoyant who earlier narrowly escaped death in a traffic accident to which he was mysteriously summoned by Duddits' astral body; somehow his near death has rendered him partially immune to the infestation's standard form – the so-called shit-weasels. Instead, he finds himself possessed, body and to a large extent soul, by an alien mentality.

This is actually one of the more intelligent aspects of Kings' book – where there are some interesting reflections that the alien may not be intelligent at all, that the thing which possesses Jones is a construct of his own mind triggered by a physical infestation – but the film discards this grace note entirely. Instead, we have a mind that talks, both to the Jones trapped within and to the outside world, in a whiny and insinuating cod British accent of a sort that many American viewers would regard as a priori evidence of faggotry. The only redeeming features of this story arc are the scenes in which, locked inside his own metaphorical sense of his memory, Jones runs around with trolleys removing files that the alien might use to his own secret chamber

– this is probably the only representation of a Memory Palace in film and as such is worth cherishing.[1]

The objective of the pseudo-Jones is to take the body of an infected dog to a reservoir and ensure the insertion of the small worms that form a part of the alien life cycle into the drinking supply of Greater Boston – much of King's work is built round the repetition of telling catch-phrases and here the key phrase, more in clear than usual, is 'one worm to infect the world'. In inadvertent alliance with it is Curtis (Morgan Freeman), a general burned out by decades of such struggle and with the habit of extremes of brutality; he is, unlike one of his formerly trusted subordinates, Underhill (Tom Sizemore), unprepared to trust Jones' best friend Devlin and the saintly Duddits whom they have collected along the way. There is a distinctly odd edge to Curtis' relationship with Underhill – he seems at the climax to be acting from an almost sexual jealousy and sense of betrayal.

The film is incoherent, while trying to be merely nuanced, in its treatment of the hawks versus doves debate. Versions of the invaders that resemble the grays of UFO mythology mouth slogans of peace and are comprehensively blasted by helicopter gunships, some of which fall victim to the alien craft when it dissolves into gouts of red fungus. Utter vengeful ruthlessness is the order of the day whenever Curtis is involved and this is shown as neither wholly useful or wholly to be condemned until the film's climax where his pursuit of Underhill nearly costs the planet the chance finally to defeat the alien invader.

There are other equally banal uses to which the invasion movie can be put, of course. M. Night Shyamalan's *Signs* (2002), which for much of its length is memorably creepy, descends into bathos at the end by making the point, for the characters, of the alien invasion and its defeat being that it justifies the incomprehensible workings of a non-denominational Providence. As the film opens, Mel Gibson's preacher has lost his faith after the death of his wife in a hideous car crash, and he lives on a remote farm with his children and his brother (Joaquin Phoenix), a failed baseball player. Something is out there in the corn fields and is making crop circles – and while it remains content to do so, and simply taunt the dwellers in the house, the film has much to recommend it. Gibson is admirable as he becomes progressively unbalanced

1. As the intellectual historian Frances Yates explains in *The Art of Memory* (1966), the mnemonic techniques practiced in classical times were refined by the neo-classicists of the Renaissance. Vast chunks of text and data could be remembered by attaching each item to an associated object, such objects being arranged in a classical theatre or a Palladian palace.

in his solicitude for his children and as they retreat further and further into the recesses of the house; there is genuine suspense here and a sense of a world coming unhinged represented by this family as a microcosm.

However, this is a plot ruined by a sudden outbreak of explicitness in which the creature in the cornfield is just one of an entire alien invasion. It suddenly invades the house and everything comes together – one child's asthma, the other's obsessive-compulsive collection of glasses of water, the habit of swinging out at any ball which wrecked the brother's career, the dying words of the preacher's dead wife – all of these come together and help them defeat the alien housebreaker. Similar things have happened all over the world. And Mel Gibson's preacher puts his clerical collar back on and rediscovers his vocation because everything is for the best in this most providential of worlds.

Setting aside the question of why aliens who are allergic to fresh water would bother inhabiting a planet as watery as Earth, and why creatures capable of travelling interstellar distances think it a profitable use of their time to terrorize individuals, we end up here with a strong sense that the only person involved in the entire proceedings who believed in any of this was Gibson himself, a man of strong religious faith. The problem is, I think, that everything ties up – that each family member has a tic and each of those tics is shoe-horned into relevance when they need to defeat the alien intruder. And the tics are arbitrary.

A trope which at the beginning of the century was a way of discussing colonialism and racism had become by mid century a way of discussing the cold war, American spy paranoia and the fear of a levelling mass culture. At the century's end, its discourse had come to deal almost entirely with a purely personal autonomy and specifically with embattled heteronormative masculinity. Women are almost entirely absent from *Dreamcatcher* and those present in *Independence Day* have no role at all in the struggle with the asexual aliens. If there is a better example of the wearing out of genre materials and their reduction to lazy clichés – the alien as bogeyman or bugger or challenge to faith – it is hard to know what it is.

5. Comedy 2

Small Soldiers
and the Joke of the Robot

Most of the time, comic SF films are, like Mel Brooks' *Spaceballs* (1986), parodies of other SF films. This is not a problem in and of itself, but often comic writers' dislike of pomposity and pretension means that they never get over the idea that this material is intrinsically ludicrous and therefore automatically funny. While there is a lot of material in the George Lucas *Star Wars* films worthy of parody, *Spaceballs* is generally crude in its comic appropriations; a good parody of *Star Wars* would understand what is loopily magnificent in the franchise as well as what is hopelessly crass.

With one or two exceptions, comic SF films rarely have anything terribly interesting to say past the jokes. Ideally, comic SF should be just as smart as any other SF; its gags and farcical situations should be ways of looking at the basic questions with which SF has always been obsessed. The fact that it is also in the business of making us laugh should not prevent its making us think. *Galaxy Quest* is a rare example of a parodic SF film that is full of ideas.

Even the most parodic of magazine SF stories, Harry Harrison's 'Bill the Galactic Hero' for example, is intelligent in its choice of things to make jokes about; Harrison is not only lampooning Heinlein's *Starship Troopers* but actually doing so far more thoughtfully than Paul Verhoeven in his film of the novel. For example, Verhoeven gets suckered into the novel's sentimental mentoring theme; Harrison mocks the overacting brutality of the training sergeant mercilessly – 'Some of you will hear stories, wicked lying stories, about how a recruit displeased me and how I killed and ate him. Those stories are true' – and shows the man as essentially a fraud: Bill later removes his trademark tusks as insignia for his own promotion to the role of recruiting sergeant.

Harrison is committed to the anti-militarism that is for Verhoeven far more a posture. When, in a late scene, a tiny alien crawls out of the human disguise in which it has been masquerading as one of Bill's comrades and grills him about why humans fight, until it is eaten by a snake, the intelligence of the comedy that has gone before has earned Harrison the moral authority to make the point.

It is interesting that so much of the most brilliant comic SF has dealt with robots, perhaps because the questions that robots provoke are so complex. Henri Bergson suggests that one of the sources of the comic is watching people behave as if they were automata. Much of the comedy of types, Ben Jonson's plays for example, assumes that individuals are trapped in sets of behaviour by their inherent psychological quirks, and *The Alchemist* is funny whether one regards these compulsive behaviours as the manifestation of ill-balanced humours, as neuroses or as programming. One of the standard jokes of SF is the extent to which automata behave as if they were people; one of its standard moments of unease is the point where humans and automata become indistinguishable.

One of the major sources of conservative social comedy is the inadequate match between aspiration and achievement – Monsieur Jourdain in *Le Bourgeois Gentilhomme* or Mrs Malaprop in *The School for Scandal* will never be all that they wish to be and are funny in their attempts; similarly, robots that try and fail to be human are at the same time comic and pathetic. The reason why, in the *Star Wars* movies, C3PO is funny and R2D2 is not is that the smaller less flighty robot is content to be a machine whereas his partner is programmed to be a sissy, not only not a man, but worse (in terms of the implicit heteronormative ideology of Hollywood) an imperfect one.

Several of the Isaac Asimov robot stories are comedies of one kind or another as well as puzzles. In 'Reason', his standard pair of troubleshooters find themselves having to cope with a robot that has logically deduced a religion in which it is the prophet of the most important thing it knows, the atomic pile which powers the remote station where they are trapped with it. There is a dark edge to the comedy here, because the machine's delusions stand to kill the human heroes and to destroy it as well. Asimov resolves the question in a neat reversal which raises important questions about religion: the robot follows correct procedure in an emergency not because it understands the danger it is in, but because it has faith that following procedures handed to it as revelation is the correct thing to do. At the time of writing, it remains to be seen how this material gets handled in the forthcoming *I, Robot*, which appears to be very loosely based on these stories.

From rather later in Asimov's career – he did most of his best and most original work when young and before developing his very public career as scientific popularizer – came the story 'The Bicentennial Man', later expanded into a novel. Its sentimental plot (a robot servant gradually transforms himself into a human philanthropist) became a sentimental vehicle for Robin Williams; the comedy here, such as it is, is mawkish.

As with aliens, part of the comic potential of robots comes from their capacity to be wiser and truer than they can know. In Philip K. Dick's underrated *Clans of the Alphane Moon*, for example, in which an off-Earth mental hospital has become a society whose social hierarchy ranks various kinds of insanity, the voice of common sense is a robot taxi-cab. In Alfred Bester's *The Stars My Destination*, the anti-hero Gully Foyle is, at a crucial juncture, influenced back towards sanity by the random optimism of a radiation-damaged robot butler. Robots are the naive observers who see clearly because they are without preconceptions; in this respect, they are a version of the child or the foreigner.

Robots, no matter how intelligent, are made things designed to be of use – their complicated relationship with humanity depends on how they mirror the fact that humans are social beings who have to find a utility for themselves. In Henry Kuttner's *Proud Robot*, for example, the drunken maverick engineer hero designs a robot when blacked out and spends most of the story discovering all the additional features which, along with a highly obnoxious ego, he built into a machine whose use he cannot remember. Brilliant and artistically gifted the robot may be – in the end, he realizes, he built it to open bottles. The fact that the particular bottles he designed it to open were the last of a brand is just an additional irony – and reflects his own redundancy in a world of reliable sober yes-men.

Robots accordingly often belong as a source of instruction in stories about coming-of-age, in which young men and women have to create an identity for themselves; like the centaur, who has wisdom because he is at the same time animal and man, and thus exists at a threshold between states, robots, particularly robots who have to some degree transcended their purely programmed origins, are accordingly often wise. It is the two robots as much as his more obvious mentor Obi Wan Kenobi who are appropriate companions to the future hero Luke Skywalker because they teach him patience and compassion; C3PO was earlier, of course, the property of Luke's father Anakin, the future Darth Vader, and Anakin's neglect of his creation is one of the first overt clues of the moral decline we know is coming. This role of mentor is particularly important in the film discussed below.

It is remarkable how little Joe Dante's 1998 comedy *Small Soldiers* has figured in recent accounts of these tropes. Part of the issue is that it is pitched at a young audience and deals in the comedy of smart young people at the brink of adolescence solving problems for adults too trapped in their own concerns to deal with what is really important until it becomes an emergency. Part too is the problem that some of its concerns overlap with those of the *Toy Story* movies, where the intelligence and socialization of toys is a fantastic given rather than rationalized back-story. And part is the knee-jerk recursiveness which is Dante's own inherent psychological trait – often very amusing if you are in on the jokes, but in this instance secondary to the film's major comedic concerns.

It is probably also the case that the fact that the robots in this film are toys, and only a few inches high, has stopped a lot of people thinking of them as robots and as part of the ongoing discourse about robots in SF. Somehow toys have never acquired the symbolic resonance of games – toys are childish things to be put away, while games are part of the default understanding of conflict and intelligence. Yet toys are the companions of childhood, the things which instruct us in love and caring; they are also the tokens with which we learn to build and manipulate, and to make sacrifices in order to acquire or dominate.

Rebellious prankster Alan Abernathy, a boy at the brink of adolescence, acquires two sets of action figures. His father runs a failing small-town toy-store and will not carry military toys as a matter of principle, and Alan, left in charge, wangles a consignment in the hope of presenting his father with sales and a fait accompli. The toys are respectively a troop of butch patriotic Commandos and their mortal enemies, the Gorgonites, variously grotesque aliens. What Alan does not know – and the adults do not fully understand the consequences of – is that the foot-high action figures contain experimental military technology, that they are for all practical purposes autonomous and intelligent.

This is in part a film about unintended consequences leading to disaster; in this it echoes Dante's earlier films *Gremlins* (1984) and *Gremlins 2* (1990), in which a harmless pet produces, and helps destroy, demonic gargoyle offspring. It is a version of the Frankenstein story, not least because the two toymakers who have created the Commandos and the Gorgonites are trapped in the final siege along with the parents of the two principals. Significantly, it is the monstrous Gorgonites who acknowledge them as their makers while the can-do spirit of the Commandos recognizes no such piety or hierarchy.

There is a distinction between the type of intelligence the two groups possess. Chip Hazard and his fellow Commandos are skilled fighters, and brilliant improvisers of military technology, but their programming limits them – they are incapable of change or growth save within rigid parameters. In no great time, they become a menace, defining as their enemy not only the

Gorgonites, but anyone who helps the Gorgonites and ultimately anyone who is not a toy commando. At the film's climax, they are ready to execute all the humans who have fallen into their power – no First Law of Robotics here. And what better name for a potentially lethal robot could there be than Chip Hazard? They are Alan's adversaries – and share his capacity for inventive use of casually found resources for mischief.

The Gorgonites, by contrast, have been given the capacity to learn and grow. Programmed to lose and to hide in dark places, they eventually overcome their conditioned fear and attempt to help Alan in his struggle to save them and his parents. Aware from Alan of the existence of things they are not equipped to feel – like the wind – they move on to a more general perception that 'You don't have to see it to know it's there' and depart on a quixotic search for the homeland Alan tells them is fictitious.

This capacity for quasi-religious faith is touching and almost mawkish – it is odd how in Dante's films it is almost impossible to distinguish between sentimental and cynical conclusions – but it is clearly hugely preferable to the fanaticism into which the Commandos grow. The Commandos are more competent but the Gorgonites are more creative and poetic – one of the charms of the film is that for once the side we feel emotional sympathy for is the one that wins. They are also the side that teaches Alan the lessons he needs to know – lessons to do with loyalty and love rather than mere cleverness.

The Commandos are the subject of much of the film's sardonic humour – they are programmed for mayhem and destruction and there are enough references to the cinema of war for their automatism to be seen as not merely robotic, but also a matter of the military mindset. Posturing in front of an American flag, in the style of George C. Scott's Patton, Chip Hazard addresses his men in a speech in which each incomplete military cliché segues bathetically into the next.

During the film's climactic assault on the Abernathy's home, Hazard flies a helicopter into battle to the tune of the 'Ride of the Valkyries' and remarks, 'I love the smell of polyurethane in the morning,' echoing Robert Duvall's Kilgore in Francis Ford Coppola's *Apocalypse Now* (1979). He is voiced by Tommy Lee Jones and his men by members of the Dirty Dozen and by Bruce Dern – this is not casting to inspire liking or confidence. The endless accumulation of movie reference jokes here reinforces the general point that robot soldiers are made more dangerous by being soldiers than by being robots.

The Commandos are terrifying in their capacity to reinvent themselves. When Alan kills one, and its comrades cannibalize it for parts, it is revealed without its face to resemble a tiny version of the Terminator – both sets of toys are designed by Stan Winston, who also designed that other dangerous robot.

Chip and his band improvise military hardware from domestic appliances, and are ludicrous less because they are small than because they are so readily outwitted by Alan, his girlfriend Christy (Kirsten Dunst) and his parents. An improvised tank lobs flaming spitballs into the house and Alan's mother, who has a fine tennis backhand, lobs them straight back out again, eventually succeeding in blowing up the tank itself. (This is a Dante trope – in the first *Gremlins* film, the hero's mother performs similar improvisatory skills at mayhem, sticking one gremlin in a microwave and another in a blender.)

Like all killer robots they keep coming back – when Christy and Alan trick a pursuing vehicle being driven by the tiny soldiers into following them across a ditch it cannot jump, all but Chip Hazard are destroyed. By this point, Alan's phone calls to the factory have borne fruit, not only in the arrival of the toys' designers to troubleshoot the situation – they are completely ineffectual like most of the film's adults – but also in product recall. Chip takes hostage the delivery driver who has collected the recalled toys and arrives back at the Abernathy house at the head of a small army.

In a memorably creepy sequence, which references the Boris Karloff version of Frankenstein both in the improvised machinery and in theremin-like noises in the score, Hazard has earlier cannibalized a dead soldier's chip to create and recruit less intelligent but potentially deadly irregulars in the shape of Christy's collection of Gwendy dolls – which are Barbie dolls in all but name. Immediately prior to Hazard's decision to do this, his men spot the dolls and suggest that they use them for Rest and Recreation – the mutation of the dolls is therefore explicitly seen as a sexual violation of them.

Hideously mutated and deformed by battlefield surgery, these monstrous dolls prattle of homecoming dances and makeovers as they turn on their former mistress and on Alan. It is not clear whether the fragments of dialogue are something which was built in to them when they were mere dolls. (In another of Dante's inspired moments of referentiality, they are voiced by Sarah Michelle Gellar and Christina Ricci, probably Dunst's major rivals among young actresses.) They are even more terrifying than the Commandos because their partial programming has left them as automata which function randomly – they are lethally unpredictable and chthonic. They are, in a sense, the Furies.

Animated killer dolls are in one sense an even more sinister version of automata than killer robots – whether in the supernatural possessed form of Chuckie and his Bride or in the inexplicable form of the deadly toys in Roger Vadim's *Barbarella* (1968). One of the reasons for this is that dolls are owned and in some sense shadow selves of their owner. When we first meet Christy, she is her obnoxious father's spoiled princess – the collection of dolls are clearly part of what he thinks it appropriate for his daughter to own – and is dating a jock who allows her no autonomy.

The jock, who has been out on a date with Christy and has entered her home on a pretext, ends up being attacked by the dolls and left to make his way home trouserless – there is a sense in which the dolls by doing this are acting as surrogates for Christy's unvoiced desires. Their murderous prattle is parodic of the conventional high school life she is almost certainly renouncing forever by hitching herself romantically – and their final kiss is very romantic – to the quirky outsider Alan – of whom her father passionately disapproves.

Early in the film, she squashes Alan's unvoiced but obvious interest in her by telling him, conventionally, that she dates older boys – by the end of the film she is her own woman, choosing to date the younger boy who is more fun. She has broken away from the programming of conventional femininity just as Alan, by wooing and winning her, has broken with the expectations implicit in his vague geekiness and mischief-making.

The violence with which, freed by Alan, she smashes the dolls to smithereens is a very clear rejection of the conventionally girly side of herself she is choosing to reject; it is also an unsuccessful attempt to repress the violent anarchic energy that she shares with them. The near maniacal glee with which she later destroys troops of Commandos – literally mowing them down with the family mower – indicates that she has, in a good way, more in common with the demon Barbies than she is quite comfortable with.

Even more than the soldiers, the dolls have a blended nature and promote and provoke the ambivalence which lies at the heart of Christy herself. The difference is that the ambivalences in Christy are part of the process whereby she grows and changes, whereas the transformation of the dolls is a one-time deal – they cannot change further. Indeed, though they are potentially deadly, the dolls become fragile again the moment they lose the initiative; like the plastic they are made of, they can only change for the worse into broken fragments.

It is their capacity for change that makes the Gorgonites more like the human characters – Archer, their leader, acquires real dignity, in particular with his actorly intonations (he was voiced by Frank Langella, one of the screen's more memorably sympathetic Draculas). The Gorgonites, the rest of whom are voiced by Christopher Guest and the other actors from the rock pseudo-documentary, Rob Reiner's *Spinal Tap* (1987), are a mixture of muscle and clown – a mute creature that is all legs and eye, a rhino man, a creature which resembles Frankenstein's monster after the soldiers take it apart and the others reassemble it, a Quasimodo-like hunchback and a twirling loon. They have a fundamental sweetness of character, all of them, and a capacity to look out for each other – it is not just that they learn, but that they have some sense of what learning things is for.

Their nature is to run and hide and be destroyed by the Commandos – after the first assault on them, which trashes the toy shop, they entirely outwit the Commandos, but only by hiding in a skip full of garbage. The Commandos' first attack on the Abernathy house has as its objective the abduction of Archer, whom Alan has taken home, and his torture for information that he does not possess, but would not give them. Part of the film's programmatic riposte to the military virtues is manifest in the fact that even before he learns and changes, Archer is capable of 'the better fortitude/ or patience and heroic martyrdom'. Alan rescues him, on that occasion, and in a piece of rough justice stuffs one of the commandoes in the waste disposal unit that was intended for Archer's grave.

When, at the film's climax, Archer buys Alan crucial time, it is less by fighting Hazard effectively than by putting himself in a position where Hazard wastes moments in petty sadism. Hazard wants to see what the aliens' guts are like and Archer replies that they are wire and plastic like Hazard's own. In a metaphoric sense, though, Archer's guts are superior to Hazard's because it takes more courage to die than to kill. Archer and the other Gorgonites are prepared to sacrifice themselves – the electromagnetic pulse Alan is trying to create will destroy them as well as the Commandos and they are content to die so that the humans who have helped them may live. In the end, Hazard becomes the thing he most feared – Alan improvises and uses him to make the connection that triggers the pulse and fries his comrades.

The Gorgonites' instinct to run and hide remains, and it is that which saves them. Earlier the rampaging Commandos have toppled the massive satellite dish which is one of the major areas of dispute between the two sets of parents. The Gorgonites take refuge under it, and it protects them from the pulse which fries the Commandos. Part of the wisdom they teach Alan is learning to change strategies at will from what is natural to you to what is hard, according to what is the need of the moment. This is a movie in praise of flexibility and multiple natures.

The adults of the film are comical because, to a greater or lesser degree, they are types and predictable because they will not change – they have become automata who need shocking out of their stasis. They need to become as malleable as Christy and Alan and to respond to emergencies; this they do to varying extents. Christy's overweening, status-conscious father, Phil, is obsessed with expensive gadgetry, toys in other words, one of which – the satellite dish – turns out only to be of real use when destroyed.

When the Commandos copy the tactics of the US army in Panama by playing very loud music ('Tell me what you want/ what you really really want') to disorient their enemies, the music they choose is 'Wannabe' by the Spice Girls, that most synthetic and artificial of groups. And what are they singing? A song about the nature of desire. This is a film in which excessive consumerism is seen as a destructive force rather than consumerism itself – the satellite dish is both a piece of excess and something which preserves, and the Gorgonites themselves were produced as a commodity, even if they become something more.

One of the things consumerism does is create and negotiate identities, both for good and ill; Alan's mother Irene talks with profound ambivalence of the career she left behind: 'The constant pressure to keep my business attire up to date and stylish – I don't miss it at all, unless you do.' This is not a film about simple dualities – her nostalgia for the life she chose to give up indicates that there is no moralistic opposition here between her choice of the simple life and Phil's desire for ever more toys. That nifty backhand is very clearly a relic of her old life rather than something she acquired along with a higher moral consciousness. She has changed, but she has kept useful things from who she used to be.

The adult who changes least is the one who is most sinisterly a joke – Gil Mars, the CEO of Globotech, who arrives in his helicopter and dishes out cheques to keep all the adults quiet. One of the most sinister moments is when he turns to his toymaker employees and tells them to make more of the Commandos, not as toys but as counter-insurgency weapons. It is worth noticing that his name references not only the God of War, but also Gil-Martin, the demonic tempter of James Hogg's *Confessions of a Justified Sinner*, whose name also means Fox; he cannot and will not grow or change because he is, unlike the merely human characters, and like Chip Hazard, a perfectly damned thing. Dennis Leary's performance has a sardonic bliss to it which enables him to walk away with some of the films' major performance honours in spite of the fact he is hardly in it.

The film may be agnostic about consumerism, but it is clear where it stands on money and greed and the eighties values that Dante had mocked in the shape of Donald Trump in *Gremlins 2*. The conversation between Irwin and Larry about the takeover of Heartland by Globotech is all about profit and loss and realism – Larry rebukes Irwin for failing to keep up with the real-world custom of making money. Given what he is shown as prepared to do in order to make money, and the fact that he creates the Commandos which nearly execute him, Larry's credentials for talking about the real world become somewhat thin. If this is the real world, then the imagined world of Gorgonia looks rather more desirable.

The scientist who designed the chip is played in a cameo role by Robert Picardo who, as the Doctor in *Star Trek: Voyager*, is one of television's most famous artificial intelligences. His presence and the film's visual references to classic Frankenstein moments – the Boris Karloff version is visible playing in the background at various points – are clues that this is a film whose director wants to place it very clearly in a tradition of discussion about authenticity and education. What makes the monster dangerous to Frankenstein is that he gives it enough humanity to learn where it is lacking – *Small Soldiers* is a comedy that is at risk in several key scenes of a far less happy outcome.

And one of its outcomes is that Alan becomes a more rounded person and learns that actions have consequences. When we first meet him, he is a clever alienated child – in one of the cut scenes, accused by a teacher of a prank, he tries to demonstrate his innocence by saying that he has far better ideas than that. This is a film which values intelligence, but not above all else – if Gil Mars is a shadow double, then it is Alan whose double he is, Alan who could choose to make the smart, safe choice and betray the Gorgonites, who could apply his intelligence to pure destructiveness rather than being prepared to learn and grow. If the rewards he gets for this are fairly conventional ones – the good-looking girlfriend and a better relationship with his parents – then this is a film set in a suburb, and its values are suburban ones, seen in a positive, but not unalloyed, light. (Dante's 1989 film *The Burbs* has a very different take on all this.)

When, at the film's end, Alan says farewell to the Gorgonites, as they set off on their impossible quest, he is saying farewell to toys, and to childhood. This is a film for adolescents, but it is also a movie about the choices implicit in adolescence, the choice to change and become who you are as an adult. If the film is also critical of adult values like consumerism and financial ruthlessness, then that is because the choices that need to be made are to be informed ones. There is no sense here that there are sorts of knowledge we are better off without – the chips that make the Commandos possible, and their remodelling by Mars as counter-insurgency weapons, also make the fey poetic madness of the Gorgonites possible, and through them Alan and Christy's sentimental education.

6. Who Are You?

Cognitive Dissonance
and Lots of Really Big Guns

Who am I, where are you and precisely what is going on?

These central questions of western philosophy are, predictably, also obsessions of science fiction, which has always been prone to latching on to good material whatever its source.

These are, after all, philosophical problems that contain an implied narrative. One of the best ways of thinking about them is to conduct thought experiments about what the consequences would be were things radically otherwise and how it would feel to be in that moment where your sense of how things are changes. And that is, by definition, story.

Comparatively few philosophers have made acknowledged use of concepts drawn from SF – Derek Parfitt is an exception in the way he specifically recognizes that SF has something to offer philosophy. Nonetheless, many of the standard tropes of SF have major philosophical resonances. It should also be acknowledged that those philosophical concerns which can handily be termed Cognitive Dissonance are also great generators of story.

The first edition of the John Clute/Peter Nichols *Encyclopaedia of Science Fiction* illustrates its article on Cognitive Dissonance with an engraving of a man sticking his head out through the appearance of the mundane world and getting his first gawking view of the planets and stars in their crystal spheres beyond. It is perhaps significant that at least two major films – Alex Proyas'

Dark City (1997) and Peter Weir's *The Truman Show* (1998) – specifically echo that image.

One of the standard philosopher's metaphors for discussing the nature of reality is Descartes' deceiver demon, who keeps your brain in a box and feeds it delusory images of reality. Another is Plato's cave, where prisoners facing away from the entrance interpret the world through shadows seen by flickering firelight. Another linked one is the Neoplatonist idea that there is beautiful music in the spheres 'but while this muddy vesture of decay/ doth hem us in, we cannot hear them'. All of these find echoes in science fiction, both in its written form and in films; the world we are shown in the Wachowski brothers' *The Matrix* (1999) is one in which Descartes' demon rules.

The stock matters of science fiction include several versions of Cognitive Dissonance. There is the world of consensual reality which breaks down under examination and proves to be a delusion and most usually a snare created to keep the reason prisoner. The classic formulation of this is Robert Heinlein's short story 'They', where everything in the universe is specifically targeted at fooling one individual who would, undeceived of his belief that he is a man who lives in America, be too powerful to control. The solipsism involved in this idea is of course also a power fantasy, one of the things to which SF has often been accused of being prone.

Another standard SF format is the world which is treated as consensual reality by the characters who live in it, but which the reader recognizes as particular and peculiar. Many stories in which the inhabitants of generation starships have lost technological civilization and fail to understand where they are fall into this category. Heinlein's *Orphans of the Sky* is the classic statement of this theme but there are many others, most recently Ursula Le Guin's 'Paradises Lost', which more subtly shows the growth of a religious belief that the ship is true reality and the worlds at journey's beginning and end delusions. Sometimes the world in which the characters find themselves is one of sensory difference – Daniel F. Galouye's *Dark Universe* takes place in a community which has never known light nor can conceive of what the purpose of eyes might be.

In all of these tales, there is an interesting dialogue between the process by which the protagonist decodes reality and that by which the reader comes to terms with what, precisely, is wrong with this picture. The equivalent process in science fiction film is even more complex since part of it is decoding which particular movie genre tropes are being invoked on screen. One of the problems for SF film is just this – that this process of decoding has to be accessible to the most naive viewer without boring the sophisticated, genre savvy one.

There is a sense in which *The Matrix* and *Dark City* both participate in this discourse of decoding and disclosure as well as a more abstract one. In both films, there is an explanation for the gap between actual and apparent reality; the demon manipulating reality has an agenda for doing so. The world invoked on screen is specific in both cases – the opening scenes of *The Matrix* alternate between the hyper-real scenes of clubbing and office life and the computer-game leaps and bounds of Trinity's pursuit by the Agents while *Dark City* specifically presents a collage of three decades worth of American urban thrillers that at once reassures with its familiarity and disorients because of its non-specificity.

The entertainment medium experienced so vividly that it and reality become interchangeable is a trope of SF that often overlaps with these themes – in many of the novels of Philip K. Dick, for example, the distinction between consuming entertainment media, taking hallucinogenic drugs and undergoing mystical experiences are deliberately blurred. There is a sense in, say, *The Three Stigmata of Palmer Eldritch* for example, that you may get lost in illusion and never get back along with a profound ambivalence as to whether or not this is a good or a bad thing.

Surprisingly, it is Dick's obsession with the difference between human beings and things that are not human, but appear to be, that has dominated the body of film made directly from his work – *Blade Runner* (1982) and *Impostor* (2001) for example – with the exception of Paul Verhoeven's *Total Recall* (1990). Perhaps the reason for this is that when film-makers feel like dealing with the nature of reality, the project almost always becomes a personal one. Most such films have a Dickian feel, but this derives as much from his influence as from direct quotation or adaptation.

Further, once you have accepted that it is possible to enter a reality you have constructed and interact with beings that believe themselves to be real, the status of your own knowledge of your own world comes up for grabs. Josef Rusnak's *The Thirteenth Floor* (1999), for example, is entirely about this question – researchers into virtual reality find themselves under simultaneous threat from an escapee from the world they have made and entrants into their world from the one which made it, who find the idea of tiered reality upsetting. Why is not entirely clear; there is the interesting implication that the murderous villain, who is also the upper world's analogue of the hero, is taking out his issues with his father-in-law, whose analogue is his first victim, and his wife, on beings who cannot fight back.

One of the points in David Cronenberg's *eXistenZ* (1999) where we start most totally feeling concern about the ontological status of what we are seeing is the point at which Jennifer Jason Leigh's game designer, pursued by terrorists, starts fondling comparatively ordinary objects in a petrol station and praising the craftsmanship of the work that has produced them. It is not clear whether she is lost in illusion or making a sardonic point about God as programmer of a game and that ambiguity is a significant part of the film's point.

In the end, she and Jude Law's character escape from one dream back into a reality that is itself a dream – and in the final reality, they are not the designers, but terrorists trying to kill them. If she is God, she is that version of God which is at once the slayer and the slain – there is no sense here that the tiering of reality ever stops, that, as in the old joke, it is turtles all the way down. All such movies are prone to slingshot endings simply because, once you have cut the assumption of consensual reality and identity out from underneath the viewer, it is possible to go on without ever definitively restoring it.

Philip K. Dick's 'We Can Remember It For You Wholesale' is, in theory, the basis for Paul Verhoeven's thud-and-blunder Arnold Schwarzenegger vehicle *Total Recall*, but the only thing which makes it through is the idea that each of the memories that an ordinary man pays to have inserted is in fact the truth. He actually was a secret agent on Mars, for example, and his desire to have a fake memory of this inserted reflects the removal of the genuine memory by his paymasters. The Dick story constantly escalates the material he asks to have added and which turns out to have earlier been removed – the film goes in a radically different direction in which the nicer man the amnesiac hero has become overcomes the ruthless thug who had his memories removed as a gambit to infiltrate the Resistance.

Yet at even quite a late stage in the film there is a profound ambiguity. One of the memory programmers appears to the hero and announces that his delusions have taken over entirely, that his sanity is crumbling; the hero responds by assuming him to be yet another minion of the villainous tycoon who runs Mars and shoots him down. (He is only comparatively nicer than his earlier self – he also kills the woman who was posing as his wife in his Earth life.) Verhoeven feints in the direction of this being a film whose narrative is intrinsically unreliable, but there is never very much risk that we will read anything that Schwarzenegger does as polysemous – he is just not that kind of actor. Even John McTiernan's *Last Action Hero* (1993), a film which exploits his persona to create a metafiction, is caught between its good intentions and his uni-directional charisma.

Nor does it help that the film's McGuffin – a hidden alien factory which gives Mars a breathable atmosphere in minutes – is so totally incredible, or that death by decompression and suffocation is represented so very crudely with pop-eyed monster make-up. Here as elsewhere – see my chapter on *Starship Troopers* – the nasty little boy side of Verhoeven's imagination gets in the way of what was good in his conception of the film.

In all of these cases, the central metaphor of the film has power in itself while initiating plots in which it influences events. To discover, in a genre plot, that the world can be understood is almost always to acquire a desire to change it – the standard assumptions of SF include the assumption that no proper person is content with abstract knowledge. Inevitably, this is even truer of SF film especially Hollywood SF film where SF is to a large extent a branch of the action adventure movie. This is why, much to the distress of purists, movies that are adaptations of SF material are prone to be considerably more crude in their appeal than the very occasional films which create original SF scenarios that are fully developed.

It is perhaps significant that all the films dealt with in this chapter are effectively new material, however much they draw on older tropes, perhaps because if the specifics of tales of this kind are to be emotionally credible, they have to be imagined in terms of the medium. *The Truman Show*, for example, falls into an extended sub-genre of SF in which people live out their lives and only gradually discover that they are a television programme or a test-bed for advertising. This was practically a cliché in the SF magazine *Galaxy* in the 1950s – perhaps the classic example of the latter is Frederik Pohl's 'The Tunnel Under the World' – and *The Truman Show* alludes to the trope as a whole rather than drawing on any specific story.

Equally importantly, though, in its final form, *The Truman Show* was a vehicle for Jim Carrey, whose hard-working comic charisma actually convinces us that this is someone whom the populace might bother watching obsessively for years. In his hands, a slick concept becomes a touching story about a person – we care as much about what happens to him after the slingshot ending as we do about the film's implicit abstract satire on reality television and our taste for it. The use of stars is one of film's useful shorthands, because they bring with them emotional baggage and expectations – to describe a film as a vehicle is not necessarily to dismiss it.

One of the reasons why some films never quite make it out of cult status and into the mainstream of hits, in spite of their intellectual and other merits, is the issue of stars. *Dark City* is entirely admirable in lots of ways, but suffered at the box office from the fact that it was full of good second-rank actors – Rufus Sewell, William Hurt, Kiefer Sutherland in the period between his brat pack status and the revival of his career in the aftermath of the television thriller *24*. People did not know where this film was going to take them and the personae of the actors involved offered them few clues.

I have always wanted to see a cut of *Dark City* which leaves off the voiceover narrative in which Dr Schreber provides us with spoilers for much of the plot – I have never seen an explanation for this opening, but it feels like a loss of nerve, whether on the part of the creators or the studio. Oh god, they thought, this is all too weird, the punters will not understand. Except that actually the punters for this sort of film are precisely the people who would understand and would have welcomed not being told in advance about the strangers and their experiments.

The pre-titles visuals start with a standard pan from the macrocosm to human scale – from clusters to stars to the upper structures of a city in darkness to the crippled doctor in a homburg hat who is waiting for something. He looks at his watch as the hands move to the stroke of midnight and around him people are travelling on the elevated trains, driving in cars coming out of a cinema that is showing 'The Evil', with 'The Book of Dreams' as a coming attraction, and suddenly they stop what they are doing and fall asleep, every one of them, except him. The two film titles are beautifully chosen for their resonance – even though *The Book of Dreams* is an early short by *Dark City*'s writer/director Alex Proyas and there may be some similar in-joke connected with the 1978 film *The Evil*.

We do not need to be told much of what the voiceover tells us. Basic movie literacy tells us that, if we start with a reminder of human and more than human scales, we are engaged in a subject of more than personal significance. The fact that this pan focuses on Schreber and his watch tells us that he is up to something – his coat and hat, and his pocket watch also indicate something about his status. We are not told specifically that he is a doctor, but he is clearly a professional. And his centrality to whatever is happening is demonstrated as the ticking of his watch is picked up by the rhythms of the score, which stops, suddenly, with everything else, except for a distant vague misty pulse.

The city revealed to us in these first shots has something of Fritz Lang's *Metropolis* (1926) about it – especially when we see the factory of manufactured memory that underlies it – and something of the Gotham City of Tim Burton's *Batman* movies. It is full of structures piled on structures and looming towers that cast long shadows into which Schreber disappears; it is the night city of Edward Hopper's paintings and the mean streets of the standard noir thriller. Yet it is not simply a city of the future or the city of the assumed perpetual 1940s of the noir film – it is, even in these first minutes, something disorientingly other.

The drawings of spirals which punctuate the titles would actually tell us something of what that might be, were we paying attention to them as something more than mere design. Spirals are labyrinths; these spirals move round slowly – they are the gears of a clock, parts of some machine. The production company for the film is called Magic Clock – and that, in a sense, is what the Dark City is. It is a magic clock which tells us what time it is not.

The narrative proper starts with Rufus Sewell as John Murdoch, with blood trickling from his forehead, in a bath. He is just awake and confused about where he is and who he is. He knocks over a goldfish bowl and he picks up the floundering fish and puts it in the bathwater. This is a good example of Proyas' economy, something he may have learned from James Cameron, because it starts William Hurt's Detective Bumstead thinking about the kind of serial killer that is kind to goldfish, but is also vaguely indicative of the film's plot – fish out of water, fish in the wrong place.

The fish moves from one state to another, from water to air to water again, under the direction of a being unknowable from its perspective. There is an interesting visual pun here – the broken syringe ignored at his feet is fish-shaped, roughly – in a film otherwise devoid of Christian reference, but which is clearly about a messiah figure, this early presence of a fish, and a fish-like item, and the later presence of an aquarium, is probably significant.

As he dresses, Murdoch goes through his case and finds a card from Shell Beach, a card which wakens memories for a second. Shell Beach is his Madeleine, but it is also, it transpires, his trigger. And hardly has he looked at the card than he gets a phone call. Schreber tells him to leave – that enemies are coming. And Murdoch breaks off the call when he sees a dead body in the corner of the room, a woman with those spirals scrawled on her in her own blood and carved into her flesh. By this time, the viewer is caught up in a sense of this as exploration of thriller tropes, even though Schreber has mentioned 'an experiment... that went wrong'; part of the strength of *Dark City* is that it draws fluently on several genre vocabularies.

The musical pulse kicks off again and we notice that the clocks Murdoch passes are just past midnight. And suddenly we see everyone wake up. Murdoch leaves, to reclaim his wallet from a diner. Three white-faced, hairless strangers turn up in his room, collecting the syringe and grilling the desk man, whom they put to sleep with a word and a gesture.

It is only gradually that we realize how strange the world is in which Sewell's character John Murdoch finds himself – there are the sudden stoppages of everything at midnight, there are the mysterious pale bald men around whom things seem to change. Buildings stretch and shrink – staircases suddenly grow beneath your feet. There is the limping man with a medical bag who walks through walls. Murdoch has memories of growing up at the beach and of bright sunlight, but in the place where he is there is never any sunlight and though there are trains and buses which say they are going to the beach of his childhood, none of them ever stop for him to get on them.

Meanwhile, Bumstead becomes more and more convinced that there is a connection between Murdoch and the killings of women while also being uneasily aware that Walenski, his predecessor on the case, went mad as a result. He visits his colleague and finds him obsessively drawing spiral mazes, mazes similar to those carved in the dead women; later Murdoch sees Walenski on the subway. He has figured the way out, he says, and throws himself under the express.

This is a film about finding the way out – and to do that, you have first to realize that there is something odd about your situation. Murdoch comes to that realization and also gradually realizes that he is neither mad nor currently a killer; to become sane, you must first acquit yourself of the guilt society and religion imposes on you. When, at one of the film's climaxes, he and Bumstead batter down a wall and find themselves looking out at the stars, they are only doing, in an actualized metaphor, what Murdoch has gradually been doing throughout the movie.

It has to be added that there is a famous work of literature whose hero wanders, with a friend and mentor, through a spiral city and ends his journey coming out to look at the stars. That work is, of course, the first part of Dante's *La Divina Commedia* – the Inferno – and in that work the city through which he wanders is Hell. There is a fantastic genre termed posthumous fantasy by John Clute whose characters wander between heaven and hell and the Elysian Fields and the Halls of Karma and the judgement seats of Minos or Horus. *Dark City* is not a posthumous fantasy, but it deals in a vocabulary of imagery drawn from the genre.

Murdoch finds out what the Strangers already know – how to tune reality so that it conforms with his desires. 'If there were gods,' Nietzsche says, 'how could I bear not to be a god, therefore there are no gods.' Murdoch does not have the option of refusing the reality in which he finds himself – his only course is first to understand the world and then to change it. The screenplay of *Dark City* alludes to much of western philosophy simply because the problems it poses are common parts of the human condition.

In much of this, he is guided, secretly, by Schreber, the quisling doctor to whom the Strangers have allowed a partial immunity to the endless experiments in identity which they impose on the inhabitants of the city, but at the cost of losing all sense of his previous self. His name, which may simply be the name he uses as a clue to himself of what he must do, is that of one of Freud's most famous patients, a man who believed himself raped by God and changing sex as a result, who saw the passivity forced upon him as a sacrifice to the divine which would make him give birth to the messiah. Which, in a sense, is what Schreber in the movie does – he is the morally equivocal mentor who guides Murdoch across the threshold into his new life.

Schreber is a liminal being like many other instructors of the newly divine and this is signalled in a number of ways – his capacity to open and close doors in brick walls makes him an opener of the way, for example. He spends much of his time in a swimming bath because the humidity is uncomfortable for the Strangers, but also because as a hot wet place where water fills the air and is surrounded by stone it is a place where the elements mix and are confused. A hot moist place is, of course, also a symbol for the womb and for fertility.

The price of Schreber's wisdom and his skills is that he has been forced by the Strangers to maim himself – he took his own memory away on their orders and somehow in the process maimed his brain so that he has a limp and a lazy eye; in many myths, mutilation is the price of wisdom because part of you is alive and part of you is dead. He no longer exists in human society and has no part in the society of the Strangers save as their barely tolerated servant – he is in a real sense a walking corpse. Like Virgil in Dante, he can only take the hero so far.

Schreber is an interesting figure because he succeeds through a piece of planning which relies on the Strangers' overweening arrogance – they know that he has been playing a double game but underestimate his ingenuity. Thus they actually force him to insert false memories into the mind of the captive Murdoch and never consider what memories he may be inserting – in fact, he gives Murdoch a reworked version of Murdoch's entire life, with Schreber there at every step of it instructing him in the use of his abilities.

Schreber is that most dangerous of their opponents – the servant who has had enough of his slavery and knows them well enough to betray them comprehensively. This is a type of worm-turning peripeteia common in heavily plotted SF like that of A.E. van Vogt: Schreber is developed thoroughly as a character right up to the point at which he has served his plot function and at that point is ruthlessly discarded by it.

Equally ruthless is the plot's disposition of Bumstead, who falls through the hole in the wall during an attack by the Strangers and dies quietly of suffocation. His purpose has been to reveal more of the world of the city than Murdoch can see by himself; in many thrillers and even SF novels, a man of his quiet intellectual integrity would be the hero. The casting of William Hurt in this part brings the sort of moral authority to the character that in an earlier generation would have attached to Henry Fonda – he has baffled hurt eyes from the beginning and they only get more sorrowful as he learns more about the world in which he is forced to live.

His search for the truth parallels Murdoch's but is from a more limited perspective – he is trying to solve a murder mystery whereas Murdoch is dealing in ultimate realities. In a film that is about becoming a god, a limited man like Bumstead, no matter how upright and worthy, is as doomed as the mentor; he is the friend who shares the human life of the hero, but cannot follow him to the end. The vision that helps Murdoch transcend humanity is merely fatal to him.

(The other reason why Bumstead has to die is possibly this: that actually he was right in the first place. One thing we are never told specifically is who the killer actually was – the issue is confused by the alien Hand's becoming the killer's copycat. The one woman we see murdered in the film is killed by Hand, who cannot have been responsible for the earlier killings. Since the thing which triggers Hand into killing is a copy of Murdoch's lost memories, one has at least the option of assuming that Murdoch, or rather the artificial set of memories who most recently occupied Murdoch's body, was the killer, at least of the girl whose corpse is in the room and who may be the only actual corpse that ever existed since we can be sure of nothing. This has a worrying further corollary – is the thing that triggered Murdoch's ability to tune in part of his forgotten experience of killing?)

Bumstead is not enough to anchor Murdoch in his humanity – that is what his wife Emma (Jennifer Connelly) is for. Emma's singing makes her the one figure around whom the remorseless pulse of the film's incidental music changes to something else; she is someone whom both Murdoch and Bumstead want to protect and whom even the demonic Hand fails to hurt. She is robbed of her identity, but not, it is clear, of her fundamental essence.

One of the film's few hopeful moments is at the end, when, robbed of her memories, she meets Murdoch again as a stranger. He does not try to force the issue by using his powers – he accepts that, if he is to have a chance at being important to her again, he will have to woo her all over again, like a normal human being, and not as a god, and they head round the outside of the city, for Shell Beach, together, at least for this moment.

Murdoch has a secret sharer in the film: Hand becomes literally this when he takes up the memories that Murdoch has lost, but he and the other Strangers who pursue Murdoch are already his demon counterparts. The Strangers are incredibly powerful aliens, and yet they suffer from a complete folly – the belief that they can understand humanity and steal some essence of it that they will be able to share as if born to it. Hand is a demonstration of the wrongness of this – no longer entirely alien but, even more creepily, not human either. What human memories teach him is just enough human malice to be a monster; Richard O'Brien, most famous for his role as the sinister butler in, and creator of, Jim Sharman's *The Rocky Horror Picture Show* (1975) was an inspired piece of casting here.

Even more remarkable, in a sense, is the casting of Ian Richardson as Book, who seems to be the Strangers' leader, unless the idol of a vast head which opens to reveal the vast central clock of this midnight world is to be taken as such. Richardson brings immense authority to the part – decades of iconic roles in film and British television are partly responsible for this – which enables him to be even more threatening than O'Brien, or the evil child who torments Murdoch on occasion. When Richardson, at key moments, says 'Shut it down!', he gives the words the full apocalyptic resonance they have here.

Dark City is one of those films where everything comes together, more or less – someone once said that a novel is an extended prose narrative with something wrong with it and there ought to be a parallel definition of film. Where Alex Proyas leaves us with mysteries, they are deliberate choices. It is a film which dramatizes the shattering of reality by making the man who comes to see clearly into something approximating a god, who kills the oppressing Strangers, brings light to the night city and creates a sea for the comfort of its inhabitants that we can see as a restoration of fertility. Like many of the best SF movies, it uses SF concepts but is also knee-deep in mythological resonance.

As of course is the other obvious good handling of these themes, the even more spectacular and considerably less thoughtful *The Matrix* and its sequels and associated material. *The Matrix* covers much of the same ground as *Dark City* with far less intellectual depth and even more style. It is significant that the CGI work in *Dark City* is vastly more interesting when setting things up than when resolving them – possibly the using up of the budget played a role here. The shots of cityscapes growing and changing, of skyscrapers shrinking and apartment blocks stretching, are what one takes away, whereas the climax consists, for the most part, of a floating Sewell sending bolts of force at a floating Ian Richardson, while the set of the Strangers' underground lair falls apart round them.

None of which is less than effective, but it never makes you feel that you have seen something entirely new in the way that the climax of *The Matrix* does, which is hardly a complaint, since *The Matrix* has scenes of violently kinetic confrontation which created a new vocabulary of action – like many of the best films, it created clichés for half a decade. Nor are those scenes of violence the only moments at which one's first watching of the film makes one feel privileged to be at the start of something: when Neo girds himself for his final battle, he asks for guns, and suddenly racks and racks of the things rush toward him out of the blankness of infinity. Never before has virtual reality been so tellingly shown.

One of the reasons why *The Matrix Reloaded* (2003) is so much less effective than the original film is just this: that, after seeing the first film, we have a new vocabulary of wonder. All that the fight scenes, or cityscapes, or shots of giant robot squids carving their way through hulls in the second film manage to do is bigger and louder and more – the Wachowskis failed on this second occasion to do new. Or better. The sequences in the third film, *Matrix Revolutions* (2003),which work best are the quieter ones. The scene where Neo is trapped in a virtual subway station unable to leave its white-tiled sterility is one of the few moments which gives us the same shock of the new as the first film.

The Matrix derived as much from comic books and commercials as from the watered-down version of Gnosticism that it espoused – it has been argued that most of its principals are there for their clothes-horse quality as for their acting ability, and if that is intended as a criticism it is more or less beside the point. The point about the movie is that its heroes and heroine look good even in the skivvies and slime of the 'real world' and in the designer suits and black leather trench-coats of the consensual reality that turns out to be the fine fakery of the Matrix.

The comic book aesthetic extends in particular to the way CGI is used – to take but one example, when Neo and Trinity attack the room where Morpheus is being held, and blast the three agents with machine-gun fire, we see in vivid individual detail the used shells plunging down to us from underneath their helicopter. This is a sinister image, but it is also a very beautiful one, and one which would not be possible without computer graphics – there are several points in this film where the sinister side of futurist aesthetics, bombs bursting so that they look like flowers, is actualized. Many of the best moments in the second and third films are likewise essentially live versions of great comic-book frames – the multiple-participant nightclub stand-off between Neo's supporters and the Merovingian's men in which absolutely everybody has at least one gun at someone else's head is a good example of this.

The movie grammar of the film's opening is simple: we watch numbers stream across the screen and those of us who grew up watching Patrick McGoohan's TV series *The Prisoner* intone to ourselves, 'I am not a number; I am a free man.' Two people have a phone conversation and it becomes clear that the numbers on screen are someone trying to put a trace on the call. The call ends – the woman thinks she has heard a trace – but they have got her location and the woman Trinity is surprised by armed police, sitting at a desk at the far end of a long room. The other participant in the conversation is an informer – this is a film in which nothing can be trusted.

The green of the computer that read the numbers is echoed in the particular shade of darkness against which this scene takes place – at several points, the film goes for all practical purposes into a tinted monochrome. Outside, sinister agents, who look like they might work for the organs of the state, arrive and are annoyed that the police, out of departmental rivalry, have gone in already. Agent Smith says, in his sinister drawl, that the arresting officers are already dead.

And instantly the film bursts into the highly kinetic action which is one of the things it is about. Trinity demolishes the police, leaving most of them dead, and exits the room and the building a step ahead of agents as superhuman as she proves to be. The chase across the rooftops is the film's calling card, far more even than the martial arts killing of the police – it announces that this is going to be either unlike anything you have ever seen, or at least a far more extreme version of it.

She talks into a mobile phone and is directed to a call box, where she picks up the receiver and disappears micro-seconds before the call box is demolished by a very large truck. The film establishes, in these few minutes, that it is about a war fought with extremes of ruthlessness – the agents mention in passing that the object of the enterprise has been less to capture Trinity than to check the loyalties of an informant.

At this point, then, we know that both sides in a war are superhuman and utterly without compunction; we know that there is treachery afoot, and someone whom people are placing hope in, and that it all has something to do with computers and phone lines. So when we meet Thomas Anderson, 'Neo', it is not just the fact that he is played by a star that makes it obvious that the film will centre around him – it is the fact that he is a hacker, and a geek, and that he has started to get unsolicited messages from his computer. He does what he is told, and follows a girl to a nightclub he did not want to go to simply because she has the tattoo of a white rabbit he was told to follow. And there he meets Trinity, who talks to him cryptically about Morpheus, of whom, as yet, he has never heard.

This probably would not have worked had the Wachowskis been in a position to cast anyone in the role other than Keanu Reeves, a slightly androgynous slacker icon whose passivity is credible. When the Oracle refers to him as 'pretty' and as 'not too bright' we do not feel that she is displaying vast insight so much as acknowledging what we have already noticed for ourselves. Reeves is a star whose screen persona has two important aspects – there is the colossal loveable dopiness that came to the fore in the *Bill and Ted* films and there is the hip competence his character displayed in Jan de Bont's *Speed* (1994). *The Matrix* successfully integrates and exploits both aspects – Robert Longo's comparatively feeble *Johnny Mnemonic* (1995) (another cyberpunk film starring Reeves, this one directly adapted from a William Gibson short story) does not manage this in any version seen in the West, though Gibson has argued in conversation that there is a superior Japanese cut occasionally available which is closer to his intentions.

Neo finds himself bullied by everyone – he is dragged out to the nightclub, he is talked at by Trinity, he is harangued by his superior about unpunctuality. When Morpheus contacts him, it is to demand of him athletic feats over a mobile phone – he is told to use a window cleaner's cradle to climb to the roof and to clamber round a cornice scores of feet from the ground in order to get to it. And then he finds himself a prisoner of Agent Smith, who demonstrates to him, when he protests about the way he is being treated, that reality is malleable. Smith causes his mouth to fuse with a wave of his hand and implants a robot insect into his navel.

By now, he and the audience are hopelessly confused – one minute he is getting the usual treatment doled out by the people they work for to the sort of free spirit people who like this sort of film imagine themselves to be, and the next he is being subjected to surreal torture by men in suits who talk to him in the same patronizing way as his superiors. One minute he is being talked down to about his time-keeping and the next he is being accused of terrorism and held down and, more or less, raped, and everyone does it in the same patronizing pompous tones. As if all this is entirely for his own good.

When he wakes up in his own apartment, it is as if all of this has been a dream – and indeed, as he learns, there is a sense in which it is. He is contacted by Trinity and met by her and some of her crew mates in a coolly noir location – under a railway bridge, in the rain. They produce a bizarre weapon and shoot electricity into the thing in his stomach and hoover it out of him, accompanied by a certain amount of his blood and a fair amount of pain. They discard it through the window where it writhes a moment, changing from the animated to the inanimate – the whole film is about the difference between the living and the never alive and the impossibility of telling them apart much of the time.

Trinity takes him to Morpheus, who tells him the truth on which the film is predicated. The world, apparently our world, in which Neo lives, is long dead and is now an illusion, the Matrix, fed to sleeping humans in their millions to keep them quiet as they generate heat and power for the Artificial Intelligences which have taken the world from humanity, who wrecked it in the process. Morpheus offers him the choice of real awakening, or of slumbering in renewed illusion, of a red pill and a blue pill. Neo takes the bait of knowledge, like Adam before him, and awakes, a bald pink squalling thing in a vat of nutrient, who is almost instantly discarded as spoiled and flushed away into a sewer, where he is found by Morpheus and his crew, brought aboard the Nebuchadnezzar, their ship, and forced to confront reality for the first time.

One of the ways in which the Wachowskis have their cake and eat it is that they make the point that living in reality hurts and then take it back again. The saviours of humanity live on an unpleasant broth – like the Spartans of Ancient Greece – and dress in tattered second-hand denims and hide in sewers from giant robot squids. Yet somehow they all manage to look good on it and look even better when they go into the Matrix and get to pick out designer clothes for themselves – they know reality and nonetheless enjoy illusion when they visit it. The traitor, Cypher, sells out his friends and humanity for illusion, but also for forgetfulness; he does not want to know the truth any more, or remember the mass murder he has done to get back into the womb of dreams.

One of the interesting things about the world of illusion is that it changes the Agents, the programs who are dedicated to hunting down and destroying the last free humans whenever they go back into the Matrix, the Agents we already met when they tortured Neo. It is clear from the rant in which Agent Smith denounces humanity to the captured Morpheus that some at least of these artificial intelligences have acquired a version of emotion. The Machines he works for merely exploit defeated humanity; Smith hates humans, regarding them as an infection for which he is the cure. He talks of their smell – Hugo Weaving is particularly good at conveying this absolute sense of disgust – and yet the more he does so, the more it becomes clear that there is a side of him which is already hopelessly compromised.

It is because of this that one of the plot motifs most overused in SF and fantasy is most plausible here. The forces of evil overreach themselves and create the enemy that will destroy them. Without the One, Morpheus and his crew will never be more than an irritant, a safety valve, and by fighting them, by trying to control every last human thing, Smith creates the adversary who is a real risk. Smith's hatred is a weakness, because it makes him enjoy the fight too much for itself and makes him lose sight of his actual objective.

The decision to make Smith survive his apparent destruction, and be reborn as Neo's ultimate opponent, a virus with the capacity endlessly to rewrite identity, is one of the two later films' most egregious failures of logic. In *Matrix Revolutions,* Neo sacrifices everything – his sight, his beloved – in order to confront the Machines and persuade them that Smith forms a serious threat to them, as well as to humanity. For reasons that are not entirely clear, they accept his argument to the extent of abandoning their assault on Zion on the brink of its final success as the price of his killing Smith for them. One can conceive of all sorts of reasons why a Matrix entirely subverted by Smith might cease to be a source of energy for the Machines, but the film does not deign to give us any.

Nor is there any very obvious reason why Neo's allowing himself to be converted by Smith into another facsimile of himself should be a way of saving humanity. It is very moving, of course, that Neo, newly bereaved by Trinity's death and blinded by the man Smith had possessed, takes this last sacrificial step. But it makes no especial sense.

This is one of several points in the two later films where there may be an agenda other than the combination of philosophy and comic book which was *The Matrix*'s strength. It has been rumoured authoritatively – his separated wife's deposition in divorce hearings, for example – that Larry Wachowski was working through gender issues during the years that the brothers were working on the later films. If this is true, as seems likely, it may be reflected in this theme of transcendence through redemptive self-annihilation. This is not to excuse the low quality of the latter films, but may at least offer a reason for it.

The thing about Neo is that he is what is known in the fan-fiction subculture attached to television programmes as a Mary Sue; he is the character in the film who is there for the fans to identify with. He is the geek on the brink of becoming a god, and he spends most of the film being taught things and told things on the audience's behalf. One of the interesting things about the film is that it has such a very passive version of heroism – the crew of the Nebuchadnezzar are determined to be impressed with the young man who might be their messiah, but the first thing they notice about him is that he can sit absolutely still, absorbing data programs through the jack in his skull, for ten hours at a stretch. It is his capacity to absorb that they wonder at before they get to wonder at his combat skills or anything else.

Anyone can be implanted with those skills, after all, so in an odd reversal it is his total passivity which renders him extraordinary. One of the most interesting things about *The Matrix* is its occasional little games with gender – Keanu Reeve's willowy, non-racially specific good looks are not radically more masculine than those of Carrie-Anne Moss as Trinity. His training fights with Laurence Fishburne as the hyper-butch Morpheus have an element of the flirtatious and seductive about them. The leathers and shades of the hyper-cool personae they adopt when they enter the Matrix to do battle are an armour, but they are also an identity; the films allude to this mutability but do not follow through on it. Again, if the rumours about L. Wachowski's personal odyssey are true, this aspect of the films may be more relevant than appeared when it was first seen.

The films are also sophomorically cutesy about names – Neo is always the One, or rather an anagram of him, who has to be rearranged to fit. He is also Thomas Anderson – at once the doubter and the Son of Man. Trinity is the goddess in the sense of being the destined consort of a god, and also has a name which implies the triple nature of the goddess. Morpheus is the lord of sleep and dreams – and, we learn in the second film, of delusions. *The Prisoner* is relevant to the name of the human villain: he wants not to be a free man, to be a number, to be in fact Cypher.

Most of the names of the beings that turn out to be Artificial Intelligences are purely functional – the Oracle, the Architect, the Keymaker; the fact that most of the human names are coded references to functions is one of many things which becomes disturbing in the second film. And then there is the rogue program known as 'The Merovingian', which could be simply a reference to the fact that he presents himself as French, or could be something rather more elaborate. The Merovingians were, after all, the Frankish dynasty made redundant and ultimately deposed by their lackeys, the mayors of the palace; in crank literature, they are the sacred kings who bear the blood of Christ. I mention these points less as serious speculation as to what the Wachowskis may have meant than as a way of pointing out that this sort of cutesiness is one of several areas of infinite regress in their work, as is the question of whether the staircase on and around which some key moments of *The Matrix* take place is intended as an echo of the staircase in their earlier noir thriller *Bound* (1996).

When Neo eventually starts kicking butt to save humanity, it is not a matter of his having lost patience, as it normally would be in action films. It is that his sentimental education has proceeded to a point where he feels able and ready to sacrifice himself to save someone else. The Oracle has specifically told him that he is not the One, and it is this certain knowledge, as he thinks, that this is the truth that makes him become the One. He sets out to save Morpheus believing that he is going to his death and that carelessness with his own life is one of the steps on his way to piercing through all illusions.

He rescues Morpheus and gets Trinity out of the Matrix as well – into a 'Nebuchadnezzar' undermanned as a result of Cypher's murderous rampage and under imminent attack. He dies at the hands of Agent Smith and the attempt to revive him seems as if it will have to be aborted in order to use an EMP weapon on the squid robots in the 'real' world. Trinity pleads with him to live and suddenly he is alive again, and enlightened, able not merely to fight effectively but to see and understand the entire Matrix as code. He rips into Agent Smith and dissipates him – the other Agents flee from him and he exits the Matrix under his own steam. He has become the One.

Which would have been a good place to leave matters, because *The Matrix Reloaded* is not merely a weak sequel but one which undercuts its predecessor. It has a number of good action and fight scenes, the first of these, Neo's prophetic dream of Trinity's death, so good that it stands up to being repeated at the film's climax. The extended battle/car-chase on a freeway between several factions including blond twin Agents is a tour de force – but it is also somehow empty, as is Neo's fight with an ever-increasing number of Agent Smiths.

The second film takes back a lot of the ending of the first. Neo's ability to see the Matrix as code seems to come and go, for example, and most of the time he still fights his virtual opponents instead of deconstructing them. Agent Smith himself is back, not deconstructed at all, but metamorphosed into a virus, the thing he accused humanity of being. Now he can rewrite any other program, and anyone who has entered the Matrix into a copy of himself, and crucially can ride the latter out of the Matrix and perform skulduggery in the real world. There is a plus side to this – Hugo Weaving's slow hostile drawl is always a joy – but it does make nonsense of the previous film's triumphant ending.

Much of the plot consists of running around collecting tokens – very much in the style of a computer game. Neo has to find the Keymaker in order to unlock a portal and talk to the Architect and has to black out several city blocks in order to get into the building where the portal is and turn off the security for those blocks and so on. The premonitory vision in which we see Trinity die for the first time is analogous to the multiple reiterations of a computer game in an attempt to avoid death as a consequence of your play actions.

It is relevant that a computer game linked to, but not duplicating, the plot of the second film was released at the same time, as was a collection of short animated features – *The Animatrix* (2003) – which deals with various sidebar plots such as the discovery that Zion is under threat from a massive drilling project. Ironically, the animated films, which can be seen as the equivalent of a shared-world anthology, as can the *Matrix* comic book, are in many ways superior to the second and third feature films.

It has been claimed by those who know that the same can be said for the game which, like the animated film, contains material that expands on plot points never seen in the three films; segments of it, such as a scene in which the minor character Phoebe necks with the Merovingian's wife, were filmed using the films' cast. It may prove to be the case that the most interesting thing about the *Matrix* franchise will be the extent to which it was always envisaged in multimedia terms.

Some of *The Matrix Reloaded* is set in Zion itself, where the common people recognize Neo's importance and the politicians and soldiers are more cynical, busy as they are with old personal feuds with Morpheus and with arguing about the best strategy for defending Zion from attack. It becomes clear – which is not the same thing as making sense – that they at once depend on and distrust machines, and that their lives – dressing in skivvies and eating pulp – are to some extent an aesthetic choice. When Morpheus addresses the masses, it is less a political speech than a sermon, and is followed by a mass rave/orgy to the drumbeats of a sort of ethno-trance music. These scenes are, it has to be said, very dull – it is also incoherent that the price of freedom should be a society so obviously stratified and hierarchical.

When Neo finally gets to talk to the Architect, he is subjected to a colossal information-dump that rewrites everything we have been told about this universe. The Machines have been in control for vastly longer and Neo is not so much a messiah as a safety valve or a Judas Goat. Zion will be destroyed, and all the humans in the tanks of the Matrix with it, unless Neo consents to become the leader of a saving remnant as his predecessors did. The Oracle is only incidentally a friend of humanity, the Architect claims, merely an AI with a more liberal policy about consent. In the event, circumstances make Neo's choices for him: to save Trinity, he has to exit the interview. She is dead and he rewrites her code so that her heart beats again. To save one life, the sages say, is to save the whole world.

And there is no special reason to privilege the Architect's version of the truth. Not only does it render all previous revelations redundant – it is almost certainly less than the whole truth. Suddenly, and at the price of great strain, Neo can effect miracles in the real world; does this mean that he can do magic or that the real world is itself another illusion which he is learning to hack? And if 'real life' is an illusion, just how far does illusion penetrate? Is it turtles all the way down? Radical scepticism is a great source of story, but in the end it reaches the law of diminishing returns.

The third film starts with Neo trapped in a subway station that exists as a point of transit for rogue programs that wish to live as humans in the Matrix – there is a touching scene in which we realize that programs mate and produce offspring and have accordingly to hide from their peers so that their 'children' can have a life. Trinity and Morpheus free him after a confrontation with the Merovingian – this whole sequence seems to exist purely in order to give that character something to do in this film, but hardly adds to our sense of who he is or what he is for. Attractive as these sequences are, they have almost nothing to do with the plot save to offer an explanation of the various children apprenticed to the Oracle.

The Oracle herself is doomed to be absorbed by Smith as he proceeds to swallow and subsume every single human and other personality in the Matrix. Meanwhile, the giant diggers and robotic warriors sent by the Machines to destroy Zion break through into a docking area and are fought in a colossal battle in which minor characters perform heroically. Neo sets off to interview the Machines – along the way he is blinded and Trinity killed by a human who has been absorbed by Smith.

Losing his eyes and his soulmate makes Neo even more totally a liminal being – part of him is alive and part dead. Without eyes, he sees the world as lines of force and communication; in a sense he sees true. He persuades the Machines to let him act as their champion against Smith, his price being that they spare Zion. He has been told, not least by the Oracle, that he will have to confront his greatest fear, and after several attempts to overpower Smith by force, accepts that this means he will have to let himself be absorbed. Given that the original blind seer of Truth was the double-gendered Tiresias, it is interesting that true heroism in the end amounts to letting himself be taken by force and rewritten in the same way that at the climax of the first film he rewrote Smith. Almost instantly, the various avatars of Smith return to their original forms in moments of blinding light.

Neo himself is left comatose in the couch/clutch of the Machines – it is not clear whether he is alive or dead, or whether, indeed, the *Matrix* franchise is done and dusted for good. Certainly the Oracle remarks to the Architect as these two unbearably smug artificial alliances strut around in the sunshine that they may expect to see Neo again. Given the hostile reception accorded to *Reloaded* and the hardly more favourable one given *Revolutions*, it seems unlikely that this particular promise will ever be fulfilled… in films at least. Still, a resurrected messiah attempting to make sense of what is still entirely unclear is certainly a direction in which the series could be taken, as is a quest for the resurrection of his beloved Trinity. These are very cheesy ideas, but hardly more cheesy than what has gone before – and it should be remembered that Orpheus became the centre of a mystery cult of initiation as well as the foundation myth of lost love. The Orphic mysteries also became one of the sources of Greek philosophy, which is, of course, where we came in.

7. The Mirrored Gaze

James Cameron's and Kathryn Bigelow's
Strange Days

Some people would argue that James Cameron, Jay Cocks and Kathryn Bigelow's *Strange Days* (1995) is not a science fiction film at all – it is a toughly romantic noir thriller set on the last two days and nights of the twentieth century – it is, for us now, set in a past that did not happen.[1] Yet the central device of the plot, far more than a mere McGuffin, is a technology that has never been invented – the recording and playback of physical sensations – which has social consequences for the Los Angeles of the film, and personal consequences for the characters. This makes it SF by any possible definition.

1. A short synopsis is in order here. Ex-cop Lenny is a dealer specializing in Playback discs; he is obsessed with his ex, Faith, who left him for a rock manager, Gant, who is helping her career. A rap artist also represented by Gant is murdered by police; this is witnessed, and recorded, by Iris, who puts the disc of this in Lenny's car before being raped and murdered. Her killer sends Lenny a playback recording of Iris' death and Lenny, who has some scruples, investigates with the help of Mace, a professional bodyguard who is in love with him, and his former colleague Max, who wants to persuade Lenny to share his cynicism. Lenny and Mace assume, after attempts on their lives, that there is a larger conspiracy than there actually is – the cops acted on their own and Gant's attempt at a cover-up is self-interested. Lenny and Mace give their evidence to the authorities in time to prevent a race riot at the millennial celebrations and their own murder by the policemen; Iris' killer was Max, who has also become Faith's lover, and murdered Gant. In a struggle with Lenny, he falls to his death.

Strange Days is most fruitfully regarded as a collaboration between all three, but especially between Cameron and Bigelow, no matter how disastrous their personal relationship may have been at the time – work on the film coincided with their divorce. It has strengths that derive from both of them: Bigelow's capacity to get stunning performances out of actors and her real flair with action sequences, and Cameron's inventive preparedness to take a good plot idea all the way.

The things which drew Bigelow to the project are obsessions she shares with Cameron. To pick on a couple, Bigelow's *Point Break* (1991) has a rather similar semi-erotic tempter/tempted relationship between its two main leads. Her *Blue Steel* (1990) has a somewhat androgynous heroine who learns a competence equivalent to that of Angela Bassett's Mace in the course of the movie, and whose competence is fetishized in rather more of the same way. Bigelow is always a sexy director even when she is not, as here, dealing fairly directly with sex and she shares Cameron's fascination with secret sharers – again, the villain of *Blue Steel* forces himself into this role – and with doubling.

The original Cameron treatment – referred to by him as a 'scriptment', because it contains a lot of final draft dialogue – is available online, as is a version of the script by Cameron and Cocks. The final film reverts in many large, and some small, details to the scriptment, and is generally tighter than either. Obvious examples of the former include the change of the scriptment's Philo Gant to the draft script's Tran and then back to Philo; Tran exists in the scriptment as a Vietnamese gangster most of whose plot functions are amalgamated with those of Tick.

Also crucial to the plot is an escalation of racial violence in Los Angeles which might have legitimately been predicted in the year 1992 when James Cameron first started working on the script, but instead levelled off during the years of the Clinton presidency. The racial politics of the film have understandably been criticized – the ending is oddly fairy-tale with everything being sorted out at the last minute by the intervention of a white patriarch, but it can after all be defended on the grounds that that is, in a sense, what happened. Similarly, the assumed economic collapse and Balkanization of American cities is a 1993 assumption that did not, in the event, come to pass.

What is also interesting about *Strange Days*' 1999 version is the almost entire absence of the Internet and associated technologies; it is one of the few films of its date whose plot makes full use of mobile phones and yet the Internet is not mentioned and seems not to exist. It is almost as if Cameron, when he first thought of the plot, made a conscious decision that the Internet and the technology of Playback and Squids (the recording devices) could not coexist in the story he wanted to tell. This refusal of certain aspects of the contemporary, far from rendering the film not science fiction – as some critics have claimed, as if science fiction had to be a straightforward extrapolation of the present into the future – in fact renders it an even more interesting consideration of the effects of technology on social and personal life.

Much of what is claimed by *Strange Days*' flawed protagonist Lenny as the virtues of Playback is after all what seemed for a while true of the Internet – it is a way to visit the dark end of the street without having to take responsibility for your actions; it is a chance to explore without commitment. What *Strange Days* does is comprehensively explore the morality of this, both in respect of the technology described and in terms of other sorts of exploration – the extreme violence of techno-noir movies like itself, for example. Many of the attacks made on *Strange Days*' morality have to do with this exploration and the fact that Bigelow forces us to look at things we would rather not have seen – it is a film about the gaze, and about not being able to look away. (It is probably simply the case that Cameron realized, consciously or intuitively, that the combination of Playback and the Internet was too much to deal with in one film – digital memories fired down a phone wire is a lethal combination.)

Its combination of tropes from noir fiction and film with near-future technology and loud rock music makes it close in many ways to cyberpunk, the movement in SF that was, when Cameron conceived the project, more or less cutting edge. Specifically, it owes some of its feel to the works of Pat Cadigan and William Gibson: Mace is the sort of tough woman with agency that both liked to use and Lenny the sort of moral burned-out case that both often used as protagonists. Lines like 'Are you paranoid enough?' have close parallels in the works of Cadigan, especially *Synners*. The film's obsessive use of mirror imagery can be related to the mirrorshade sunglasses that were for a while part of the stock set-dressing of cyberpunk stories and lives.

The running argument about whether the raw and unmediated material involved in Playback is inferior to the considered nature of art or the more natural processing of memories through gentle fading indicates that the technology here is an actualized set of metaphors. This set of metaphors is thrown into interesting dialogue with techniques like twinning and doubling in the plot and with the existence of twins, doubles and secret sharers among the characters. This play of metaphor and the concrete is one of the things that SF at its best is defined by.

There are, of course, things which were true in the real 1999 which could only have been predicted from the standpoint of 1992–1995 with great difficulty. The music of the film, for example, is a mixture of rap, grunge and thrash without a hint of the bubble-gum boy-bands that were to be a significant feature of the end of the millennium. The film shares its title with a Doors album, and the portentous apocalyptic polymorphous music of Jim Morrison is a significant part of the sound that Faith, the film's rock singer, makes; the actual Doors song *Strange Days* occurs twice on the soundtrack, first as Lenny gives Tex his disc[1] of running and takes in exchange the disc that will be one of the film's major McGuffins and fading into Faith's first solo number, and secondly as Lenny and Mace arrive at the hotel for their final confrontations.

What follows is a close consideration of *Strange Days* as a woven interplay of themes and metaphors and characters. An analysis of it in terms of acts, or of the pursuit of goals by the central characters, would be another perfectly legitimate procedure, but has, in my view, less to do than is ideal with the actual experience of the viewer, particularly the repeating viewer. None of the four central characters are precisely clear about their goals, for one thing, and their relationship with each other constantly changes and is constantly subject to revision. An analysis which assumes a straight line can be drawn is going to misrepresent the film's feel, because *Strange Days* is a film whose effect on first viewing depends on a series of revelations, and whose effect on second viewing depends on seeing how each of those revelations is carefully set up either literally or symbolically.

The exposition of the world Lenny lives in, and the goods he sells, is handled extremely effectively – the opening is a classic piece of SF exposition where we are not told everything at once and are instead shown it several times over before a final expository chunk for those members of the audience who really have not been paying attention. The film starts with titles, with a date, with a shot of an eye and Lenny's voice saying 'Boot it' and then moves to a long jerky shot from the point of view of one of a group of young thugs. They put stocking masks on, discuss guns and raid a restaurant; in the ensuing chase by the police the viewpoint character fails in a leap from one building to the next, is briefly caught by one of his friends and then dropped – to his death. At no point in any of this has the innocent unprepared viewer any sense that this is not part of the main thrust of the film's plot – though retrospectively the single shot of Lenny's eye is a useful instruction that this is a film about the gaze and about points of view.

Until, that is, the screen flashes red and we move to Lenny pulling off his headset and rejecting the disc:

1. Throughout what follows, I have referred to these as discs in spite of the fact that in both versions of the script and a couple of times in the film itself, they are referred to as tapes. The description in the script is of something that looks like a DAT tape and the product in the film itself is clearly a disc.

Lenny	Goddamnit! You know I don't deal in snuff. How many times I hafta tell you?!
Tick	Don't have a fucking coronary, Lenny.
Lenny	Well you could've at least warned me. You know I hate the zap… when they die. It just brings down your whole day.

The entire shooting style changes from crude and jerky and POV to a more finished camerawork and the viewpoint of an omniscient third person.

Suddenly the narrative rules have started to change – the change to a conventional movie style makes us realize that we are dealing with a narrative in which there is a privileged view and we have just moved to it. It is a move from the subjective to the objective and it means that we examine anything Lenny says or does with a critical eye. On the one hand, he does not deal in snuff – which we realize instantly means that there is a commercially available form of whatever we have just witnessed which involves the death of the viewpoint character – and that Lenny lives in a world where there are other people who will deal in it. At the same time, his entirely selfish attitude to the dead robber means that our sense of him as having scruples is instantly qualified by a sense that he is a deeply selfish man.

The reference to snuff does double service – establishing clearly that there is material out there which deals in recordings of death and dying and making explicit the analogy between Playback material and pornography, and thus establishing the extent to which this is a film which engages with discourses around pornography. (It is, indeed, a film some sequences of which have been angrily accused of being pornography, of being snuff.) Significantly, once this has been established, the conversation moves to discussing death recordings under the alternative term 'blackjack clips', thereby clearly defining that particular piece of imaginary slang.

The ensuing conversation between Lenny and Tick gives us most of the information we need. Lenny is a man producing material for customers and it is clear that what is wanted is radical sensation – a teenager quarrelling with her boyfriend is not enough – but not so radical that it involves death and dying. He talks to Tick about his scruples and his need to cut the recording – and this proves to be in large measure a way of talking the price down. Later on, in his car, he offers the disc to a client and there is no talk of cutting it:

Lenny	I just got something in, Bobby, you might appreciate. A 211 at a Thai joint goes south, and these three

> scuzzballs end up in a gun-and-run. It's a beauty, two
> thumbs up. Parental discretion advised. I'm talking it's
> the master, not some stepped-on copy. One of a kind.

We have had the analogy between Playback and pornography made explicit; the phrase 'two thumbs up' – the catchphrase of real-life movie critic Roger Ebert – and the implied joke about ratings makes an analogy between Playback and movies which will become progressively important as the film proceeds.

While Lenny moves around his city, recruiting participants in his schemes, sampling and commissioning other tapes and reinforcing our knowledge of what precisely it is that he sells, we see in the streets he drives through and listen to on the car radio he largely ignores the racial tension, the arbitrary police violence and apocalyptic black political hopes that are another crucial aspect of the film's plot. The movie's first shot included a date and time – much of the radio dialogue focuses our attention on the fact that it is now after midnight and it is two days before the end of the millennium. This is effective movie-making, establishing a lot of plot points, among them the mere fact that Lenny ignores everything going on around him.

He is, in this respect, the noir hero who 'sticks his neck out for nobody'; we know because this is a movie set in the darkest of nights that he will come good in the end, like Bogart, but we do not even begin to know how long it will take him.

As he drives, we get the first of many sequences in which the endangered society Lenny lives in is shown as background. We see a street life full of images of the young, black and white, confronting or running away from usually white police; we see the flames of Molotov cocktails; we see roadblocks. Similarly, in the various night-club scenes, we see images of violence as entertainment and of gender ambiguity and of sexual excess, and of all three in various combinations; when we meet Philo Gant and his courtiers, they do not particularly stand out from their context.

And suddenly Lenny stops being the focus of our attention – instead, we see the character we come to know as Iris running from two cops, Steckler and Engleman, and exercising ingenuity to avoid their merciless attention. One of the things that makes Iris' eventual death so shocking is that we have got used to the idea of her as someone who gets away from dire situations, as someone who is competent in a thriller plot. These scenes combine a sense of LA as city of dreadful night with a very real sense of it as a city of the future – when the film was shot, the new LA metro was open only from Union Station to McArthur Park, though scheduled to open as far as North Hollywood and beyond by the year in which it is set.

The fact that, a few minutes earlier, we have seen Lenny explain to a possible Playback performer the wearing of a wig with a Squid recorder under it means that when Steckler tries to pull Iris through a subway train window, and ends up with her wig in his hand, we know what it is that he has just found. We know that Iris has seen something that the cops do not want made public and that she has it on disc. By the time we see her stuff it in through the roof of Lenny's car some scenes later, we know that her disc is the McGuffin round which the plot of *Strange Days* is going to turn.

Lenny gets home, just missing her phone call and neglects to listen to it in favour of his nightly routine of Playback-induced nostalgia – in one of the film's trademarks, a plot point which functions as a metaphor, this is a failed connection. This is the first we know of Faith, the first hint that Lenny has something else seriously wrong with his life – the Playback sequence of her and Lenny rollerblading establishes tellingly how they think of their relationship. Faith cruises through life competently using her body, while Lenny is too busy looking at her to be able to cope. Alternatively, he relies on her to catch him before he falls and she is too concerned with her own elegant movements to remember to care for him – either way, and probably both, the rollerblading sequence is an apt establishing symbol of their relationship.

The Playback sequences into their love-making; significantly, they are looking at themselves in a mirror. Faith says, and she will say other things which both counter and amplify it: 'I love your eyes – I love the way you see.' As cannot be stressed too often, *Strange Days* is a film full of mirrors and of twinned events – it is at the point when Lenny again experiences a Playback in which someone is making love to Faith and looking at themselves in a mirror that he will come to realize how totally he has been betrayed by almost everybody he cares about. The young thug's fatal fall turns out to be another twinned event – this is a film in which Cameron, Cocks and Bigelow manage to make most things that happen do double or triple duty.

Unlike the other Playback clips we have seen and will see later, Lenny's memories of Faith are in something like real colour values – there was an overlit washed out quality to the robbery clip and a subsequent porno clip is overlush in its colour to the point where skin-tones are almost orange. The clips sent to Lenny anonymously by a killer are more or less monochrome, leading Tick to speculate that the killer is seriously colour-blind and possibly brain-damaged. The two shots we get of the damaged brains of Tick and Gant are psychedelically over-coloured and full of distortion. The only clips we see that approach Lenny's for realism are the clip he makes for the amputee DJ Tex, and Iris' clip of Jericho's assassination – and that is because the first is an act of kindness and the second is the truth. (It is established in Lenny's sales pitch that Playback technology started off as a means of gathering police evidence.)

The flashback to Lenny and Mace's first meeting, when he was still a cop, and her husband was arrested by his colleagues, and he was kind to her son, is in real colour values. It is, of course, a real memory and not a Playback.

In the moment of stillness at the end of the Replay, we see just how vulnerable Lenny is and are reminded that he is not only the slick dealer we have seen playing games with everyone he meets; he is also a sad man, a loser, and it is his sadness that makes us like him. In this, as at various other moments of stillness in this highly kinetic film, Ralph Fiennes oozes a vulnerability that makes us sharers in his flawed humanity. The film is all about sharing – and secret sharers and about the difference between the raw feelings of Playback and the controlled feelings of a movie audience, feelings that have been mediated by Art.

The death of the black singer and activist Jericho is mentioned on television as Lenny breakfasts on an ice lollipop; he ignores it as he ignores almost everything that is truly important in his world in favour of food without nourishment. The popsicle is, almost inevitably, red, white and blue – in case we had not noticed, Lenny *is* White America. He continues to suck it as he prepares his outfit for the evening – Lenny ignores essential things for appearances. In case we were wondering how we should take not only his revisiting of the relationship with Faith, but that relationship even when it existed, we have been told.

When we next see him, he moves almost at once into his sales pitch to a potential client – we have seen how phoney he is in many respects and yet he is a believer, an evangelical believer in what he sells:

> Lenny   It's my job to know people and what they want… what's behind their eyes…

and:

> Lenny   This isn't like TV only better. This is life. It's a piece of somebody's life. Pure and uncut, straight from the cerebral cortex. You're there. You're doing it, seeing it, hearing it… feeling it…

and:

> Lenny   I'm your priest, your shrink, your main connection to

the switchboard of souls. I'm the Magic Man, the Santa
Claus of the Subconscious. You say it, you even think it,
you can have it. You want a girl, you want two girls?

Lenny is so deluded himself about what he wants and completely fails to
understand this fact; he is the priest in need of salvation, the psychiatrist who
needs to cure himself, the giver in need of a gift. He thinks of himself as the
'main connection to the switchboard of souls' and yet he constantly makes
false connections.

At the same time, his acceptance of everything he sees in his rounds gives
him a curious capacity for forgiveness and love. In his treatment, Cameron
is quite specific about this: 'Christlike, in a strange way, he understands all,
forgives all.' Fiennes's performance captures this gentleness and this capacity
for taking endless punishment. Lenny's casual attitude to routine beatings
never seems masochistic to us – just an acceptance of how things are.

At this point, Tom Sizemore as Max breezes into the film. Almost everything
about Max is a double or a triple bluff – our first impression is that he is a
cop out to roust Lenny for dealing, and then we are told that it is his idea of
a joke to disrupt Lenny's sales routine and scare away his clients. Max mocks
Lenny for his clothes, and most especially for his highly coloured ties, and for
the humiliation of having lost Faith, and for having been thrown off the force,
all of which tells us something very worrying about Lenny and Max's ideas of
what male friendship is supposed to be like. It is, of course, true that Max is
just as brutal about himself and the bullet in the head that terminated his own
police career.

The two ex-cops are twinned with each other (and as a pair are twinned
with the nightmare cops Steckler and Engleman, who for most of the film
we assume to be its principal face of evil). Lenny is the vice cop who grew
too fond of the dark end of the street and the things sold there; Max, as we
eventually learn without being encouraged to think about the implications of
this, was a homicide cop who learned the hard way about homicide.

As we are shortly to learn, Max is seriously wrong about one or two
things:

Max   I mean sure, Faith was by far the most outstanding
           woman a guy like you could ever hope to get, I mean
           it's completely and deeply humiliating that she's gone,
           but it's over, campadre.

Lenny could, if he were not blind to his own real needs, get a woman far better than Faith; nor is it, as we gradually realize, entirely true that Lenny and Faith are over – every time Faith swears it is over, we see the lie in her eyes.

The two short sequences that follow make important plot points, but are got through in an almost perfunctory fashion. Iris turns up, tells Lenny she and Faith are in trouble and takes him out to his car. She sees what seem to be police and runs away from the peril they represent. It is in fact a repossession truck taking Lenny's car away; Lenny tries and fails to bribe the repo man with a fake Rolex, which Lenny replaces from a seemingly inexhaustible supply. Lenny is not actually very good at being sleazy and even minor players like a repo man can see through his act; his minor incompetences, like failing to make the payments on his car, turn out to have terrible consequences. Iris mistakes the repo man for the cops and runs off to what she thinks is safety and is actually her death.

It is only at this point in the film, well past its first half hour, that Mace appears or is even mentioned. She rightly resents the way Lenny exploits their friendship to get her to drive him around, all the more so because she has strong views about Playback and its effect on him; she specifically raises the point of the potentially racist element in his exploitation of her with the flip joke 'Driving Mr Lenny' in order that it can be dismissed, but there is nonetheless a real bitterness in her tone. She constantly lectures Lenny on his inadequate perception of the nature of friendship, but he knows, without quite understanding why, that she will always forgive him.

The similarity in names between Max and Mace have to do with the simple fact that Mace is Lenny's Good Angel just as Max is his Evil Angel. She hates the fact that he feels unconditional love for Faith, but identifies with that love, because it is what she feels for him. Interestingly the script improves the draft on this point – her line 'the only thing worse than a junkie is a man in love' becomes 'the only thing worse than a junkie is someone in love'. She is another of Lenny's secret sharers. She tries constantly to remind him of simple verities – like 'A friend is more than one person constantly doing favors for another' – just as Max tries to convince him of his absolute nihilism.

> Max   To the end of all things!
>   (*slugs down the shot*)
>   You know how I know it's the end of the world? Because
>   everything's been done, every kind of music's been tried,
>   every government's been tried, every fuckin' hairstyle.
>   'Ow you gonna make it another thousand years, for
>   Chrissake?'

Max is reacting to a television broadcast about Jericho's murder in which the dead rap singer and activist refers to the LAPD as an occupying military force. Jericho also refers to the authorities as 'rearranging the deck chairs in the Titanic', ironically, given that Cameron's future projects were to include his Oscar-winning *Titanic*.

Importantly, the house to which Mace's client Mr Fumitsu takes Lenny, having been persuaded by Lenny to become his client as well, is where we first meet the icily hostile Commissioner Strickland, whose combination of rectitude and loathing for Lenny sets up important plot points for the last act. He refers to Lenny by his surname, Nero, neatly establishing Lenny as someone whose footling corruption is a part of the apocalyptic.

We see Lenny at his worst when he is riding around with Mace, and yet we also see how much she loves him against her better judgement. Mace does almost everything to refuse to facilitate Lenny's going to the Retinal Fetish night club – a name which is as expressive of the content of the film as is 'TechNoir' in James Cameron's *The Terminator* (1984) – save actually not take him. She tries to throw him out of the car; she rebukes him for abusing her friendship, but in the end she not only takes him, but waits around.

Mace's job as a security driver – a combination of cab-driver and bodyguard, whose car is bullet-resistant and who has martial arts skills – is part of Cameron's vision of the end of the century and a city in meltdown. The whole point about Mace is that she is not extraordinary – she is an ordinary working mother who has found a job niche and filled it; Cameron's assumption is that security drivers are, in this world, routine.

It is only at this point in the film that we actually see Faith in the flesh – a slicker and at the same time more battered Faith than we have seen in Lenny's Playback clips – and meet Gant and his posse of thugs. The sequences involving this group have the repetitious feel of a dream or computer game – Lenny does the same thing time and time again and is thrown out and beaten up and comes back for more. He lets himself be mocked by Gant for being a loser, in spite of the fact that Gant is, from his perspective, just another punter, someone as obsessed with Playback as he is himself.

Gant has Lenny thrown out of the club by his hired muscle: Lenny breaks a window with his reinforced briefcase and is back in the club in seconds. The case is one of his accessories – one of the more expensive things he owns – and he uses it here as a blunt instrument and later as a shield. Unlike his watches, it is durable and the real thing.

In a throwaway moment, Lenny gives the amputee Tex a disc of a runner pacing along Santa Monica Beach and flirting with women as he runs; Tex gives him a disc which has been left for him anonymously. Part of what makes

Lenny vulnerable is that he really is, some of the time, a good man – he claims to know what people need and in the case of Tex it is arguable that he is right. And before we see one of the worst things Playback can be for, we see an almost entirely benign use of it. The contrast with movies is further set up at this point – Tex moves rapidly between decks and monitors from which he is projecting video clips to the walls of the club.

Lenny guesses that Faith does not love Gant and is using him for the sake of her career, that Gant is using her as an accessory, whose sheer rawness as a singer makes her at once both an impressive performer and something rather less than a saleable commodity. Cameron's description of Faith's singing in his original treatment is impressive and also makes explicit that her singing is one point along the continuum of the real in this film about authenticity: 'She seems like a force of nature.'

Maybe for the first time we see in Faith what Lenny sees: her energy, her talent, the life force flowing strong through her like a river. Her movements are fierce and unchoreographed, exploding toward the audience and then folding in, as if wrapping around some deep inner pain:

> Faith doesn't play to the audience, or engage them in any way. She is merely taking what's in her head and letting it out. She could give a shit if they are there or not.

Juliette Lewis' performance is at its most impressive when she is playing Faith the singer – she has a strong sense of precisely what it is that Cameron and Bigelow want from her and she gives it everything. She is also good in the scene with Lenny in which she tells him to go away and leave her alone – there is a brittle edge to her which might mean that she is lying or might simply mean that she has had enough of him. Lewis is good at playing Faith the performer of utterly sincere emotional truth and Faith the accomplished deceiver – we never entirely know where we are with her, which is as it should be. This was one of a group of similar roles she played in the mid 1990s – she may not have exhibited much range between this and Dominic Sena's *Kalifornia* (1993) and Oliver Stone's *Natural Born Killers* (1994), but she had a sleazy intensity that scorched the screen.

Fiennes is also at his most impressive as he stands, watching her, a solitary motionless figure shot by Bigelow in near-silhouette, and contrasted with the complex motion of Faith's dancing and the cavorting of the fiddle player who is part of her band. Meanwhile, he is being watched by both Gant's entourage of thugs and by one of the two cops we saw chasing Iris earlier.

He follows Faith into her dressing room where they talk, and she repairs her outfit in various mirrors, which frame them together much of the time; he pleads with her to come back to him and she refuses. The script's constant comparison of Playback and movies is made explicit during her rejection of Lenny:

Faith   You know one of the ways movies still have Squid beat? Because they always say 'The End'. You always know when it's over. It's over!

One of the film's neater ambiguities is that Faith uses cinematic language here to tell one of her more blatant lies – Lenny 'knows' she is lying because she has told him in language which, in a film, would always be a lie.

Faith also tells Lenny that Max is trailing her for Gant; Lenny confronts Max about this within moments of leaving her and forgives his friend in a moment of male bonding that is considerably more unpleasant in its implications than Lenny even begins to realize:

Lenny   Watch her for me. Stay on her.

Max   I'm on her.

Like much else in this film, this exchange means a lot more the second time we watch it.

He is thrown out of the club again by Wade, who this time gives him a perfunctory beating – Lenny asks for, and gets, a moment of grace to remove his expensive jacket and asks, 'Not the eyes'. From the way he is rubbing his jaw when we see him, it is clear that Wade complies with this. Throughout the film there is a steady escalation of the violence doled out to Lenny – he finds himself in jeopardy a piece at a time.

One of the most disturbing aspects of the scene where Lenny witnesses the stalking, rape and killing of Iris is that he thinks when he slips the disc into his player that he is safe. He is riding in the back of Mace's car and is getting away with doing Playback there even though she disapproves of his doing so – he is with the strongest woman he knows. Suddenly he is in a monochrome nightmare.

This is the sequence over which Bigelow has been most denounced – it has been claimed both by some feminist critics and by some male critics not normally noted for their feminist sympathies that it is an example of her buying into the boys' club of action directing by betraying women. It is certainly one of the most upsetting representations of rape and murder in mainstream cinema – like similar sequences in the equally condemned Michael Powell film *Peeping Tom* (1960), it needs to be. The killer's gaze concentrates almost exclusively on Iris' blindfolded face and though it is clear he is doing something with a knife we never see exactly what it is.[1] We never see genital contact, but the killer's bucking motion against Iris' body is almost more upsetting – a piece of pure male aggression that has nothing to do with even the pretence of pleasure. The most hideous aspect of the scene is that Iris is made to witness her own death through her killer's eyes and other senses; he not only records her death but broadcasts it to her as she dies.

Not only is the killer making Lenny the sharer in his killing – he is making an explicit link between sharing and death and sex; Lenny is at once made complicit in Iris' death and seduced. And in case we had not noticed that what is on offer is an explicit linkage of ideas about rape and murder with ideas about the cinematic gaze, and the feminist argument about them, one of the killer's last acts on the disc is to frame the dead Iris' face with his hands as if in a camera shot. (This framing is absent from Cameron and Cocks's script and is one of the points where Bigelow returns to Cameron's original vision in the treatment.) Lenny is in a very real sense both rapist, because he shares his sensations, and raped – because this sharing is against his will; significantly, he watches to the end only after telling Mace to drive to the hotel where it happened in the hope that it had some other end than it has. (The hotel is the Sunset – a perfectly plausible LA name and yet usefully linked to the film's millennial theme.)

Fiennes's performance during this sequence entirely answers the charge that the cinema audience is meant in any way to experience Iris' murder as anything other than an obscene violation. He collapses vomiting at the end of it and interrupts it before he knows for certain she is dead to tell Mace to drive to the hotel where the killing took place. It is, of course, arguable that any representation of rape and killing is inevitably compromised, but Bigelow goes to significant lengths to try to make this otherwise.

In another of the scenes that plays very differently when we watch it for the second time, Lenny and Mace go to see Max, who watches the disc and then persuades Lenny to talk his way through its implications. Yet again, the two men share things, from the tequila they drink to their meditation on what they have just witnessed:

Lenny   He stalks her. He rapes her. Then he does her…

---

1. There may be a horrific implied pun in that the sort of small knife used is sometimes referred to as a boxcutter.

Max	And he records it. Thrill kill. Wants to see it again. And again.

Lenny	He records himself raping and killing her –

Max	But at the same time he's sending the signal to her –

Lenny	So she feels… what he feels… while he's in her. The thrill while he's killing her… is sent to her, heightening her fear… which in turn heightens the turn on for him. (*turns to him*) I've seen a lot, Max.

Max	So've I. Too much.

Lenny	But this is a bad one.

Max	Top ten.

Lenny	He makes her see her own death, feeds off the reaction… killer and victim merging… orgasm and agony merging. And he records it all.

The two men discuss the murder and their discussion becomes ritual behaviour in itself until Mace interrupts them with one of the most important considerations of all – they need interrupting because otherwise they would go on being caught in this moment of rapt contemplation of the horror – by pointing out that the killer sent the disc to Lenny. And suddenly Lenny is confronted with his good and evil angels both making him see his complicity with the killer to an extent that he finds unbearable:

Max	He's skull-fucking you, bud. Trying to get a reaction. Maybe pushing you to do something.

Mace	Maybe he just figures Lenny will appreciate what he's created. It's the dark end of the street, Lenny. How do you like it now?

Max has just walked Lenny through the rape and murder a second time so that first he experiences it as Playback and second as the memory of Playback turned into a narrative; if the one is a skull-fuck, what is the other? Again, this is a scene with a radically clearer meaning on a second viewing as is Max's final comment: 'Keep moving man; someone's thinking about you a whole lot.'

Lenny's response to the situation is to go and see Faith *again* and to appeal to her again to leave Gant; her refusal to leave, and ostentatious display of loyalty to Gant, is, as we are told almost at once, false. Gant knows she still has feelings for Lenny, and he beats her for it in a moment of savage misogyny.

Downstairs, Lenny is getting a beating of his own, one which is explicitly an attack on his masculinity – 'We tried to find a smaller girl to beat the shit out of you, but it was short notice' – and his lack of authenticity – when he tries to buy them off with his fake Rolex, one of them takes it, asks if it is impact-resistant, and uses it as a knuckle-duster. The beating that Lenny gets from Gant's courtiers leads into the far more efficient beating that they get from Mace, with some assistance from Lenny. Up to this point, we have seen Mace as moral centre and as someone on a very short fuse with Lenny – what we have not seen is Mace as the very effective professional dispenser of violence. For Gant's little posse, beating up Lenny, or anyone else on whom they are let loose, is a hobby – something they do because they enjoy it; for Mace, violence is something for which she has no especial taste, but which she is very good at.

Especially since she is protecting the man she wants. In one of the film's regular touching moments of stillness, she tends to Lenny's wounds back at his apartment and as he falls asleep, cradles him in a pose which represents her as a *pietà*, as the virgin mother cradling the dead Christ. This reflects how Lenny sees her almost until the film's end, because he cannot let himself see her as a sexual being.

Lenny wakes to a phone call from Max, who is watching Gant and Faith at Jericho's funeral. It is as the call ends that he discovers another disc – this one recording the killer's visit to his apartment during the night when he was asleep. It is only after seeing the killer touch a knife to his throat that Lenny finds the scratch it left there – again, he is being told by the killer, but also by the film's auteurs, that he is a blind man who knows nothing of his own fate. He hears a noise and scrambles for his gun, only to find Mace making coffee in his kitchen; Lenny is here, as so often, confused about who his friends are.

They take the discs to Tick, who gives them crucial information about the killer – that his monochrome vision is a symptom of brain-damage. In one of many effective pieces of misdirection, our attention is diverted from this to his mention of a visit from Iris before she was killed; she copied a disc. Mace talks Lenny through his memories of his last meeting with Iris and he realizes that she had put this other disc in his car.

Though this is a film much of which takes place at night, it is only at this late point that it becomes explicitly a night journey, a ritual quest for knowledge. The trip to the junkyard with its dog is in a real sense a trip to the Underworld – a place of dead things with a demonic guardian – and Lenny receives a message from the dead Iris in the shape of a note asking him to help her. He is not yet ready to acknowledge his failures as a human being and the extent to which they led to Iris' death and when Mace asks him what the note said, he says 'Nothing'.

The attempts by the killer cops to rid themselves of Lenny and Mace partake of shared ritual initiation. Explicitly, their firing of the car, and Mace's saving of her self and Lenny by driving into the sea, and then, once the fire is out, breaking free and swimming to safety is not only the hugely enjoyable action sequence that it is, it is also an ordeal by two of the elements, fire and water. (Three if you count the breath they have to hold while escaping.)

Even more than in the earlier sequence of Lenny's beating by Gant's posse and Mace's rescue of him, he is entirely passive in most of this. It is Mace who knows what to do and all he can do is follow her lead. This is one of several moments at which their relationship reverses standard action-adventure gender expectations; this is a film in which the woman is the action hero and the man her untrustworthy but attractive beloved who has to be rescued all the time. She even gets a distinctively female version of the usual stock macho line: 'Calm down, baby. This is what I do.'

The one really positive action Lenny performs in all this is his deception of the cops, giving up to them what they think is the disc they are after, but is in fact one of his discs of Faith. For the first time, Lenny gives up a little bit of his past for the greater good and for his and Mace's survival. He shows her Iris' disc with a grin and asks 'Are you impressed yet?' and for once she is.

Lenny has recognized the two policemen for what they are and warns Mace that she has to move her family to safety. There follows one of the more problematic scenes of the film – the quick dip into Mace's other life, a life of family and community, is perhaps too crude in its portrayal of an upper working-class black milieu as held together by mutual regard rather than atomized and mutually exploitative like Lenny's social world. Cameron and Bigelow sentimentalize Mace's family and friends a little too much – this may not be racist, but it is certainly naff.

Lenny watches the disc and finds out what it is that is so important that his life is being wrecked as a side effect of it – something so important that his sheer seriousness about it makes Mace break her firmest resolve and experience it directly. Earlier, when selling the whole wirehead experience to the lawyer Keith, Lenny smiled salaciously and talked about Keith's 'virgin brain'; here he apologizes to Mace for a negative first experience: 'Sorry this has to be your first Playback.'

Iris is with Jericho and his friend Replay when they are stopped by the two cops Steckler and Engleman, who start throwing their weight around; Jericho responds with threats of exposure – they have stopped and brutalized the wrong people this time – and they murder him and Replay and Iris' friend Diamanda, just like that. Iris runs and escapes them – we know how that story ends. The effect on Mace, both of what she has just seen, and of losing her Playback virginity, is devastating; here, as at several other points in the film, Bigelow relies on a moment of stillness and the absolute intensity of Angela Bassett's look to convey this.

They arrange to rendezvous with Max and find Tick with his brain blasted. Lenny works out that the two cops are too unsubtle to be the killer – he has started using his intelligence again. Unfortunately, this does not extend to ceasing to trust Max, who talks them out of taking the evidence to the police with claims that he has heard there is a death squad. Max and Mace have, at this point, one of the crucial debates of the film – should they release the disc to the media and risk an apocalyptic bloodbath, or suppress it by using it as currency? Significantly, the film offers no very obvious answer to a question out of which it will inevitably have to cop.

Mace and Lenny attempt a rescue of Faith, who this time is willing to come with them; she talks of Gant's paranoia, how he burned the other copy of Iris' disc and how scared he is that knowledge that he tapes his clients will destroy his career. Everything she says is true – and everything is also, as we find out later, a lie. In the event, the rescue attempt fails; its most important aspect is perhaps that when Faith wants to tell her story to Lenny alone, he insists on including Mace in the conversation.

This foreshadows and precedes what is, perhaps, the most important single scene in the film. To recap, we have seen different sorts of sharing of experience. On, broadly, the negative side, we have seen the reflexive voyeurism that Faith loves and hates about her relationship with Lenny; the discs from which he endlessly revisits the raw and unprocessed form of that relationship; the discs he sells and his relationship with the clients to whom he acts as priest and analyst; the discs with which the killer has invaded the minds of Lenny, Iris and Tick; the sharing of police habits of analysis by Lenny and Max and the macho camaraderie at the surface of their friendship. On the positive side, we have seen the bonding from shared adventuring that has linked Lenny and Mace and the moments of tenderness in which he allows her to care for him. More neutrally, we have seen the frenzied nightlife of clubs and the passionate communication that is Faith's singing; we have been reminded that we are watching a film, and films have been distinguished, clearly, from Playback.

Lenny announces his intention of going to the hotel after Faith, and Mace refuses to go with him. Now, we have moments of emotional nakedness between Mace and Lenny. She tells him what she really thinks of Faith – 'that toxic-waste bitch' – and tries to smash as many as possible of his tapes of life with Faith by stamping all over them. She rages at him – 'pussy-whipped sorry-ass mother-fucker' – and warns him that going to the hotel is just a trap:

Mace   This is your life, Lenny! Right here. Right now. This is realtime... not playback. Real... time. Time to get real. Understand what I'm saying... she doesn't love you. Maybe she did once, I don't know, but she doesn't now. These are used emotions. It's time to trade them in. Lenny, memories were meant to fade. They're designed that way for a reason.

Her plea to him makes no reference to her own feelings, but rather to authenticity and emotional honesty, to the right kind of sharing. He replies in kind and they share their feelings in terse dialogue that is the closest either has come to admitting what she feels for him:

Lenny   Have you ever been in love with somebody who didn't return that love?

Mace gives him a look like, jeez Lenny, are you dumb sometimes.

Mace   Yeah. Lenny. I have.

Lenny   It didn't stop you from loving them. Right? Or understanding them, or being able to forgive them...

And he goes on to talk to her about his feelings for Faith in absolute honesty with tears streaming down his face and talking about his love for Faith, the artist of truth and intensity:

Lenny   She could take all the hurt and rage of the entire world and lift it up to heaven in one voice. I helped her. And I promised her that I'd always be there... to protect her. (*long pause*) See? It's not about what's in her head. It's what's in mine. I can't let go of the promise. It's... like... it's all I have left.

She tells him that it is not all he has left, and kisses him, and agrees to come with him to the hotel. Both abandon their trademark cool for an intimacy that touches us deeply.

People who do not like this film feel this moment to be grandiose sentimentality; people who admire it think otherwise. Bassett and Fiennes certainly give it their all – modern film actors rarely get the chance to deliver Hollywood romantic dialogue so entirely full-blooded. The scene is a remarkable one to find in the middle of a film made, let us remember, during the divorce of its director and its principal writer.

What follows straight away is pretty standard passage work: Lenny and Mace have simply to be moved from her friend's home to the interior of the hotel through a crowd less obviously angry, more clearly caught up in the spirit of the hour. It is carnival (which is also, in case we forget, a time of saying farewell to the flesh) and the streets are full of streamers and ticker-tape, like the stage when Faith performs. Mace has abandoned her trademark efficient androgynous uniform for a sequinned outfit and an elaborate hairdo, but she retains her deadliness, with a gun in a garter holster. Faced with security at the door of the hotel, she looks round in momentary panic and Lenny echoes her earlier quiet boast of competence: 'This is what *I* do.'

Mace has still not started to suspect Max; she sees Faith as the betrayer even though it is Max that has suggested using the disc for a trade. The confrontation between Lenny and Mace about the use of the disc is one of the points at which *Strange Days* makes its clearest references to the history of noir in film. He talks of using it as currency, with which they can buy safety for themselves and, of course, Faith; for him, it is the equivalent of the letters of transit which act as McGuffin in *Casablanca*. For Mace, on the other hand, the disc is something much too precious to be used for barter – it is simply the Truth, 'a lightning bolt from God':

> Mace   It can change things. Things that need changing before
>   we all go off the end of the road. And you do not have
>   the right to use it for currency. You go… you go alone.
>   This is where I draw the line. I care about you Lenny…
>   a lot more than you know… which makes us both
>   pretty stupid. But you pawn that tape, you mean
>   nothing to me.

Faced with this direct appeal from her as his conscience and the woman who loves him, Lenny seems to fail the test and walks away from her. She turns to leave, then breaks and comes back, only to bump into him returning to give her the disc. It is a nice touch that Lenny's moment of truth coincides with Mace falling short of her own standards of rectitude; she is the voice of righteousness, but she is also someone in love hoping against hope that Lenny will suddenly make the relationship between them right.

(I have mentioned earlier the extent to which Lenny is a darker, more ineffectual twin of Rick in *Casablanca*. The parallels extend further: Rick too has a genially corrupt secret sharer in the shape of Reynaud. More interestingly still, though he turns out to be a force for righteousness, Strickland, as head of an occupying army, who despises the film's protagonist and struts around in absolute certainty of his own right to rule, has interesting parallels with Colonel Strasser.)

After their moment of sharing, the film's two central characters pursue parallel but separate storylines. Mace confronts Strickland, whose reaction is to threaten to arrest her for possessing illegal material; she is grabbed by one of his officers and fights her way out. She is attacked again, this time by Gant's coterie, and fights free of them as well. Now she finds herself pursued through the crowd by Steckler and Engleman and metaphorically menaced by a clock-faced mime and by a leering Death. She successfully evades them for a while and they start shooting randomly into the crowd; at which point, she attacks and disarms them with their own weapons. All of this is perfectly competent by-the-numbers action stuff of a sort both Bigelow and Cameron can do in their sleep.

Meanwhile, Lenny has confronted Wade in the corridor and repaid his earlier beating with a swingeing violence that foreshadows his next confrontation. In Faith's room, Lenny finds broken glass, disorder and another envelope addressed to him by the killer and starts to play back the disc he finds in it as if he already knows what he is going to see. It is almost a repeat of the Iris tape – except that Faith clearly knows who the killer is – and he watches in despair as something that almost recapitulates the murder of Iris follows. He wanders through to the bedroom and finds a shrouded body – only it is not Faith as he has assumed but Gant, who has had his brain fried by a booster box.

Lenny watches the rest of the disc at this point and discovers that the killer is, and always has been, Max. Whereas in the murder disc, the killer looked into a mirror to show that he was masked, now he looks into a mirror to reveal his identity. It is never explicit that Faith knows she is recapitulating Iris' killing, but she is doing rather more than play out a rape fantasy, she knows Max is Iris' killer and enjoys being a sharer in his sexual fantasies. When she says, a few minutes later, that Lenny taught her to enjoy being watched, it becomes explicit that his actions and tastes may have prepared her for this ultimate corruption.

Lenny watches the burning of Gant's brain and takes off the headset – to discover that he is not alone in the room, that Max is doubly reflected in the mirrors. Max no longer needs Lenny as a sharer – the double image implies that he has become his own sharer – and utters a line classic in its cool ironic betrayal: 'Don't make any assumptions about our friendship, Lenny.' Lenny talks him into sharing one last time – the standard riff in which the villain explains the plot is for once plausible here – and a lot of the loose ends are elegantly tied up by a man who loves to boast and loves to demonstrate how clever he is.

Some of the plot points raised here are worth commenting on. In a superior piece of misdirection, we have avoided thinking of Max as the killer simply because we know both from watching his Playbacks and from Tick that the killer has monochromatic vision and Max has commented negatively on Lenny's ties: now we are told the truth:

Lenny   I didn't know you were colorblind, Max.

Max   Only way I could stand your ties.

In a superb piece of economy, this turns out not to be the last use of the ties in this very thoroughly written plot.

So much of the plot turns out to have been Max setting up a situation in which he could avoid killing Faith by killing the man who has hired him for her murder – which means in turn that he has had to find a patsy for the other killings he has ended up doing along the way:

Max   And who better than his girlfriend's loser ex-
          boyfriend... a known criminal... who has been seen
          hassling them in public numerous times.

Lenny   And who was, regrettably, also your best fucking friend.

Max   No plan is perfect, Lenny.

Lenny learns the hard way about the problems with a model of friendship which includes making use of your friends – at this point as at so many others the script goes out of its way to make him a man who is punished in order to see the error of his ways.

Max uses the fireworks displays of the imminent millennium to cover the gunshot when he kills Gant and plans to do the same when he shoots Lenny. The millennium also serves as part of his justification for his endless betrayals

– he echoes his earlier nihilism about the millennium being the end of the world through exhaustion of experience: 'Hey, cheer up. World's gonna end in ten minutes anyway.' He also makes explicit the linkage between that nihilism and his feeling of entitlement – his own past suffering legitimizes anything he now chooses to do:

> Max   Hey… nothing means nothing. You know that. Look around… the whole planet's in total chaos. You gotta take what you can, while you can. Cause some shitbird can come up and put a fuckin' .22 in the back a your head any second.

It is also during this prolonged gloat that the script makes explicit that the pervasive paranoia of the plotting, so memorably expressed by both Max and Gant, is in fact a delusion – that Max has talked not only Lenny but also Mace into avoiding the cops with his talk of a death squad, and that going to the police would have been the sensible thing in the first place. By the same token, it never occurs to him that they have gone to the one policeman they know to be incorruptible – Max's own paranoia ensures that he does not understand that a virtuous person like Mace will, even when tricked into paranoia, find a way around it and that Lenny is enough of a realist to have worked out what that way would be – the man who loathes and despises him above all others.

Lenny knows that the moment Max stops talking and gloating he is dead, and manipulates him straight back by asking him about his relationship with Faith – Max is so used to the secret sharer role and so enjoys the sexual humiliation of the friend he loves, hates and plans to kill that he allows Lenny to buy time by persuading Max to talk him through the deal Max and Faith struck. Previously, Max has kept separate the roles of friend and killer; now the two roles are united.

Lenny thinks he can bear what he is about to be told – Faith's entry and insistence on acting out the dialogue between her and Max makes for a sharing too far. It is also a rehearsal of the past, another form of Playback, from which Lenny learns things he did not necessarily want to know and gets his nose rubbed in the moral mess he has helped to create:

> Faith   And I said, 'That's good, because I like the feeling of someone watching me. I acquired the taste from Lenny.'

We have seen enough in earlier scenes that we know what, at this point, Lenny does not: that Faith has some feelings for him and that he has, ironically, always been right to believe this, though wrong to think it mattered. Faith takes part in Max's extended humiliation of Lenny because she needs to do this in order that Max trust her – and then betrays him to save Lenny, or at least by grabbing Max's gun hand to allow Lenny to save himself. Or perhaps the habit of betrayal has gone so deep in her that it overrides her survival instinct.

In the ensuing fight, random shots destroy the room's mirrors – given the importance of mirrors actual and metaphorical throughout the film, mirrors had finally to be broken at its climax, both for the sake of the metaphor and because, in a film about violence that has mirrors in it, there is always going to be damage before the film ends. Lenny and Max are no longer to be secret sharers and the film's obsession with doubling and twinning is in its last minutes – but not before, just as happened with Iris and the killer cops, Max's long hair is pulled off and revealed to be a wig with a Squid inside it – interestingly, it has never been especially plausible that it was his real hair, but we have thought of it, have been misdirected to think of it, as there to hide his head injuries.

Finally, Max is suspended from the room's balcony by Lenny's tie, one of the ties he so despised, and is trying literally to do what he has been doing throughout the film – drag Lenny down with him into the darkness. Earlier in the fight he has stabbed Lenny in the back – again, he has done literally what he has been doing throughout. And in an economic piece of plotting replete with metaphor Lenny pulls Max's knife from his shoulder and uses it to sever the tie between them – Max, who has all the way through the film been so much the manipulator and the puppet-master, sees his own death coming for him and can do nothing whatever to prevent it.

The camera follows him all the way down in long tracking shots whose entire artifice does not even slightly weaken their effect; Lenny and Faith watch him fall and it is the last thing they ever do together. At the beginning of the film, we witnessed through Playback the death of a young thug we hardly knew – here we see the death of a man we have come to hate. The one was a jerky sequence of images that meant almost nothing to us; the second a composed piece of art that enables us to luxuriate in death. The twinning here is a handy way of making us consider the morality not of Playback, but of our own movie-going habits; Lenny may not deal in snuff, but Bigelow and Cameron do, in a sense, and are prepared to remind us of the fact by making us cheer a violent death.

Lenny knows the whole truth about Faith, a truth that includes her unpreparedness to see him killed by her new lover – and he quietly and without appeal rejects her. He leaves without a second glance, nor does he spare her much more of a look when she is taken away by the police at the end of the film. (One of the film's several loose ends is that it is not entirely clear what she has been arrested for.)

This last sequence of the film is efficient rather than memorable – there is a very real sense in which the film ought not to have a happy ending. It is not, for example, especially plausible that Mace manages to overpower both of the killer cops, nor that the subsequent attack on her by a mob of riot police leaves her with so few injuries. There is a sense in which what ought to happen is that Lenny loses her and has to learn to live with real memories instead of Playbacks. That, realistically, is not a film that would have been made in the mid 1990s, and at least what happens is attractive and uncynical.

As it is, the cops hunt her down and she turns the tables on them; she is attacked by riot police who in turn come under attack from the onlookers, black and white, who are in turn attacked by more heavily armed police. For a moment, the massive riot Max warned them to dread seems to be coming about. All of this is interrupted by the police commissioner who descends in one of the film's omnipresent helicopters, saves Mace and orders the arrest of the guilty men. This is the stuff of melodrama and fairy story – a deus ex machina that has, at least, been carefully set up, but which really will not entirely do.

Much of what follows is a by-the-numbers denouement: one cop grabs a gun, and blows his brains out; the other, covered in his blood, has to be shot down before he can kill Mace. At Strickland's behest, the LAPD bloodily cleans its own house – this is, after all, a science fiction movie. This renewal of menace after the apparent ending is more or less a cliché of the action film of the 1990s – John McTiernan's *Die Hard* (1988) for example – but at least here it serves a purpose other than playing games with the audience's nerves. Lenny performs perhaps the only heroic act of which he is capable – he interposes his body expecting to take a bullet for Mace – and it is a passive one; his momentary heroism is compromised by the fact that he almost immediately faints. In his relationship with Mace, he remains the girl even when he manages to do the right thing.

He and Mace are taken away separately at first – both have many questions to answer – but Lenny insists on reclaiming her so that they can kiss the new year in, both wincing with the pain of their injuries. It is perhaps a cop-out that they are together and that the New Year passes on an image of interracial romance than on the bloodshed that has seemed likely throughout the film; at the same time, we have been shown enough darkness throughout the film that the happy ending seems almost perfunctory.

The clock-faced mime counts down the seconds and it is the new millennium. Mace and Lenny kiss and they are only one of many couples, mixed-race and same-sex, kissing, in a public act of open sharing. The camera zooms away from them and they are lost in the crowd of kissing couples, and then it zooms upwards, and the crowd is replaced by paper party-favours, falling like white flowers or snow against the darkness, a final image of embattled purity and celebration. It is one of the most attractive moments in the careers of either of the film's auteurs.

8. Creation as Product

The Paradox of Franchises

Many of the distinctive traits of science fiction as a literary form and in particular the things that separate it from SF film derive from its collegiality. Science fiction, especially in the USA, was, from a fairly early stage in its history, written by people who had graduated to writing it from reading it – a significant number of the writers of the so-called Golden Age of the American SF magazines had started off as fans who wrote letters to magazines and corresponded with each other. There is an extent to which the writing of science fiction was a continuation of that correspondence about science fiction.

Examples of this collegiality can be multiplied endlessly. To give but two examples: several young writers and editors of the 1940s, notably Cyril Kornbluth, Frederik Pohl and Damon Knight, moved into a shared apartment and held open house there; other fans who turned into writers – notably Isaac Asimov – spent much time with them even if they did not share the group's radical politics. Robert A. Heinlein was famously generous with patronage, time and money to those he regarded as his colleagues – he jobbed various other writers into his war work at the US Navy Yards, and he gave not only money, but story ideas, to the very different writer Theodore Sturgeon when the latter was blocked and broke. Again, this collegiality transcended strong political views.

It is useful to compare the attitude of the great precursors of SF to each other with those of their literary descendants. Verne mocked Wells, regarding the idea of gravity-screening material in *The First Men in the Moon* as mere fantasy, and the space gun in his own *From the Earth to the Moon* as hard fact; ironically, the science of the situation is that Verne's gun would work after a fashion, but smash the passengers in the capsule it fired to jellied bones, whereas there is a slim possibility that anti-gravity is a force in the universe. Later generations tended to argue these things out in fictional form as well as by grumbling to their immediate friends – indeed stories were often a way of grumbling to those of their close friends who had become editors and writers.

One of the determining traits of Anglo-American, commercial, genre SF is this tendency to echo earlier texts in order to have an argument with them – from the 1940s onwards there has been a constant examination of the implications of stock themes which has been a collective enterprise. (It is useful to distinguish this dialectical metonymy from that echoing of earlier texts, also common, which is purely ludic.) Do humans as we know them have any traits which might not be shared with alien life forms, such as a sense of humour, a capacity to lie, immortal souls? Is time travel possible and, if so, what happens when you kill your grandparent? Can societies be based on bizarre arrangements and still be stable and just?

Many of these questions are by way of being thought experiments as much as literary conceits, which is why they have often been considered useful by philosophers such as Derek Parfitt, or by scientists and technologists – some gadgets in the real world, like waldoes, the manipulators used to handle atomic waste, take their name from the SF in which they were originally described (Heinlein's novella *Waldo*). Occasionally, the speculations of SF writers have influenced the way technologists think about a whole enterprise – William Gibson's novella *Stealing Chrome* and novel *Neuromancer* had a real influence on the development of virtual reality as well as coining the term 'cyberspace' for the virtual universe created by computer interconnectivity and creating many of the visual clichés of the 1990s.

The reason for this is not just that individuals have good ideas. It is that, for the most part, those ideas have hinterland – they have a context in an ongoing dialogue that has endlessly refined them. Gibson crystallized a lot of ideas about virtual reality in his fiction, but he was drawing on a whole body of literature about artificial dreams, say, that vary from the shared hallucinations of Philip K. Dick's characters to the chill machine-mediated utopia of Arthur C. Clarke's *The City and the Stars*. Gibson drew on the styles of his predecessors as well, notably on the moody noir cityscapes of Alfred Bester and the jagged expressionist gimmickry that Bester used to represent the conversations of telepaths or the rapid visual cuts with which he described teleportation. This is by no means to say that his, in fact very original, work was derivative; it is rather that much of that originality was made possible by reacting to that hinterland of influences.

Sometimes as an exercise in mutual influence and playfulness, sometimes as a purely commercial enterprise, most often as a combination of the two, one of the standard forms of published SF is the shared-world anthology – George R.R. Martin's *Wild Cards* series, for example. Themed anthologies are even commoner – and also occur in crime fiction – but the point of the shared-world anthology is to set a group of rules and then play with them, whether those rules be a fairly complex set of parameters for life on an alien planet or something looser like a ages-old conspiracy of shape-changers living among humanity. The point is not that ideas be new; it is that they be explored.

Because magazines have played a large part in the history of science fiction, and editors need to be able to persuade their readers to come back loyally every month, series of stories by a single author were always a significant part of SF magazine content and this continued when book publication became progressively the dominant norm. Whereas series stories in the thriller genre have tended to feature a character or group of characters – Peter Wimsey or Modesty Blaise and their galleries of friends and allies – many SF series have been centred on a universe as much as on characters within that universe: Heinlein's Future History, Niven's Known Space, Asimov's long sequence that includes both his robot stories and the *Foundation* novels in a well-worked-out stream of continuity.

Continuity in SF is therefore not only about the biographies of characters; it is about the historical process, whether at the macro-level of statecraft or the secondary level of the history of a technology. Moreover, the greater involvement in SF of its consumers/fans means that authors are rather more likely to have any gaping holes in the logic of their continuity pointed out to them and either to expend ingenuity on trying to fix it or simply to go back and alter the original text – Larry Niven had, after criticism, to revise the orbital arrangements of his high-tech *Ringworld* sequence.

Of course, one of the reasons why written SF has proliferated series is that, both in magazine and book form, series are a sound commercial product; ironically, a form dedicated to the new can often be quite conservative in its preparedness repetitiously to service audience expectation. Similarly, SF movies have proliferated series because a series that works is a sound investment for the studio lucky enough to have one on its hands. One of the reasons why we refer to such series as a franchise is the proliferation of other products – models, spinoffery, T-shirts – that a successful SF movie series is even more likely to generate than a successful series in other genres. (A successful thriller series like Richard Donner's *Lethal Weapon* (1988–1997) may generate action figures or possibly novelizations, but its detectives use real-world cars and other consumer durables – models are less the point here than product placement.)

Much filmed SF fails to work as SF simply because it lacks contact with a broader context of influence – with one or two exceptions like Leigh Brackett, who wrote the script for *The Empire Strikes Back*, and had a long career in the SF pulp magazines and as a screenwriter, few scriptwriters have this sense of the hinterland of the ideas with which they are working and even fewer directors and producers. When playing with ideas, they are not going to know what is a cliché and what is an interesting new twist, even when they come up with one. This in turn means that comparatively little filmed SF has the resonance that comes from being one point in an ongoing collective dialogue. This would not matter were these films noticeably engaged in dialogue with other sorts of film, but with a few exceptions – the Hitchcock references in Terry Gilliam's *Twelve Monkeys* (1995) and Steven Spielberg's *Minority Report* (2002), the noir and expressionist gestures of *Dark City* – this is not interestingly the case.

The one place where SF film might have been hoped to build up such a dialogue is perhaps in the various SF franchise series. After all, the sheer process of making a sequel ought to concentrate the creative mind on what worked in the first film and what did not, on how to say things in a second film in a way that does not merely recapitulate the first and cash in on its success. It should be possible for an intelligent writer and director to use the first film of a series as the hinterland that gives the later films ever greater richness of texture, rather than as a template of which they are ever thinner and greyer xeroxes.

This ought to be the case, perhaps, but with one very major exception, and a couple of special cases, this has not been even slightly what happened. One of the obvious special cases is Peter Hyams' *2010* (1984), which sensibly imitated its predecessor, Stanley Kubrick's *2001* (1968) by involving Arthur C. Clarke as an advisor on the project; another is the Zemeckis *Back to the Future* trilogy, where the theme of time paradox is played with with real elegance, perhaps because the theme's discourse has entered into the popular imagination rather more than other similar preoccupations of SF. The second film's dystopian alternate future is in any case a clear nod to the alternate present shown us in Frank Capra's *It's A Wonderful Life* (1946).

The sequence of *Alien*, *Aliens*, *Alien³* and *Alien Resurrection* is, as I shall demonstrate, the exception, partly because of the utter excellence of the original and the real thoughtfulness which James Cameron brought to the question of making a sequel. Though there is much to be said in criticism of both David

Fincher's *Alien³*, which tries in effect to be a sequel to the first film and not the second, and the Jeunet/Whedon *Alien Resurrection*, where an imperfect match between the visions of director and screenwriter produces some unsatisfying compromises, at the very least this was at no point a franchise series which stumbled because of lack of thought.

One of the reasons why SF cinema has so often consisted of a quest for franchises – some singleton films, like the sub-standard Stephen Hopkins' *Lost in Space* (1998), were consciously trial runs for a franchise – is that the return of SF cinema as a serious genre in the late 1970s was sparked by the creation of one of the most commercially successful cinema franchises of any kind – the *Star Wars* sequence. That sequence's failings, particularly in the later films of the twenty-first century, derive in part from their auteur George Lucas' long-term failure to engage with the material he colonizes in any very serious way.

Specifically, the films fail to engage interestingly with the idea of historical process – the best space opera has tended to be about history, and has dealt with Galactic empires in order to show them rise and fall. For Lucas, history is entirely a function of biography – the Republic falls and is replaced by the Empire solely and wholly because Palpatine is, and Anakin Skywalker becomes, a bad man. Compared to even the best pulp magazine treatments of this sort of material – Isaac Asimov's original *Foundation* sequence, say, though not his later additions to it – this is infantile; *Foundation* discusses the predictability of human affairs and the wild cards that sooner or later distort any plan or prediction in terms that include morality rather than being limited to it.

Nonetheless, the bliss of seeing *Star Wars* for the first time in the 1970s should not be underestimated. It was, primitive as its CGI now looks in the original, unimproved version, the first time most SF fans had seen the things that they had spent their lives imagining, the first time that many other viewers had come into contact with a stock of images that feel like the folk memory of a genre. Its opening is almost impossible to better from that point of view – a starship looming into the screen from over their heads firing wildly at what is following it, a starship of immensely greater size. Part of the effectiveness of that opening and of the film as a whole comes from John Williams' score, which is not any the less an exemplary piece of film music for its enthusiastic plundering of Korngold and Arthur Bliss.

There were a lot of delightful throwaways – the animated chess-pieces, the floating spherical training robot, the space-port bar – and moments of utter wonder – the long shots down the internal shafts of the Death Star – many of which were cheerful renditions of stock material from SF illustration. (To give but two examples – the shafts resemble many of the covers Kelly Freas drew for

Analog SF and the stormtroopers' quasi-robotic carapaces resemble those John Schoenherr drew as illustrations to Frank Herbert's *Dune*.) The echoes were here, but we waited in vain for much in the way of argument or originality.

In fact, there were many points at which Lucas' work even then failed to make sense in its details – but we swallowed Republican forces led by hereditary aristocrats and the mysterious Force and farms in the middle of desert and barren hills where nothing seems to be being grown because of the sheer gusto of what was on offer. After all, galactic empires are a great cliché of bad space opera and part of the fun of goodish space opera has always been watching authors try to make sense of the concept. We assumed that Lucas, having appropriated so much else, would have also acquired a sense that apparent logical flaws in continuity need explaining and the capacity to make up an interesting explanation.

And we went on swallowing it in Irving Kirshner's *The Empire Strikes Back* (1980), because Leigh Brackett was on hand to give us a sombre sense that the destruction of evil was not going to be as simple as all that, to give us cool moments like the tripping of the giant walking combat machines and our first sight of Cloud City. The revelation of Luke's parentage was genuinely impressive and the carbonizing of Han Solo a moment of real terror. While Luke's loss of his hand is present partly because losing a body part is one of the things that happens to the Hero with a Thousand Names, the actual sequence is gripping and gruelling; it is more than a good idea competently executed.

On the other hand, there was Yoda and all his Zen-ish cuteness and distorted sentence structure, the first sign of the hideous cuteness of which Lucas proved capable and which was to inflict on us the Ewoks in *Return of the Jedi* (1983) and, later on, Jar Jar Binks. Part of the trouble is that he enters the plot in order to teach Luke the use of the Force and it was to be twenty years before Lucas made up his mind about what the Force was. This in turn meant that Yoda had to be at the same time vaguely impressive and impressively vague, a character created by sampling a selection of martial arts mentors and, specifically, one also influenced by the guru figure in the US television series *Kung Fu*.

One of the few strengths of the later films, it has to be admitted, is their presentation of a younger (though still ancient), more dynamic Yoda, though it is worrying that one of the few characters in Lucas' oeuvre to have undergone interesting character development should have been a puppet. The fight between Yoda and Dooku (Christopher Lee) is one of the best moments in *Attack of the Clones* (2002), simply because Lucas finally acquired a screen icon with enough gravitas to make us swallow it.

There is nothing wrong in principle with small furry horribly cute aliens, or gangling amphibian ones, as long as you do something with them to add a touch of acid to the sentimentality. The Ewoks have a strong family resemblance to the Hoka in Poul Anderson and Gordon Dickson's stories about brilliant and charismatic teddy bears who frighteningly fail to distinguish fact from fiction and make life difficult for their human allies. They also resemble the Fuzzies of H. Beam Piper's stories, creatures whose defenceless cuddliness made them ideal test cases for a legal definition of the borders of sapience.

Lucas, though, saw them as an excuse to have small creatures with a lot of fur speak in high-pitched voices and drive flying motorcycles. By this third film, his failure to do anything interesting with the material he appropriated was starting to become glaring – in spite of wonderful little throwaways like the small malignant creature which lives as a parasite on the vast Jabba the Hutt. The same was true of his broader appropriations – the confrontation with the Emperor and the redemption of Darth Vader was material which had mythic scope, but not mythic depth. The reason why the third of the original trilogy was the least liked was that it was the film in which Lucas' failure to deliver on all that the first film had promised became most blatant.

The Empire, and those who serve it, are evil because they have turned to the power of the Dark Side of the Force – or to be more precise, they are evil because they are evil. The portrayal of Vader and his Emperor as physically corroded by their power was simply not enough in spite of some real efforts by the two actors involved to provide the portentous dialogue with charisma and vitality. If, as we can assume, the climax of the third prequel will show us how Anakin Skywalker's moral corruption caused physical damage which necessitated the protective suit that gave him Darth Vader's distinctive heavy breathing, say, it is unlikely that, even if it makes sense as plot, it will work as a piece of moral symbolism.

There was then a gap of almost two decades in which we saw a lot of SF cinema and most of us believed that Lucas would never deliver on the promise implicit in the first film's title *Episode IV – A New Hope*. The news that he had finally delivered the first episode was greeted with some enthusiasm by the generation that had grown up with the first three films as a part of their childhood, and rather more scepticism by those of us for whom they were a partial fulfilment, ultimately betrayed, of what up to that point we had hoped for from SF cinema and never got.

His perpetual tinkering with the earlier films as the possibilities of CGI expanded were an index of his weaknesses as a creative force. Alterations like the insertion of Jabba the Hutt into *A New Hope* were serious mistakes – the whole point about Jabba was that he sounded interesting and we were made to wait some serious way into the third film to encounter him, a point which is lost entirely if a not especially interesting CGI version of him crops up early on in the sequence. Lucas was also in the habit of second-guessing his own best instincts; it is important to our sense of Han Solo that he is prepared to shoot first pre-emptively, and Lucas spoiled this by inserting a first shot from the bounty hunter he kills.

The Force had always sounded more like a fantasy concept than an SF one, even in the looser intellectual manners of space opera, and the announcement here that contact with it depended on the presence of 'midichlorians' in the blood stream of the gifted sounded like a clumsy way of fixing the unfixable. One of the problems was simply that the word sounds like a garbling of mitochondria; another that the concept has not so much been rationalized as moved sideways. Instead of individuals being in touch with the infinite, small creatures in their bloodstreams are – which is even more of a problem.

There were now too many paradoxes in Lucas' world to make it even slightly plausible that sense would ever be made – we are supposed to believe in the preternatural goodness of the Jedi Knights and yet at the same time watch them operating without a sense of moral incongruity in a world in which slavery is common. When Obi Wan and his mentor Qui-Gon Jinn discover the potential of young Anakin Skywalker (the future Darth Vader), they ship him off for training without bothering to free his mother from bondage. Now, if this failure were to be portrayed as the fatal flaw which helps trigger his corruption, that might be forgivable, but, on the contrary, her death in *Attack of the Clones* triggers, not rage at his masters, but genocidal fury against the sand-dwelling raiders who killed her.

Quite suddenly and arbitrarily, we are told, as late as *Attack of the Clones*, that Jedi Knights are supposed to be celibate, or at least to avoid serious emotional entanglements. Part of what estranges Anakin from the order is this rule, which has not been mentioned in any of the previous films; moreover, since his break of these vows begets Luke and Leia, it is hard to see it as a corruption. Had Lucas been smart enough, he could have portrayed this as paradox – his great sin produces the ultimate remedy to his crimes – but that really is not how any of this works. He wants his Jedi Knights to be perfect paragons, and yet their fall is precipitated by what looks uncommonly like their own failures and their own fault as much as by their betrayal by the nemesis they have fostered and trained.

The portrayal of alien life forms in these first and second chapters is quite remarkably offensive in its recycling of racist stereotypes. Anakin's slave-master is portrayed as avaricious and hook-nosed, for example. The CGI-character Jar Jar Binks has the vocal mannerisms of the servile and easily scared African Americans of 1930s cinema as well as some of the physical mannerisms of contemporary baggy-trousered hip-hop kids; the ruler of his people, when we meet him, is an equally offensive stereotype of bullying, superstition and a readiness to be cowed by harsh language. To make matters worse, it is, of course, Jar Jar Binks in his later incarnation as political representative of his people who is tricked into proposing the emergency powers that Palpatine will abuse in due course to become the Emperor of the original (but chronologically second) trilogy. It is not good enough for George Lucas to claim innocence or attribute racism to those who read these things as racial abuse in the light of incontrovertible screen history; it is hard to say whether his blitheness or his self-serving ripostes are the more offensive.

The first film in the sequence, *The Phantom Menace* (1999), has little to recommend it. Lucas suffers from the delusion that it is enough simply to construct Obi Wan's character from a lot of dramatic ironies – this brash young man will grow up into the old sage and this is amusing – and he never really thinks of a character for Qui-Gon Jinn to have. McGregor has clearly studied not only Guinness' performance in the part but other performances by a younger Guinness – he puts more into the part than Lucas has written. Neeson has even less to work with and, like other actors who found themselves in these films, relies on screen presence and authority to do most of the work for him. Other actors – Natalie Portman for example – have equally little to do, and don't do it. About the only pleasurable part of the experience of *The Phantom Menace* are the various architectures and, I suppose, the battle with killer robots in long art-deco galleries and the garden spaces and squares that surround them.

Attack of the Clones was not as bad as *The Phantom Menace*, but to say that is instantly to damn it with the very faintest of praise. Again, the characterization was thin in the extreme and actors as excellent as Christopher Lee and Samuel L. Jackson found themselves with almost nothing to do. Yet the seascape and the floating platform where the cloned stormtroopers are being made is not only gorgeous to look at but, like Cloud City in *The Empire Strikes Back*, a thoroughly imagined locale that only partly derives from previous film and fiction. The arena scene is a set piece that has to stand up beside, on the one hand, the fight with Jabba's pet monster in *Return of the Jedi* and such more recent arena fights as the ones in Ridley Scott's *Gladiator* (2000) and it can be said that it is not a disgrace, that the monsters are not especially clunky and the combats with them flashily athletic in just the right way – and the Jedi beat their animal opponents through intelligence as much as through skill.

The politics of the first film made very little sense – an attempt by a group of traders to take over Naboo, a planet which refused to accept their terms and conditions, precipitates enough of a crisis that Palpatine, who has actually instigated the whole thing, manages to look statesmanlike enough in his handling of it that he is voted in as Chancellor of the Republic's Senate. The second largely recapitulates this – Palpatine has instigated a separatist movement and gets voted supreme power, including the right to use an army of cloned stormtroopers he has covertly created, against the separatists.

There is a minority view among critics and fans that all of these inconsistencies are in fact subtleties – that Lucas shows the Jedi Knights as wantonly quietist because he wishes us to see them as irresponsible, that the process whereby Palpatine comes to power parallels other such processes – that of Hitler or Caesar – with remarkable accuracy. This might be true were it not for the strong element of occultism involved in Palpatine's rise. Certainly the creation of genuine threats as a way of having extraordinary powers voted to you to oppose those threats is a technique with historical parallels, but the parallel breaks down – the members of the secret Thule Society may have had something to do with the early Nazi Party, but they did not grant magic powers to Hitler.

Palpatine is not just a machine politician, but a Dark Lord in the manner of Tolkien, and his corruption of Anakin Skywalker to the point where he becomes Darth Vader parallels the seduction of the human kings who became the Nazgul. It is too early at time of writing to be absolutely sure of the process whereby Anakin is corrupted – but the attempted seduction of Luke by the aged monstrous Emperor that Palpatine becomes gives some hints. Emotionally, Anakin's capacity for murderous rage will be played up to; physically he will be horribly scarred inside and out so that he needs the body armour that is the manifestation of his corruption. One of Palpatine's other acolytes, Darth Maul, resembles the standard iconography of the Christian Devil – red skin and horns.

Ultimately, the problem with the *Star Wars* films is that George Lucas has rarely listened to his critics. It took a monomaniacal vision to get the first of the films made against the scepticism of the studio system, and indeed part of the film's importance, for good and ill, is that it helped give independents some real clout. At least in the early days Lucas paid attention to the comments of his actors – Harrison Ford's remark to the effect that you could type the dialogue, but not speak it – and hired a competent SF-savvy scriptwriter (Leigh Brackett) for the second film. The continued success of the franchise, however, and of his other business ventures in the field of cinema sound made Lucas progressively impervious to negative comment – he had done so much right that he felt entitled to assume he was doing nothing wrong. A one-man band has no collegiality.

The other successful franchise SF series also relied heavily on a writer-director; James Cameron differs from Lucas in imitating not merely the garish surface of science fiction but at least some of its attempt to make sense of the ideas. We know, from his instruction to the cast of *Aliens* that they should read Heinlein's *Starship Troopers*, that Cameron has read at least some science fiction; the extent to which his script for Kathryn Bigelow's *Strange Days* draws on the work of the cyberpunks in general and Pat Cadigan in particular indicate that he has gone on doing so past adolescence.

Cameron has said that the first *Terminator* film (1984) was written as the embodiment of a nightmare – the sense of being pursued by something unstoppable and inexorable. The fact that writer Harlan Ellison ended up claiming damages for the use of an idea he had put into a television show is almost beside the point (the case was settled out of court and a credit to Ellison inserted in subsequent prints of the film) – the Terminator is not the first killer robot warrior from the future and neither was Ellison's 'Demon With a Glass Hand' or 'Soldier' in *The Outer Limits*. Cameron's decision to flesh out his nightmare with an SF vocabulary rather than a horror one had the consequence that he could play the drama out logically; the strength of the first film and the second is that the premise develops organically throughout the film.

The idea of warriors from the future battling to ensure or prevent a moment that appears trivial, but is actually significant, goes back at least as far as Jack Williamson's *The Legion of Time* (1938). The human warrior, Reese, is unaware of precisely the contribution he is to make – he knows that he is to protect Sarah Connor so that she can give birth to his leader, John, but is unaware that he will be John Connor's father, and that John Connor has always known this; this has no specific debt to previous SF, but is of a piece with the paranoid plotting of Van Vogt and with various time paradox stories, notably Heinlein's 'By His Bootstraps'. The Heinlein story features a man kidnapped into the distant future by a mysterious older man – the main point of his presence there is to age into that man and kidnap his younger self. The extreme neatness of this knot of paradox is paralleled closely in Cameron's two films.

Also very much in the spirit of Heinlein is the way that the killer robot's attempts to murder Sarah Connor force her to become the warrior woman who will train the leader of the human resistance who will ultimately defeat its AI master, Skynet. The Terminator and Skynet fail by overreaching; their meddling with destiny produces a colossal ironic knot.

There is a non-ironic counter-knot; in the future, after her death, Sarah's son John gives Reese a photograph, with which Reese falls in love, motivating him to be the man John sends back to save her. The photo itself is destroyed in a fight with another Terminator, so that by the time Reese meets Sarah, he is in love with his memory of the photo. After Reese's death, on her travels in

Mexico and pregnant with John, Reese's child, Sarah in the last moments of
the film has a photograph taken by a child with a camera and buys it from him;
it is, of course, the photograph she has never seen. Does she buy and preserve
it in the sure and certain knowledge that to do so closes that particular loop?
Cameron makes this unclear, in one of his occasional moments of tact.

Another such moment of tact has to do with a third knot which existed
in late versions of the *Terminator* script. In the final version, Reese and Sarah
make their final stand against a Terminator stripped of its human semblance
in a factory full of robotic machinery; in the earlier versions, they had gone
to the factory specifically to blow up Cyberdyne long before it could build
Skynet. Ironically, their destruction of the Terminator at the cost of Reese's life
leaves fragments of it to be found and developed by Cyberdyne – the future
technology creates a precondition for its own development.

Cameron cannot have known that he would be able, a few years later, to
develop a sequel, though it is possible that he realized that, should a sequel
ever become possible, this would be a perfect premise for it. More probably,
he realized that two complicated paradoxes was quite enough for one film's
audience to wrap their heads around.

The second film, *Terminator 2: Judgment Day* (1991), accordingly starts
with this paradox as its premise – Sarah realizes that her failure to destroy every
part of the Terminator created the possibility of Skynet and the destruction
of humanity. Accordingly, she sets out to become the perfect terrorist and
becomes less human in the process, thus alienating her from the young John,
who believes her to be a maniac and has become, by early adolescence, a cynical
petty thief and hacker. The arrival of two Terminators, one programmed to
kill her and John, the other to save them, ironically creates a counter-process
whereby Sarah relearns compassion, and John idealism. They have become the
softer gentler people that they will need to be in a world which will not know
any apocalypse for which they need feel responsible. It is the 'good' Terminator
itself which realizes that, to close the loop, every piece of future technology
must be destroyed – including itself – and plunges self-sacrificingly into the
metal in which it has eradicated its technologically superior opponent.

All of these paradoxes and oppositions relate to a visual language of
doubling that we know well from Cameron's other films and scripts (*Aliens,
Strange Days*). In the first film, the Terminator adopts a pair of dark glasses
when the destruction of part of its face reveals the robotic nature of its eyes; in
the second film, Sarah at her most murderous adopts a pair of similar glasses;
the eyes are, of course, traditionally the window of the soul.

At the start of the Terminator's murderous rampage in the first film, it
casually destroys a toy truck in a suburban street; in the second film, Dyson's

child is playing with a toy truck as Sarah arrives at his house with murder in mind. Both toys are also paralleled by the larger vehicles that the duel between these adversaries will destroy. Similarly the opening sequence of *Terminator*, with its animations of a dark robotic future full of killing machines rolling across fields of human skulls, segues into a momentarily sinister, actually innocuous, shot of a dump truck. Where the future machines are creatures of darkness and greater darkness, illuminated only by gunfire and explosions, the dump truck inhabits a human world of colour and dirt, the grey metal that provides a visual pun with the machines giving way to yellow paint.

This is part of a more general opposition in the film between darkness and light, between the shadowy reflectiveness of gunmetal surfaces and the brightness of day and California. The bar where the Terminator tries to assassinate Sarah is called Tech-Noir, which is a handy summary of this aspect of the film. In a future that is all darkness save for the occasional glint of flame from derelict televisions turned into stoves, Reese briefly owns a window into the sunlit past via the photograph of Sarah. The film ends with the taking of that photograph – for the moment at least colour and complexity have won.

One of the intelligent things about the sequel is that Cameron only intermittently and in the last phases of the film returns to this opposition – appropriately, since the vision that haunts Sarah is not one of the dead mechanical future but of the atomic firestorm that destroys suburban normality. Even those scenes that take place at night in public and domestic interiors tend to be brightly lit by comparison with their equivalents in the first film. One of the reasons for this de-emphasis of the noirness of night-time may simply be restrictions on the extent to which the young Edward Furlong as John Connor could work late, but it helps make the second film gentler in feel. Even its horrors are softer and more whimsical; when one of the hospital orderlies is confronted with his own murderous double, at least part of the joke is that it shares his plump, apparently benevolent, aspect.

Obviously the film's two climaxes – the invasion of Cyberdyne by our group of righteous terrorists and the police siege of the building, and the final destruction of the two Terminators – operate with a palate far more like that of *The Terminator*. The climax of the first film briefly involves the flames of the exploded tanker which burns away the Terminator's human outside; the second involves a far greater interruption of the darkness of its closing sequences by the sombre light of flames by being set in a foundry, where both Terminators are dissolved in molten metal.

The first film's image of the final destruction of the monster was that of a red electronic eye finally fading to black. In *Terminator 2: Judgment Day*, as the T1000 dissolves, it recapitulates the distorted faces of the victims it impersonated. The implacable and inexorable has been replaced in the next generation by something which writhes and cannot escape. Both are contrasted with the fate of the 'good' Terminator which lowers its crippled body into the flames with quiet dignity. Nothing so interesting happens with either good or bad Terminator at the end of Jonathan Mostow's *Terminator 3: Rise of the Machines* (2003).

In both films, the Arnold Schwarzenegger character arrives from the future naked and acquires his characteristic outfit in scenes which by the second film have become part of the films' schtick. In *Terminator*, he takes them from a group of young punks whose presence at the viewing platform of the Griffiths Observatory in LA links them, and him, to James Dean in Nicholas Ray's *Rebel Without A Cause* (1955), a key scene of which takes place at the same location, except that a machine can be so much more nihilistic than any human. In *Terminator 2: Judgment Day*, the 'good' Terminator invades a biker bar and so has sunglasses and a motorbike from the outset – this time Lazlo Benedek's *The Wild One* (1954) is being referenced. It is important to remember that, at this point, we do not know that he is in the present on a mission of protection – the fact that the people he hurts are hyper-aggressive outsiders makes his fight with them less full of moral cues.

One of the many problems with the inferior third film – not written or directed by James Cameron – is that this schtick is reduced to burlesque. The jokes made in the first two films at the expense of the naked hunk were finely judged so that they include a level of aggression from the men he asks for their clothes that makes us at least partly complicit in his violence against them; the third film's positioning of him in a bar full of women watching a gay male stripper is a far cheaper joke, made almost homophobic by his trashing of the stripper's distinctly unbutch sunglasses.

There are other repeats between the films, which in the case of *Terminator 2* add something, and in the case of *Terminator 3: Rise Of The Machines* are merely repetitions. In the first film, the presence of Earl Boen's Doctor Silberman offers a rational commentary on what we know to be true – for him, the very coherence of Reese's story is proof that he is insane. He is the only survivor of the precinct house because he leaves just as the Terminator arrives, passing him in the hall. He is thus well placed to be the psychiatrist in charge of the hospitalized Sarah in *Terminator 2*, to explain to her constantly that her concerns are chimeras, and to keep her away from her son.

He is also of course overdue for a comeuppance and one duly comes when he witnesses the more advanced Terminator walk through iron bars; the crumpling of Boen's already crumpled face is an eloquent portrayal of a man who has just walked off the edge of his world. The brief reappearance of

Silberman in the third film adds nothing to this – it is just there as one of the things which happens in a *Terminator* film.

Terminator 2: Judgment Day adds value and ups the ante – the Terminator has been superseded by the fluid T-1000 which is smaller, capable of impersonating anyone it sees, male or female, and of changes of shape and colour that allow it to meld with the chequered lino of a floor in order to ambush. It was a smart move to have the massive Arnold Schwarzenegger thrown around by the considerably smaller Robert Patrick.

Having done this, of course, little was added by the arrival of the specifically female TX. It was an inventive move to have her capable of interfacing with computers and directing machines against her victims, but this merely results in more car chases and collisions. It seems possible that at one stage in the development of the script, she was supposed to be responsible for the implantation of the virus that triggers the coming to genocidal consciousness of Skynet, but if so, this is a good idea that got lost in the rewrites – as it is, the virus is never explained at all.

After Arnold Schwarzenegger's remarks to Arianna Huffington during his gubernatorial race – he sneered that he had a perfect role for her in the next *Terminator* film – it is difficult not to see the TX as in some respects an expression of the star's misogyny; in a key moment in one of their fights, he gets to stuff her face in a toilet. However gratifying it may be to see Schwarzenegger thrown around by Kristianna Loken, it adds no joke that was not already implicit in his fight scenes with Robert Patrick. Some of the jokes about the TX's shape-changing abilities are laddishly sexist – shortly after her arrival, she consults an advertising hoarding and inflates her breasts by several inches.

Another weakness of the third film lies in its handling of braided story arcs. Both of the Cameron films are exemplary in moving us rapidly between several centres of attention. The first half or so of *The Terminator* keeps our viewpoint jumping between the unknowing Sarah, the Terminator and Reese, and the activities of the Terminator as perceived and investigated by two doomed police detectives. Particularly in the case of Sarah and the detectives, it is a complex picture of little lives with non-apocalyptic concerns – Sarah jokes with her flatmate and plays with her iguana and one detective mocks the other's tie. Gradually the film's focus narrows down – the detectives are slaughtered and Sarah and Reese become a partnership, and the vicarious complicity of the audience in the Terminator's mayhem is reduced by seeing it increasingly from the potential victims' point of view.

Similarly, the early stages of the second film moves between the two Terminators, Sarah and the young John Connor. Cameron deliberately defers our knowledge that the Schwarzenegger Terminator is to be John's protector this time until a scene in the mall which echoes the scene in which Reese saves Sarah in the disco-bar Tech-Noir – indeed almost the only cue that he is not as entirely sinister as the shape-shifter is hyperbolic overstatement on the soundtrack. As he leaves the biker bar in his jacket, boots and sunglasses and drives around LA on a spiffy motorbike, he is accompanied by the hard-driving rock anthem 'Bad to the Bone'; at the point where vicarious complicity topples over into fetishism, an ironic hint is being dropped.

The early sequences of the film deliberately undercut what we think we know from the first film in another respect. In the first film, John Connor is never seen even in Reese's memories; his messianic qualities extend even to the initials he shares with the film's director. In the second film, we see him unromantically as a young punk with few loyalties, who believes that the mission into which his mother has tried to train him is so much moonshine. He uses his abilities as a hacker for petty computer theft; even his ride is unheroic – a motor-scooter. The contrast between this and the Terminator's large bike is made explicit at the point when John is snatched from the one to the other for safety on the brink of being squashed.

At this point, their storyline is braided together. Their attempt to rescue Sarah is counterparted by her attempt to escape and the T1000's attempt to get to her in the mental hospital and kill her; this sequence, cutting between these three protagonists, is particularly impressive. Sarah, reunited with her son, is almost at once off again by herself as she sets out to assassinate Miles Dyson and John sets off in pursuit to stop her; this section of the plot recapitulates the whole plot in miniature, as Sarah tries to make herself a killing machine.

The relationship between the young John Connor and his inhuman servant is shown as a way in which the future leader learns responsibility. He is given to understand that he has an absolute power to give orders to the Terminator and briefly abuses this by making it stand on one leg and so on; rapidly he realizes that he has to give sensible orders. As with Ripley in *Aliens*, Cameron shows responsible leadership in terms of being a good director of your followers' actions.

The compromise whereby Dyson is recruited to the assault on Cyberdyne is a neat expression of the entire point of the film. Unlike even a 'good' Terminator, which can be ordered not to kill humans, but will regard this as carte blanche merely to maim them and shoot out the kneecaps of a precisely monitored group of besieging policemen, Dyson can be reasoned with.

The interlocking narratives of *Terminator 3: Rise of the Machines* are far less interestingly managed. The connections between the characters are almost arbitrary – Kate may be destined to be John Connor's future wife, but she knows him because they were at high school together. The TX has come back as much to assassinate his future lieutenants as to kill the elusive John himself. Kate's father happens to be the senior officer in charge of Skynet – this is a convenient rather than a particularly plausible plot given. There is no excitement to the process of storytelling itself.

Some of the more interesting aspects of the plot are thrown away in exposition. After John's death in the future, a future Kate, his wife, has reprogrammed his assassin to act as their protector – this is the stuff of high drama, but not when explained briefly by Arnold Schwarzenegger during a car chase.

The third film also suffers from some profound incoherence in its plotting of time paradox and in its reinvention of the films' premise. In the first two films, Skynet is a colossal piece of hardware, a single unit which contains an artificial intelligence designed to run the US nuclear weapons system, a doomsday computer that becomes aware and destroys humanity. It is because it is a single unit that it is possible for John Connor and his army to take it and destroy it.

In the third movie, partly because of the delay in developing a single large unity caused by the successful trashing of Cyberdyne, Skynet has been reimagined as software that runs on the US defence intranet. It is given total control as part of the fight to stop that intranet being corrupted by a virus; it is a synergistic effect between it and the virus which creates the artificial consciousness that decides to destroy humanity.

There is, of course, a crucial incoherence here. A single unit might destroy humanity because it felt threatened by humanity's ability to blow it up or indeed unplug it. An endlessly self-replicating piece of software, however, has no particular reason to do so. It most especially has no reason to destroy humanity by starting a nuclear war, since vast parts of its habitat would be destroyed at the same time by the electro-magnetic pulse effect. Indeed, the interests of a being made of software are entirely a matter of the continued existence of humanity to build more *Lebensraum* for it. Of all the stupid bits of scientific rationalization in SF movies, the *Terminator 3* version of Skynet has to be one of the stupidest.

It was only through some very fancy footwork that *Terminator 2: Judgment Day* managed to make it remotely plausible that Skynet had sent a second machine to a later date. Since Skynet is presumably aware of its own origins, this makes the first film marginally less plausible. Either Skynet was primarily interested in ensuring the planting of the technology which ensures its existence and was prepared to create its future adversaries as a by-product, or it was making a serious attempt on Sarah's life and John's existence of which its own genesis was merely a by-product – neither of these responds to unpacking especially well. The only real way to make sense of any of this is to assume that the principal time line is supplanted by each set of paradoxes – Cameron, however, knows that film-making, as opposed to SF, is ultimately about sensation and keeping the audience involved, rather than thinking. Fine as the handling of this material in the first two *Terminator* films is, there are limits to their sophistication.

The third film comes into its own, a little, in its last act; Kate's father turns out to have sent her and John not to a place where they can prevent the apocalypse but to a place where they can survive it. After the high-tech of the particle accelerator and the Skynet control room, the 1960s technology of the shelter they find themselves in is genuinely shocking – this scene intelligently exploits the history of computers and just how far they have come in a very few decades. The problem still remains that any later film in this franchise will have to take place after the atomic war and deal with John and Kate's struggle against Skynet, a struggle which, since their characters have been so formed by Skynet's attempts to extirpate them in the past, they can hardly lose.

The third film suffers hugely from the absence at its helm of Cameron, who clearly felt that two of these films was enough. His involvement with the Terminator ride at Universal Studios[1] gives us some idea of what a third or later film with him as creator might have been like – derring-do across time and in the heart of great machines. The most pressing reason why this franchise is unlikely to continue further is the career change of Arnold Schwarzenegger, who shortly after the release of *Terminator 3* was elected Governor of California; it has to be added that, by the third film, his remarkable physique was starting to show the wear and tear of age as well as the digital consequences of the film's ever-escalating mayhem.

Cameron has always been a competent director of his casts – his decision to cast Schwarzenegger as the Terminator rather than as Reese was one of the most intelligent second thoughts in the history of movies. The Terminator will always be Schwarzenegger's classic role partly because the two Cameron films are among the classiest he has ever been in, and partly because they make excellent use of every aspect of his distinctly limited range. Blank menace is something he can do, and sinister comic lines – his appearance in Cameron's worst film the sub-Bond *True Lies* (1994) indicates that there are some things neither man can do.

Linda Hamilton has not been praised enough for her role in both Cameron

1. This ride starts as a presentation in the offices of Cyberdyne interrupted by emergency sirens and moves the viewers rapidly through corridors to a theatre where they witness a confrontation between the Connor family and a hologram representation of the embodied Skynet.

films – she makes a solid fist of Sarah's evolution from suburban airhead waitress to competent warrior in the first film, and from unbalanced sociopath back to something like normal humanity in the second. The luminous Claire Danes is one of the best things about the third film, in spite of the unlikely jump into action adventure from sensitive serious roles like her part in Daldry's *The Hours* (2003). When Nick Stahl's John Connor says, admiringly, 'You remind me of my mother,' audience laughter is in part an acknowledgement of how intelligently Danes makes Kate's evolution parallel Sarah's.

Apart from Schwarzenegger and the plot premises, the principal thing that unites the films is the design work of the excellent Stan Winston. Too little consideration is given by serious critics to the role of creators like Winston, partly because of the absence of a vocabulary with which to work on him – it should never be forgotten that one of the things that decides which SF movie becomes a successful franchise is the quality of the design work. One of the few moments of real delight in *Terminator 3* is his reverse-engineered small prototypes for the machines we saw in the opening moments of the first film. When Claire Danes shoots down a miniature aerial Terminator, part of the charge we get from her action comes from the accumulated good will of the franchise – we care about the moment because it has hinterland both in terms of story and of the look of things, a hinterland that only a franchised series can give us.

A Franchise Case Study

Alien and its sequels

Alien

'We live, as we dream – alone.'

It is important, sometimes, to sit down and watch a film as if it were for the first time, as if you knew nothing about it at all, not even the hints you get in reviews or the spoilers you get from your friends – to turn back the clock so that 'Rosebud' is a mystery and you do not know whom Ms Lund will choose. Some movies are so much about the unfolding of circumstance that it is important to let them move at their own speed and wait to tell you things.

Alien was not, when it opened in 1979, the first of a franchise starring Sigourney Weaver; it was a stand-alone film in which she was only one of a talented ensemble. In his commentary to the DVD, Ridley Scott claims that he meant the audience to think of her as no less likely than some of the other characters to get killed – after all, in 1979, the slasher film had not evolved to the point where Ripley is instantly recognizable as the Final Girl, the androgynous female without vices who will always make it through to the last scene.[1] Ripley is in fact one of the templates for the Final Girl.

Ridley Scott[2] was a director who had previously made one film and a lot of commercials; he was not someone who was necessarily expected to make a masterpiece. *The Duellists* (1977), based on a Conrad short story – *Alien* has,

1. See Carol J. Clover, *Men, Women and Chainsaws: Gender in the Modern Horror Film* (BFI, 1992).
2. Of course, in all of that follows, the contribution of the various screenwriters, perhaps especially Dan O'Bannon and Walter Hill, who originated and worked on the project, is crucial as is the work of designers, cameramen and cinematographer. It is clear though that Scott, while not in any real sense an **auteur**, brought many of his own people to the film as well as his considerable controlling intelligence.

of course, its own Conrad references – was a period piece which got respectful reviews, but no more, partly because of its deliberately off-key attitude to its not especially likeable characters, who use Napoleon's campaigns as a mechanism for pursuing their own constantly interrupted feud. Because it follows them over a number of years, as they age, and are disillusioned by personal and national setbacks and failures, it has a pace alternately sluggish and frenetic that is entirely at odds with the easy steady progress of a conventional commercial film.

Alien too is a film which has its own pace – it, daringly, opens incredibly slowly, after a title sequence in which geometric shapes leisurely evolve into the title over a background of a ringed planet and its moons, the camera takes us slowly through the corridors and rooms of the Nostromo, an ore-refiner and freighter, as it wakes slowly and brings its crew back from cold sleep as one of the last stages in its waking. Mobiles twist, and the pages of an open book flap, in the breeze of a suddenly restored atmospheric circulation; plastic birds dip their heads into a glass of water. A computer starts to run through its routines, its screen reflected in the visors of emergency helmets slung above the chairs opposite it. The Nostromo is not, at the film's start, a bad place – we are not getting any particular clues as to what sort of film this is, except for an undercurrent of unease in the music and ambient sound.

What Scott is telling us in this scene is that this is a mundane future – this spaceship is a place in which people work; we are taken around the corridors precisely to demystify the whole idea of being on a spaceship. Scott has described Kubrick's *2001* as one of his favourite films; Kubrick had done the spaceship as object of romantic wonder so totally that it could not be done that way again and Lucas had, in *Star Wars*, played the card of sheer size. The point about the Nostromo is that it is not beautiful or elegant – parts of it do not even work that well.

He is also establishing the geography on which the later more urgent stages of the film will be played out. One of the strengths of this film as opposed to its successors is just this – by the time the characters are fighting, or running, for their lives down these corridors, we already know where exactly they are at a given moment. Cameron manages to establish something rather similar about the interior of the troop carrier in *Aliens*, especially its loading bay area; he makes a virtue of necessity with the larger spaces of the base and the power plant once the characters are trapped on the planet's surfaces, not least by taking the crude but effective route of having them look at maps and blueprints when necessary. The spaces in Fincher and Jeunet's films seem far more arbitrary, far less given – anonymous corridors, or work-spaces whose relationship to the rest of the location seems almost contingent.

The camera takes us into a darkened room full of a brooding presence that gradually becomes a room full of light; the presence proves to be the support system for the cold sleep pods where the crew are just waking up. The pods are spherical, with transparent lids; in a film in which eggs are to have a crucial role, it is important that there be these good eggs at the film's beginning and end to counterpose the evil eggs which we are going to see in due course. Nonetheless, that first sight of the sleep system is not without its sinister side...

The first of the crew we see in focus is Kane (John Hurt), whose tousled features inspire instant affection as he rubs sleep from them and sits, semi-naked, as consciousness slowly comes fully back to him. This sequence is incredibly important simply because, as it happens, Kane is going to be the first of the crew to die, and this sequence gives us an emotional investment in him. For a British audience at least, Hurt's earlier roles – as the flamboyant Quentin Crisp and the deranged Emperor Caligula – had identified him not just with decadence and depravity, but with the hurt innocence with which he drew sympathy for his victim and his monster. He was the actor Scott could trust to make us care. It is also interesting and perhaps a deliberate miscue, given the ambiguities of Hurt's screen iconography, that the man who is to be the first victim should have almost the name of the biblical first killer.

The other thing that needs pointing out about the scene is that Scott and his team took one of the stock pieces of convenient furniture of SF and said something important about it. In most SF from Wells and Bellamy onwards, suspended animation has been a convenient mechanism for getting your central character forward into a utopian or dystopian future, or across the galaxy; what Scott points out not least through the semi-nakedness of the characters[1] is how vulnerable sleepers are, how vulnerable and how innocent.

There follows a breakfast scene in which we start to get to know the crew as an ensemble without getting any very clear sense of any of them. Scott deliberately mixed the sound so that none of the dialogue comes across especially clearly – the point was to tell us that these seven people work together and know each other really well, but also to imply certain failures of communication. As gradually emerges, most of the relationships between this crew are antagonistic and most of them are alone on this ship – any sense that the breakfast chat was actual communication rather than phatic gestures would have weakened this point. The Nostromo takes its name from a novel by Joseph Conrad and the June 1978 draft of the script has, as one of its epigraphs, Conrad's aphorism 'We live, as we dream – alone.'

---

1. He would have liked them to be entirely naked, but the producers would not let him.

The other effect of the breakfast scene is to establish sheer normality; these are ordinary, rather dull people having rather a dull meal on a spaceship that is as close to being just a place as any in the literature or filmography. This is one of the strengths of this film, and to a lesser extent of its sequel, *Aliens*, one largely neglected by the third and fourth films in the franchise – this is about terrible things happening to people who might be our neighbours.

As the officers go about their duties, it is only gradually that they appreciate that they have been woken too soon – they sleepily expect to be in the home stretch of their return journey and only slowly realize that there is no solar system traffic control to be contacted. They reconvene to discuss what this means – a fragment of dialogue between Brett and Parker, the two non-officer crew members, establishes our sense of the nagging class hostility that is one of the many undercurrents on the ship. They resent the fact that as non-officers they get half the bonus the other crew members get; they also resent that they get ordered around.

The pecking order among the crew is far less obvious than it at first seems – Dallas is the captain, but when science officer Ash explains that they will not be paid unless they follow the distress call the ship has picked up, it becomes clear that Dallas has very little power. Tom Skerrit makes Dallas a figure of appealing weakness – he is likeable but a company man. This is one of several points at which we start to realize that much of the real power on board rests with Ash – and one of the first hints that the company is not benign. (The first hint about the company comes, of course, from the ship's name; the novel *Nostromo*, after all, deals with the machinations of a mining company whose intentions to its workers are anything but good and with mined silver that brings death to all who have anything to do with it.)

Dallas goes to work in the computer room which is, claustrophobically, almost spherical in shape – another egg or womb. The computer is called Mother, but is not personalized; Scott decided not to go where Kubrick had gone and the computer here is a big smart machine with no autonomy. Given what we know by the end of the film, this is lulling us into a false sense of security; this crew will not be betrayed in the way the one in *2001* was betrayed by Hal, but that does not in fact mean that they will not be betrayed.

The lander part[1] of the Nostromo separates itself, letting us know that this is a ship that comes apart – as we learn, there is a lander that detaches itself from the refinery/freighter, which has room for all of the crew, and also

1. In some versions of the script, the Conradian reference is continued by calling the shuttle the Narcissus (after *The Nigger of the Narcissus*). Presumably someone who actually knew their Conrad realized that, given the general stroppiness of Parker, this reference became invidious the moment the African-American Yaphet Kotto was cast in the role.

a smaller three-person shuttle. Part of the film's determinedly anti-romantic attitude to space travel comes in what follows – the moderately bad landing in which the lights flicker and people have to use a fire extinguisher has become sufficient of a cliché in, for example, the *Star Trek* series, later than 1979 that one tends to forget that it is an SF cliché which *Alien* largely invented. Parker and Brett report, and inflate, the damage; it is important for us to remember that the shell which protects these characters is itself fragile.

Kane, Dallas and Lambert suit up and head off for the alien distress beacon. It is typical of what we come to think of as Ripley's combination of the gung-ho and the sceptical that she refuses to take Ash's word for it and subjects the beacon's message to a translation algorithm; this is one of the most transparent pieces of gobbledegook in the film, but little enough stress is laid on it that we hardly notice it as such. Somewhat later, she announces to Ash that it seems to be a warning beacon rather than a distress call; he replies, seeming sensible, that communications are down and there is no point in her following them to the alien ship since they will be back before she can reach them.

As with so much else in the understated dialogue of this quiet film, there is an undercurrent here – an undercurrent of her suspicion that Ash knows more than he is telling and his suspicion that she is guessing too much and too accurately. We have seen the odd little jigs and shakes Ash goes in for when he is alone – we are conscious that something about him is not right, but have no idea what that might be.

In an interesting counterpoint to this, Ripley progress-chases Brett and Parker who make so much noise with what appear to be part of the lander's malfunctions, but is actually a jet of gas they can turn on and off, that she cannot make them listen, and is forced to listen to one of Parker's diatribes about bonuses. In a scene removed from the film's final cut, Parker talks to Brett about his desire to do violence to Ripley and Brett accuses him of being attracted to her – this was a sensible cut simply because the theme of male violence is more shocking when it does emerge later for not having been paralleled here. The hostility between Parker and Brett on the one hand and Ripley on the other has this much in common with the mutual dislike of Ripley and Ash – it is a dislike of people from two worlds for each other. Yet, at this point, we have no sense of how different the worlds are that Ripley and Ash inhabit.

Meanwhile, on their way across the small planetoid and at the ship, Dallas, Kane and Lambert move from one world into another, from the grimy industrial design of the Nostromo to the unpleasant organic flowing lines of the alien ship. One of the many intelligent decisions made by Ridley Scott and the producers was to hire two completely different designers – the original drawings for the Nostromo were done by the radical political cartoonist Ron Cobb and those for the alien and the ship where its eggs are found were by the Swiss visionary Giger; it is hard to imagine two graphic artists with less in common.

It is Kane who finds the desiccated titanic corpse of the alien pilot and notices that something has burst from its chest; he is a man who sees the double of his own death and does not know what it is. The fact that we never see the alien pilot especially clearly – nor even entirely work out which bits of what we see are him and which his chair? bed? coffin? – is one of several points in the film at which the gap between living thing and machine are deliberately blurred.

They spot a hole in the dais on which the pilot lies and Kane is lowered through it into the hold, which, he remarks, is unpleasantly warm – we see the condensation start to build up in his protective suit and realize yet again that this is a human future in which things work, only not necessarily especially well. He follows a blue light to the vat of water in which eggs are sitting, a blue light which proves to be some sort of force field protecting what is in the vat from the outside – or perhaps the outside from what is in the vat. He slips in; he observes the eggs with wonder, particularly when the one nearest to him suddenly opens its four toothy-looking flaps; the interior of the egg pulses gently – and suddenly something flies out of it and hits him straight in the faceplate.

This is almost the first point at which anything sensational happens in the film and it has taken well past the half-hour mark to get here; one of the reasons why this, and various other things still to come, are such shocks is that we have been lulled by Scott's leisurely pacing into a false sense of security and started to think of this as a film in which we get to observe the future in a realistic way and without much excitement.

It is also at this point, or perhaps at the point of their entry into the alien ship, that the film in some important aspects switches genre; we have moved from the solid logical world of a future of dirty technology, personal bickering, company politics and class hostility into a world where unexpected things happen when you transgress rules you never thought of as important. The blue barrier is, it turns out, like the warning beacon, something whose implications got ignored. The alien ship turns out to be the Bad Place of horror films and is to change the Nostromo, by contagion, into another one; the egg is a Malign Sleeper, the thing you awaken at your peril.[1]

1. There has always been, of course, a strain of SF which played with these fantasy motifs – Martian psychic vampires with snake-like tendrils for hair, say. A book often cited as an influence on the film – the fix-up *The Voyage of the Space Beagle* by A.E. van Vogt – deals with a sequence of occasions on which the eponymous expedition gets itself variously infested by dangerous aliens found floating in space or marooned on planetoids. The Beagle's crew are smarter in their ways of dealing with the creatures than the Nostromo's, but not so smart that things don't keep happening to them.

The next thing that happens is that Dallas and Lambert arrive back at the lander with the injured Kane and Ripley refuses to let them in, even when ordered to do so by Dallas; she cites the regulations about quarantine and he argues that Kane will die if not given medical attention. In the event, Ash gets up and opens the airlock manually. Ripley is at this point doing the right thing in terms of good sense, at the expense of a certain humanity – this is in line with a tradition of hard-edged SF stories of the 1950s like Tom Godwin's 'The Cold Equations', where the captain of a ship carrying plague vaccine has to kill and jettison a stowaway whose additional weight jeopardizes his mission. We are being told that she is sensible, but not that she is deeply likeable – in fact, somewhat to our surprise, it is the apparently logical and rule-oriented Ash who breaks this particular rule.

The fact that, when Ripley confronts Ash about his behaviour, she makes her argument in terms of rank and the chain of command makes some interesting points about the way she sees the world – again, she is not being positioned as a sympathetic character. What is also interesting about that sequence is that, in it, we hardly see Ripley as a whole person at all – she stays on the edge of shots which centre on Ash and his attempt to justify his breaking of rules which he above all should be dedicated to keeping. We are being told visually, yet again, that she and Ash in some sense inhabit different worlds and different discourses.

In one of the scenes cut from the theatrical version of the film (and restored in the 2003 cut), Lambert confronts Ripley and puts the pure human case against the decision Ripley made. Lambert tries to attack Ripley and has to be pulled off her by Parker and Brett. Dallas shouts through to them that he ordered Ripley to let them back on the ship – and Ripley maintains the rightness of her position. Interestingly, at this point, Parker in particular backs Ripley up: he is pragmatic about the danger that breaking quarantine might have put them all in even though he dislikes Ripley. This is a film in which their self-interest is always a crucial factor in our understanding of the interaction of the characters.

It is worth commenting at this point how the cuts made to the film's final version, while clearly made for reasons of pacing and length, generally work against Veronica Cartwright's finely nuanced performance as Lambert. Choices always have to be made; one of the advantages of DVD and the availability of these sequences is that we can experience a possible alternate cut in which Ripley is more balanced by Lambert, in which the rational level-headed brunette is more completely set against a more fragile and elfin woman who argues for more human values and who crumbles almost completely at the film's crisis. Given that, in some early versions, it is explicit that Ripley and Dallas had had a past, and that there is some emotional connection, never made clear, between Dallas and Lambert, it is probably sensible that this opposition be played down. The 2003 cut largely achieves this.

In the first versions of the script, all of the crew are male, though it is specified that they don't have to be cast that way. Scott tells us in his commentary that there was a stage in which past romantic involvements were made explicit – and in one of the deleted scenes Ripley and Lambert discuss whether either of them has had sex with Ash as part of the process whereby Ripley struggles to establish what it is that she suspects about Ash. The final film is one in which the gender of the two women is relevant but down-played; several of the men – Parker, Brett, Ash – are far more obviously and crudely male than either Ripley or Lambert is conventionally feminine.

One of the ways in which the film can be read as feminist – it has, partly on the strength of elements in its sequels, also been read as misogynist – is in its anxieties that a woman like Ripley, who passes as equal in a male-arranged world, will always be at risk of being betrayed or threatened. Parker and Ash, for very different reasons, loathe her and Dallas does not respect her enough to pay her attention when, as it happens, she is right to question his decisions.

The sequences in which Ash explores the capacities of the face-hugger while trying to remove it from Kane's head is a masterful piece of exposition – we get shown rather than told just how impossible the medical situation is. First we see that, when an attempt is made to loosen its grip, it merely tightens its tail's stranglehold on Kane; then, when an attempt is made to cut its finger-like arms, it bleeds an acid which eats its way almost instantly through several levels of the shuttle. Finally, during the scan, it is made clear that this deadly threat to Kane's life is also the only thing keeping him alive – that the thing which is suffocating him is also feeding him oxygen.

At the same time as providing medical attention to Kane, Ash is exploring the nature of the creature. His lack of real concern for Kane's welfare, as opposed to his real intellectual curiosity, strikes an odd note even at the time, but one whose implications we do not think to explore. Here as with much else in the film, the film plays absolutely fair with us – giving all the information that will prove to have been relevant but which we never get round to reading properly.

One of the paradoxes that not just this but also the other films of the franchise explore is that the creature and its kind are not only destroyers and devourers, but also, in an entirely self-interested and exploitative way, nurturers – they preserve the humans that they are using as prey. One of the reasons why Ripley's relationship with the cat is so touching is that there is nothing in it for her – it is one of the few entirely selfless relationships in the film. The fact that she is capable of this, even if it is not her default mode, is the thing that makes her the creature's opposite.

The sequences that follow – the disappearance of the face-hugger, the search for its remaining husk, its dissection and Kane's apparent recovery – are a set of false leads and false starts. We know that this is not all there is going to be to it, because we are outside the fourth wall and know that some bigger shock is coming – we take malicious pleasure watching each of the occasions on which the crew of the Nostromo are made to jump out of their skins because we know that there is a bigger shock coming even when, on a first unspoiled viewing, we have no particular idea what it is going to be.

The search for the husk is literally a sequence of false shocks – one of them as crude as Dallas knocking over a piece of medical equipment making us and him jump from the sudden bang. We get used to seeing bits of medical equipment dangling from the ceiling in this sequence, so much so that we do a double-take when we gradually realize that the thing unfolding near Ripley's head is the tail of the face-hugger, which drops onto her shoulder like a tarantula in a Bond film. This is one of the few points in the film at which Ripley shrieks or reacts in a 'girlie' way; more usually she mutters under her breath. Ash prods the husk with his probe and we jump a little bit when it tenses round it – but he explains this as reflex and for once turns out to be telling the truth. Or part of it.

The dissection of the face-hugger is one of the film's more inventively disgusting sequences. Ripley complains that a creature which bleeds acid should not be allowed to decay on a ship, but this is a murmured counterpoint to Ash's exploration of what at this point is revealed to be only too vulnerably fleshy. Scott explains that, when filming this sequence, they simply filled up the creature's shell with fresh shellfish every day – its inner organs are oysters and mussels – one of the points of this is to make us entirely believe in the creature as organic and evolved. We are allowed to see the face-hugger most clearly and as a whole at this point, when it is dead and an object of contemplation rather than a process of menace.

Perhaps too much so – Scott makes clear in his commentary that he always intended us to read the creature as designed as well as evolved. Though this is never explicitly stated, the creature's partial artificiality makes considerably more sense in SF terms than the alternative – because an evolved creature needs a regular habitat and a prey that has evolved along with it, whereas a creature that is in large part the product of design is more plausibly a universal devourer that can wait for aeons and eat what comes its way.

Kane's apparent recovery mirrors, in Hurt's look of battered innocence, both when he is still comatose and when he is up and about, that vulnerability which we saw in him in the awakening sequence at the start of the film. He and the others talk as if the whole episode were over, as if they can just climb back into the innocence of their mechanical eggs and have done with the problem. Before they do this, though, they sit down for a meal, for Kane's last supper.

It is not that the scene in any explicit way mirrors any particular portrayal of the Last Supper, so much that any scene of intimate convivial eating is liable to echo that whole strain in western religious art. As opposed to the earlier shared meal, relief makes the characters relax with each other – sitting next to Kane, Parker smiles with genuine good humour as opposed to the slightly predatory glint that is his default mode. We are still aware of how much tension there is between these characters but for a few moments of grace we like them more than at any point in the film.

What follows is horror – Kane starts to choke and retch and jokes about the poor quality of the ship's food are instantly stilled as he starts to convulse and the food is swept aside so that the table can be used as a makeshift bed. What is truly horrible about the scene is that for a few moments neither crew nor audience fully understand what is happening – this is a meal where he is not eating, but being eaten, from the inside out. The creature that bursts out of him is like a human foetus being born; it is like a poisonous snake that uncoils; it is like a rat that has gnawed on his bowels; it is the eel or the lamprey that feeds on corpses. It is one example of the Worst Thing one can imagine.[1]

The crew pull away from the man they have been trying to help and huddle together for the one and last time – Parker gestures with a piece of cutlery as if there were something that could usefully be done with it and is waved into not doing anything. And, with a hiss that we hear as a hiss of malice, the creature races across the table and is gone. There is something fiercely unnatural about the speed with which it moves – in fact, Scott tells us, it was mounted on a small dolly on a model railway track; even though it is tiny, we experience it as infinitely formidable.

There follows one of the relaxations of tension which are part of Scott's technique in this film – Kane is given a funeral of sorts, wrapped in a shroud and jettisoned from the airlock. The funeral is not shown as being religious in any way – as far as we are aware, no one prays or says anything over the body – this is a world in which the human characters are on their own and know it. The thin white line of his corpse turns over and over and drifts out into space – this is one of those shots which reminds us how the Nostromo is big compared with humans and tiny compared with space. Our very last

1. When I saw *Alien* for the first time in the autumn of 1979, I was recovering from surgery, and had had stitches out earlier that afternoon. My guess is that this made me the ideal audience for this scene.

sight of what was Kane just echoes the vulnerability always associated with him. In earlier versions of the script, the corpse is not jettisoned so efficiently and turns up floating alongside the ship, hideously distorted by vacuum for a cheap shock effect; the decision to leave it behind and avoid these effects is a good example of the tasteful reticence which makes this a great horror film.

The improvisation of weapons and techniques for searching for the creature is all based on the assumption that it is still tiny – they are hunting with electric cattle prods and zap guns and a direction finder that is hardly any good until you are right on top of it. Of course one of the first things that happens is that Ripley's team find the cat[1] and Brett fails to grab it – it also has to be said that Ripley is not quick enough to say that it needs to be grabbed. The point about the cat is that we are still thinking of the alien as roughly cat-sized.

Brett goes off by himself to find and catch the cat – even though the creature has killed Kane in being born, none of them think of themselves as being at risk, so going off into the dark room where the monsters eat you is only a moderately foolish thing to do. Brett sees a fragment of dead alien skin and fails to think about what it might mean; it looks like a piece of dried gut, or a condom – it is the piece of garbage that you look away from. It is, of course, also the shed skin of the serpent.

There follows one of those moments where the film's symbolism has a strong religious resonance. Brett follows the cat into a room where the ship's interior weather has produced a shower of condensation and for an extended moment of bliss he lets the water run onto his head and down his face and stands in the shower wrinkling his eyes against it in a moment of pleasure and grace. Then he puts his baseball cap back on and continues to stand there with the water rattling on its peak.

Harry Dean Stanton makes Brett quietly likeable – he is Parker's sidekick who makes a joke out of hardly saying anything except to answer whatever people say with a laconic 'Right'. As with Kane, there is a sweetness to Brett in this last moment before his death; he bends down to take the cat out from where it is cowering and takes a while before he realizes why it is panicking and turns around to face his death. We do not see the creature clearly at this point – we get a sense of spikiness and of darkness and of that terrible mouth with the secondary jaws that unfold from within to be followed by an even

1. There is probably no particular resonance to the cat's name, Jones, except that it is just another very simple obvious name like those of all the other crew members. On the other hand, it is possible that it refers to the cat's running away from the people who want to protect it and inadvertently getting them killed: 'Something is happening, but you don't know what it is/ Do you, Mr Jones?'

smaller, even more vicious set. It is not even clear to us what the creature does to Brett, just that it is awful.

There is an inevitability to what happens next. Dallas goes into the ship's service ducts with a flame-thrower and the others track him with a sensor and with an audio-visual link that makes them as much the helpless spectators and sharers of his death as we are. He scrambles around futilely for a while in a space that in its high-tech way – tight steel doorways iris shut behind him like sphincters tightening – is little more than a cave in which he cowers with a flame-thrower for a torch to scare off predators. One of the ways in which the film earns its Conrad references is this sense that there is no real progress – that in crisis we regress to humanity's past.

He puts his hand on some slime without recognizing the implication of it, and then the creature appears on the sensor – it is, in a piece of nightmare logic, almost as if you come across evidence of its presence and fail to recognize it. Ash watches with an inhuman passivity and a secret smirk. Lambert cries out to Dallas but there is no time for him to avoid it – again, we do not see what happens to him, which makes it more dreadful, just a flash on the video of claws and teeth and then interference and nothing. Parker goes to look for him and sums the situation up – 'No blood, no Dallas. Nothing.' Usually, in films with the 'Ten Little Indians' plot, there is some obvious logic, punitive or otherwise, to who gets killed and in what order; one of the unsettling things about *Alien* is that there is no simple logic.

In fact, of course, there was a sequence in which we did find out what happened to him and Brett which was filmed but did not make it into the final cut; since the cocoon sequence is imitated in the sequels, it is perhaps the most important of the deleted scenes. In her travels around the ship, Ripley finds Dallas and Brett tangled up in cocoons – Brett already mostly devoured and Dallas already aware that he is past saving. He pleads for death and Ripley gives him the mercy of a quick burst from the flame-thrower. This was cut from the film late enough in the production process that it found its way into the novelization – but, as with all of Scott's cuts, it is obviously the right one.

Just as we do not need, in this first movie, to see the alien clearly too soon, so we need to have a sense that its victims are softly and silently vanished away,[1] rather than knowing too clearly what their fate is. Scott is able to make a classic horror film in the manner of Val Lewton in which we do not see too much too soon; his successors in the franchise did not have that option. The slowness and stumbling that comes over Dallas in the moments before his

---

1. In the original Dan O'Bannon treatment, the Nostromo was called the Snark.

death is one of several points at which the horror of the creature is conveyed not only visually but because time and movement suddenly work against the next doomed person when it is in their vicinity – this is a great horror film in part because it understands what happens in nightmares.

Dallas' death means that Ripley inherits his command – the casual informality of much of the behaviour of this crew does not mean that there is not a structure of command here. She listens to what the others have to say – Lambert suggests simply leaving the ship in the shuttle. She asks Ash what information he has and mocks him sceptically when he says that he is still collating. She takes Dallas' key and goes to check for herself on the computer, Mother, what information is available. It is at this point that she discovers that her control of the computer has been pre-empted – that there are secret orders and that its objective is now the preservation of the alien creature and that the crew are now regarded as expendable. Ripley, herself no stranger to cold logic, discovers a colder logic at play and turns to find Ash has entered the room silently behind her and has sat down quietly next to her.

The sequence that follows is one of the most humanly upsetting in the film – we have thought we understood the tension between these two but in fact we know nothing. Earlier, Ripley used the door controls to stop Dallas walking away from an argument with her; now she finds the same controls used to trap her with Ash. He attacks her viciously and demonstrates a level of strength which surprises us – this small man is capable of throwing the quite tall Ripley across a room. It is only when he starts to perspire with the effort and his sweat is a creamy white that we begin to suspect the truth.

The attack is very slow and measured; Ash stands watching the semi-conscious Ripley, considering his next action, his face framed by little mechanical birds suspended from the ceiling on springs – automata that offer a clue to his real nature. Ash's anger at Ripley's curiosity takes the form of a quasi-rape in which he slowly and with deliberation rolls up a magazine and forces it into her mouth as a surrogate for the penis he presumably does not have. This is an act of aggression against Ripley as a woman of question-asking intelligence; it is also an act of male aggression – Ash's artificial perspiration has the appearance of semen and his name is that of the First Man in Norse Mythology.

Various critiques of the *Alien* films have seen them as expressions of a gynophobic male paranoia about birth and pregnancy and certainly elements even of this, the most measured and sane of the sequence, can be seen in this light. Kane's death is an obscene birth, for example, and the creature can be seen as a combination of very pronounced male and female characteristics – the face-hugger's underside, probed by Ash, is fleshy, pink and moist, whereas the chest-burster is small and phallic and grows in size and dangerousness with extreme rapidity. The final form of the creature has a large phallic tail and a set of telescoping jaws which manage to be both phallus and vagina dentate at the same time. The film explores these areas of body horror so comprehensively that it is almost impossible to map any one interpretation of the creature as a single correct one – were it possible to accuse *Alien* simplistically of gynophobia, Ash would offer a useful balancing paranoia about male violence.

Ripley is helpless against Ash; it is the one time we see her without resources, and indeed it takes both Parker and Lambert to destroy him. Parker hits him with a pipe and discovers, when his head flies off in a spurt of the white liquid, that Ash is in fact a robot; the decapitated Ash still struggles to choke Ripley and throttle Parker and it is only when Lambert impales him with one of the cattle prods that he shorts out. One can read this as simply literal; or in sexual terms; or one can try and work it out in terms of the stronger members of the crew being vulnerable to Ash and the weakest capable against him with a weapon bequeathed to her by the dead Brett. There are times in this film where mythic resonances are so strong that it is almost beside the point to try and decode them.

Though in a sense no surprise – we find ourselves remarkably unshocked by the revelation that Ash is a robot – this scene offers another significant down-turn in the fortunes of the survivors – one of whose number is revealed as effectively the creature's ally. The screws just keep tightening – the fact that one of the crew is a robot who has actively or passively hindered the struggle is a further refinement of the Ten Little Indians aspect of the plot. This sequence of scenes is the last time that any of the characters is shot in a well-lit room – when later on Ripley is running through the ship to get to the shuttle, when she crosses a well-lit room, she is mostly shot there from the darker room she is coming into. With this betrayal, the characters generally, and Ripley in particular, move into darkness and twilight for good.

It should also be added that Ash is a counter-revisionist robot. In early SF, both in fiction and film, robots were competitors with humanity who would sooner or later turn on us, as they do in Capek's *R.U.R*, or pass for human and mislead us, as the false Maria does in Lang's *Metropolis*. Then there was an era in which robots were our friends, inaugurated by Asimov's Three Laws of Robotics, the idea that robots could be hard-wired out of being dangerous – and which include such cinematic icons as *Forbidden Planet*'s Robbie. The fear of our own creations turning on us got diverted from robots and androids on to computers. Ash on the other hand is a menace precisely because he has been programmed, programmed to act as the perfect company man who will always do as he is told.

What follows is a scene entirely presented in SF terms – Ripley and the other two rewire Ash's brain and run his mostly severed head off the mains – and yet we are back in the mists of mythic time, where a severed head is asked to prophesy – Bran in Celtic British mythology is perhaps the most apposite. One of the first robots in literature is Friar Bacon's brazen head, which utters elliptical statements about the nature of time… As Ash's eyes open, more of the white semen-like fluid gushes from its mouth, as if the presence of its life force guaranteed the truth of its prophecy.

What Ash tells them is bleak: they have no way of beating the creature – 'I can't lie to you about your chances, but you have my sympathy.' Asked disgustedly if he admires it, he says in the flat tinny voice that is all he has left to wound them with that 'I admire its purity. Survival unclouded by conscience, remorse or delusions of morality.' We see Ash as a monster; to himself he is a chimera, radically compromised by his appearance of humanity and capacity to pass. We are never explicitly told that the creature is artificial in origin – but Ash's near-worship of it, and the assumption by the company that it can be exploited, implies something of the kind.

As they leave Ash, Parker turns and destroys him with the flame-thrower. This is powerful in itself – an expression of Parker's angry need to fight back effectually even if it means attacking an already defeated menace. What is particularly interesting about the shot, though, is an example of how *Alien*, one of the finest of all SF films in its creation of a nightmarish future world, was shot without CGI. In those scenes in which Ash's head was not speaking and moving its eyes, Ian Holm was replaced with a model head, and, once the film crew were sure that they had finished with this prop, they simply set fire to it.

It is at this point that the internal geography of the Nostromo becomes the enemy of the three survivors – in order to leave in the shuttle, they have to perform a variety of tasks in a variety of locations with time and a fast-moving alien enemy against them. The ship becomes the playground of anxiety dreams – unwieldy cylinders of coolant have to be loaded on to a trolley which cannot conveniently be negotiated through doorways and constantly tips and spills. Ripley has, in order to free the shuttle, to go to the control room of the lander to fiddle with one set of controls; in order to set the Nostromo to self-destruct, she has to go to another location and go through an elaborate set of procedures she only half-knows with her eye on the instruction manual. Along the way, she finds herself carrying a flame-thrower and a box with the cat inside; no wonder she puts her hair up.

It is interesting that the film establishes very precisely why Ripley is not with the other two when they are killed – most people I talked to when writing had misremembered this as her going off to look for the cat, as opposed to finding and boxing the cat while engaged on other tasks. She hears Parker and Lambert come under attack over the intercom and runs to find them – but she is much too late, as one always is in nightmares. Lambert is utterly paralysed by fear, Parker fights back bravely – none of this makes a difference to the creature which punches a hole with its telescoping jaws in Parker and does something lasciviously unpleasant to Lambert with a tentacle that snakes up her leg. Ripley finds them dead and realizes that she is on her own – and that the creature is somewhere between her and the shuttle.

For a while, music disappears from the soundtrack to be replaced by Ripley's amplified heavy breathing and muffled curses; crashing chords return when she finds the monster waiting near the shuttle and disappear when she races back to the auto-destruct controls. There is a sense now that everything is turning on her – the gusts of CO_2 that were Parker's way of avoiding talking to her now become the way the malfunctioning ship operates all the time and the auto-destruct mechanism is so complicated that she marginally fails to turn it off in time.

Scott plays games with time in this sequence – the first two minutes of the countdown go by in just over twenty seconds of film time and the next two only just over thirty, but then the final thirty seconds before the point of no return happen in real time. Time then speeds up again, but not to the same breakneck speed as at first – the nine-minute point in the ten-minute count comes at just past the six-minute count – and then slows down to real time for the last minute. Nothing, at this point, is going right for Ripley.

The creature has not even pursued her – it is too interested in the cat, offering a major false lead and additional area of suspense when she returns to find the creature gone and Jones the cat safe. By the slimmest of margins, she gets the shuttle away from the Nostromo before the triple explosion that marks its end. 'I got you, you son of a bitch,' she mutters at the creature she believes herself to have killed.

Though far from unheard of, the multiple and false ending was less of a cliché in 1979 than it was to become over the ensuing quarter century when it became less a cliché and more an expected formal gesture. Ripley puts the cat in its cold sleep coffin and prepares herself for sleep, rendering herself more and more defenceless by taking off layers of clothing and relaxing, now she is alone, out of the aggression that has been her stock way of coping with her not especially beloved, and now dead, colleagues. Strings start to swell on the soundtrack instead of the pizzicato and woodwind snarls that have promoted unease up to this point.

In a wonderful visual double-take, we and she notice a grey ovoid stacked behind one of the racks in the crowded shuttle; and then a claw leisurely unfolds and tries to grasp Ripley and we realize that the grey ovoid we have looked at, but clearly not seen, is in fact the top of the creature's head. It reaches for her slowly and lazily – she is the last survivor and it has plenty of time because she has nowhere to run.

She shrinks back from it and finds herself brought up against her salvation, the spacesuit that is hanging in a closet – her near-nakedness is almost an advantage as she steps very slowly into its legs, and pulls it up over her and pulls the helmet down over her. She moves from being almost naked to being clothed in a white spacesuit – practically the armour of light since the point at which we know she is safe inside it is the point at which the helmet's interior electronics come on. There is a wonderful shot of her turning her face so that half of it is obscured by the back of the helmet and watching the creature as it lunges towards her without panic or alarm. She moves from a position of ultimate vulnerability to being protected – not from the creature, because we have no illusions that the spacesuit proofs her against it, but from what she will do to it.

We saw how the Nostromo, perhaps under the influence of Ash, gradually became an environment more favourable to the creature than to the crew; the shuttle is under Ripley's control – the creature is on her turf, now. For a while, at least, she even provides her own score – the breathy tuneless version of 'You are my lucky star' which she mumbles to herself as she moves around the cabin. She has moved through seconds of despairing collapse like Lambert's to a place beyond that, a sense of things coming together.

There is a wonderful rightness to what follows: she confuses it with gusts of gas – presumably the internal fire extinguishers? – opens the airlock, shoots it with a grappler gun and incinerates it with the shuttle's drive. Parker was in the habit of tormenting her with noisy sprays of CO_2; Brett improvised weapons from ship's equipment; Kane was last seen tumbling out into vacuum; Dallas pursued the creature with flames. By observing them and their failures against it, Ripley has learned how to kill it. When she finally kills it, as opposed to when she thought she had done, she has no need to say so.

Goldsmith's evocatively unsettling score is replaced by the music whose sound world it has constantly frustrated and subverted, Howard Hanson's lush Second Symphony, 'The Romantic', a gloriously anachronistic twentieth-century score. Ripley makes her report and settles into her cold sleep coffin, this time safe and invulnerable. Her face is finally entirely relaxed – the music swells and dies around her, with a particularly poignant shot of her face at peace at the point when its slow unwinding suddenly pauses for a moment and then goes on; Scott mentions in his commentary how much he loves that moment in the score and then the credits.

Aliens

'Get away from her – you bitch.'

As the writer and director of two of the best sequels ever made, James Cameron speaks with some authority on how sequels work and ought to work:

> You can take that mental programming that the audience has from the first film and work little twists and turns on it, and play against their expectations… but not in a hostile way… What I try to do in *Aliens* is make the scenes function if you haven't seen the first film, but have a second layer of resonance for those who have… It goes back to the idea of film being a participatory experience rather than just a passive one.

His views imply a contract with the audience – what will be on offer will be faithful to the original in big things, but constantly offer new takes on those things and on a variety of minor points. His admiration for the Ridley Scott film is immense, but he wants and needs to do new things – it is not that *Aliens* defines itself against *Alien*, but that it will not simply repeat what has already been done. Everything that happened in *Alien* will be the case, but will be subject to expansion and to tricks.[1]

1. When Ripley awakes, it is decades later. At first disbelieved by her employers and forced to work in menial jobs, she is reinstated when the colony that has been established on LV-426, the worldlet where the crew of the Nostromo found the alien, goes offline and persuaded by company man Burke to go there as civilian advisor to a detachment of Marines led by inexperienced officer Gorman. She befriends various Marines, among them Hicks and Vasquez The colony has discovered the alien eggs, and has been slaughtered or taken as hosts, all save a child, Newt. The over-confident Marines die one after another; Burke tries to use Ripley and Newt as hosts for aliens. Ripley takes charge and rescues Newt when the child is captured. They and two other survivors – the android Bishop and Hicks – are menaced by the alien Queen which has escaped the destruction of her nest, and Ripley defeats it in hand-to-hand combat.

In the discussion that follows, I start by discussing some of the differences between Scott's procedures and Cameron's, and only after establishing the very different atmospheres of *Alien* and *Aliens* do I proceed to discuss the film in a linear fashion. It is important, as Cameron demonstrates, not to do the same thing twice in quite the same way.

For example, when we find ourselves with Ripley going back to LV-426, the Marine ship is called the Sulaco. This is a tricksy reference by Cameron to the Scott film – Sulaco is the port city in Conrad's novel *Nostromo*, which gives its name to the ship in *Alien*. It therefore serves as a reference back to that name's meaning – that corporations cannot be trusted – and also implies that the Marines may be unduly subject to the Company's influence as well. We are never shown direct collusion between Lieutenant Gorman and the schemes of the company man Burke, but we remain aware of its possibility.

Cameron is fond of such games – Bishop, the android member of the Sulaco's contingent, is distrusted by Ripley, but is in fact benign. When she explains her hostility in terms of the Nostromo crew's betrayal by the android Ash, his explanation as to why this sort of thing could not happen nowadays is, in its description of his programming, a homage to the Laws of Robotics, as devised by Isaac Asimov and John W. Campbell. Bishop prefers the term 'artificial person', a joke which at first sounds like a slur on 'politically correct' diction, but has a gratifying turn when it becomes clear that his standing on his dignity is entirely justified – Ripley comes to regard Bishop as one of the few of her new companions that she can entirely trust. Her escape plans rely entirely on him both as pilot and as capable of calling down a shuttle.

However, Cameron can be a little too fond of tricks. The company that builds both Bishop and Ash is referred to as Cyberdyne, the company which, as discussed above, in scenes cut from the theatrical release of Cameron's *The Terminator*, cannibalized the Terminator's parts to build Skynet, the entity which destroys humanity and sends the Terminator back through time, and which features heavily in the sequel, *Terminator 2*, that he was to make some years after *Aliens*. There is a fine line between this sort of extra-textuality and entire self-indulgence – and Cameron does seem to cross it here.

One of the most obvious differences between his film and Scott's is that, whereas the Scott film was an ensemble piece from which the character of Ripley (Sigourney Weaver) eventually emerges as protagonist by dint of survival, here she is the centre of our attention from the beginning. Cameron's film is an ensemble piece, needless to say, but it is in large part about Ripley's relationship with the members of that ensemble – the complement of the Sulaco – individually and severally. It is a film which draws on the iconic imagery of Sigourney Weaver as Ripley – at once deeply vulnerable and an efficient and effective agent – that the first film created and gradually builds it to a point where she becomes almost a demi-goddess.

Ripley's new status as protagonist is signalled by her role as the possessor of knowledge and wisdom about the aliens and by the fact that she has become, in a variety of ways, a liminal being who inhabits the threshold between worlds. She is uncanny – her survival of extended hypersleep was a thousand-to-one chance, her recovery another. She is born again, and gets second chances – she is therefore in a sense innocent, making her a secret sharer of the child Newt's combination of innocence and experience. She has awakened from long sleep and her attempts to do good precipitate that which she most dreads – she has a weird oppositional kinship with the alien Queen.

It is perhaps helpful to see both Newt and the Queen as shadow doubles of Ripley. Newt has like her lost everyone she has ever known and experienced terror beyond bearing and come out the other side as a possessor of unpalatable harsh truths. When Ripley suggests to her that she would be safer with Ripley and the others, Newt shakes her head very slowly and deliberately; 'It won't make any difference', she says with an experience beyond her years. She is at the same time the good girl Rebecca with clean hair and feminine dresses and the waif Newt – the name she prefers; the fact that she is a being with two names and two natures makes her uncanny in the way that Ripley is.

The Queen is uncanny of her essential nature – she is a monster, but she is also a reasoning creature in a way that we have only intermittent evidence that the lesser aliens are. It is possible to communicate with her – Ripley threatens to burn her eggs unless the warriors give her and Newt safe passage. It is also possible to lie to her and betray her – Ripley burns the eggs anyway. The Queen feels emotions that are vaguely parseable – she displays rage and spite – whereas the lesser aliens are merely predatory and malevolent. She is also capable of altering her nature for a greater purpose – she tears away her egg-laying organ in order to pursue Ripley. She is a beast that is capable of using tools – she takes a lift and she understands enough to hide in the landing gear of the shuttle. Like the other two, she has two natures.

Self-sterilized and monstrous, the Queen can also be seen as the Crone, the dark aspect of the triple goddess. Critics have overstated the extent to which Ripley is the Mother and overestimated the extent to which her protection of Newt is solely and wholly a matter of paying her debt to the daughter whom she inadvertently abandoned – Newt is also another self who has experiences more like Ripley's than anyone else's and has to be protected for that reason. Newt is, needless to say, also the Maiden, the triple goddess' third aspect. The final conflict of the film ignores the male principals almost entirely – Hicks is unconscious and Bishop, dismembered by the Queen's lashing tail, is quite literally less than half the man he used to be.

It is arguable that, as part of her education in competent violence, the woman Marine Vasquez is another of Ripley's doubles. If, as I argue in the previous section on *Alien*, Ripley's final victory depends on things she has learned from each of her dead crewmates, it is from Vasquez and from Hicks, of all the Marines, that Ripley learns most. Hicks takes the time to teach her the mechanics of using the weaponry; from Vasquez she learns the attitude – the systematic aggression and the fearlessness beyond despair that is the only way she stands a chance of rescuing Newt and surviving herself.

Vasquez is also important because she is a woman whose motivation for fighting comes from the selfless love of her comrades and of her own competence as a fighter. Without her presence, the film would be far more open than it is to the accusation of only legitimizing female violence if it is in defence of your child, or someone you have identified as your child. Vasquez dies defending the retreat of people many of whom she does not know or like because it is her job to do so; at the film's climax, Ripley fights the alien Queen not only to save Newt, but also to protect the blinded Hicks and the helpless android Bishop. She learns that commitment to the team partly from Hicks, but mostly from Vasquez's example.

There exist two versions of *Aliens* – the original theatrical release concentrates rather more entirely on the viewpoint of Ripley and plays down somewhat one area of Cameron's conception of the character. He sees Ripley as in part motivated by her feelings of guilt over her failure to get home before her daughter, whom she last saw as a child, dies of old age; some viewers have seen this as evidence for the reading of Cameron that it is only in defence of motherhood that he is prepared to allow women to display violence.

I would argue that this is fair comment, but an oversimplification. He has to make Ripley at least somewhat more likeable and reconnect her with humanity; one alternative would have been to involve her romantically with one of her new crewmates, but he does not choose to go down that path, instead making her relationship with Hicks very much a comradeship and a partnership in arms, in which he teaches her to use big guns and agrees that they will kill each other rather than become bait for aliens. To have replaced this image of men and women working together with a minimum of flirtation with conventional romance would have been far less interesting.

Ripley needs to have a motivation that has shadows and ambiguities to it – and protective motherhood links her to the new version of the alien we meet in the course of the film. Part of the point of the sequel was to up the ante on things we have already been shown – and part at least was to cover one or two areas in which the first film had failed to be absolutely and consistently logical.

In *Alien*, we see a part of a life cycle – egg to face-hugger to chest-burster to full-grown alien warrior – but it makes no sense that this be the whole story; eggs after all imply something that lays them.

Cameron has said of Ripley in this film that 'her experience is a long dark tunnel' out of which she comes at the end. In other words, she is taking a Night Journey, a quasi-mystical trip through the darkness in order to come through at the other end to the light. Newt too goes through a journey from being the happy child of the first scene in which we see her to being restored to innocence at the film's end, to a place where it is safe to dream, a place at the end of night.

Where the title of *Alien* came up as blocks of white on a dark background which gradually mutate into the letters, the blocks of the title *Aliens* come up as ovals that alternate a pale blue light with the dark background that they lie against. (The blue is, perhaps coincidentally but perhaps not, almost exactly the shade of the force field that protected the eggs in *Alien*). They then transform, first into roughly oblong blocs and then into the letters, at this point losing the stripes and becoming pure blue light – the 'I' expands and acquires curvature before filling the screen and vanishing into pure bright white. This is replaced first by the emptiness of space – much of which is here also a very dark blue – and then the dark blue and black interior of the Nostromo's lifeboat. Gradually the darkness and shadow is punctuated by the warmer colours of yellow and white lights on the instrument panels; the first and only sustained pale colour we see is Ripley's face as she sleeps in her hypersleep casket.

Cameron's film plays much more than Scott's did with light and darkness, heroism and villainy, often in the same person; his is a less pessimistic view than Scott's in that even the entirely incompetent and somewhat venal officer Gorman finds a sort of redemption in his death. Of the human complement of the Sulaco, only Burke, the company man, is beyond redemption – he is the one person whose behaviour throws the worth of human beings into doubt: Ripley says to him: 'I don't know which species is worse. You don't see them screwing each other over for a fucking percentage.'

Where Scott's visual palette depends largely on a contrast between the lit and unlit areas of the Nostromo, much of Cameron's takes place in dark spaces fitfully but harshly illuminated – he is fond of a chiaroscuro, of dark objects finely picked out by unnatural light. He is also fond of reminding us that the flesh is weak and the universe dark and hostile. The aliens love it where it is dark and warm and cthonic; they are the thing that lives in the dark room. Conflicts that take place in their territory are ones in which they have an advantage – Ripley takes that advantage back in her first confrontation with the Queen by using a torch and her second takes place in comparatively well-lit human space.

The other major difference between Scott and Cameron is this: Scott establishes plot points by slow accretion where Cameron is obsessed with foreshadowings and with putting, in Chekhov's terms, the gun on the wall in the first act so that it can be fired in the third. He is far fonder than Scott of mythic resonances. Scott's film is in many ways simple and austere where Cameron's is rich and noisy. The dialogue of the Scott film is utilitarian, where Cameron gives his characters lines that have potential life beyond the text – the Marines in particular have an idiolect sufficiently recognizable that it has been casually parodied in a Terry Pratchett novel (*Reaper Man*), on the assumption that Pratchett's audience would automatically get the joke.

James Horner's score for the title sequence is admirable at conveying both unease and threatened vulnerability, building up from a bass line that, as we look out into the empty reaches of space, is not going anywhere except a momentary snarl and from drumbeats that prefigure the martial airs that dominate much of the rest of the score but here just say mourning and unease. Over it there is a noise of wind – a wind inappropriate in space but which we come to recognize when we eventually reach the colony world of LV-426.

In Ridley Scott's film, Goldsmith reassured us after a score of appropriately sinister hoots and twitters with a big four-square triumphant tune – a fragment of Howard Hanson's 'Romantic' symphony – as Ripley prepared for her long sleep. The music that Horner gives us for the sleeping Ripley is equally lush, but edgier; it is a constantly repeated lullaby refrain with an edge of threat that inhabits a sound world similar to the slower numbers from Khatchachurian's ballets. There is no triumph here, just a sadness that is interrupted by distant snarling calls, by a lower strings counter-melody, the bass line we heard earlier and by the returning drumbeats. Lastly the title tune reappears briefly, in woodwind rather than strings, and is then silenced.

Horner's award-nominated work on *Aliens* is one of the best modern American movie scores, even though he and Cameron appear to have disagreed about how much of it should actually be used – the two men did not work together again until *Titanic*. Perhaps the most important thing about it is just this – that he wrote something with this degree of complexity and subtlety for a genre that had hitherto tended to be accompanied by the rather cruder scores of, say, John Williams. And one of the reasons is that both he and Cameron saw the film as one which transgressed obvious genre boundaries – it is a science fiction film and a horror film and a film about soldiers and a film about the stresses of surviving trauma.

We see a menacing shape that turns out to be nothing more sinister than a robot camera and a salvage crew find Ripley still asleep in the Nostromo's shuttle, the cat Jones still cradled in her arms, with the deep blue of a scanner's light playing across her features; she is posed between life and death, between human and animal. Just to remind us that we are still in a world in which the cash nexus is everything, the comments of the men who find her are appropriately cynical and commercial: 'Lights are green. She's alive. Well, there goes our salvage, guys.'

The next shot is of one of the things we need to remember is at stake – Earth itself – but it is only what we look at for a second; there gradually moves into shot the threatening spiky lines of Gareway, the company's space station. It is almost as if the planet has railings round it, the mark of being owned by corporations and powers. The shot moves sideways and proves to be the view from Ripley's window as a nurse talks to her; our view, not Ripley's. One of the things about Cameron is that there is something deeply maverick and American populist about his radicalism – it is almost as if he has never got over the fact that the frontier ended up being fenced in.

In the ensuing sequence, we are introduced to the superficially charming company man, Carter Burke: 'I work for the company, but don't let that fool you; I'm really an OK guy'. And at first, he seems to be the friend Ripley needs – he brings her Jones the cat, he helps her prepare a statement for her hearing, he offers her sympathy. But there is always something slightly off about everything he says and does – he would, for example, have been prepared to keep the news about her daughter's death from old age until after the hearing.

He lacks affect – it comes as no surprise when he is identified as the man who sent Rebecca's family to their doom rather than risk spending money on sending trained personnel. Cameron's deep hostility to this man – the film's human villain – is for a long time demonstrated in small touches: Burke has one or two very neat tells – he is always at his least trustworthy when he covers his mouth with a loose fist, when he replaces his verbal dexterity with an implicit threat of force.

Ripley is only just starting to realize how long she has been asleep – in one of his typical moments of misplaced spin, Burke tries to get her to concentrate on the idea that she is lucky to have survived at all rather than unfortunate to have slept through the lives of everyone she knew – this is true, but inappropriate. Suddenly her heartbeat accelerates; the cat snarls and pulls away from her; she starts to convulse and spills the water Burke offers her – she stares with horror as one of the creatures starts to emerge, not from her chest, but from her abdomen, in an even more nightmarish parody of birth. And then she wakes up.

Part of this is just Cameron waking us up – nothing much has happened in the film yet and he needs to promise us that, as in Scott's film, the deliberately stately pace will culminate in breakneck action. For those people who saw *Alien*, her convulsions have an extra resonance because they recapitulate Kane's; the bulge in her abdomen tells us that it is all starting again. Yet a viewer who knows nothing, will still get a sense of her real jeopardy. Her dreams again pose her between life and death; the presence of the company man Carter Burke in what proves to be a dream prefigures his eventual attempt to implant her with an alien – her dreams are lies that include truth.

Her contemporaries are as dead as her fellow crew-members – since humans are social beings, she experiences a kind of civil death, while alive. Before the board of inquiry, we find her sitting in a peaceful garden which proves to be an electronic fake – in the screenplay it fools the cat Jones – this signals to us yet again that we really need to not trust Burke who joins her there just after she has turned it off. For a moment she appears to be in touch with the world of nature and then we discover that it is just another comforting lie.

The committee of inquiry is all about ignoring her and brushing her under the carpet as an embarrassment. She stands with photographs of her dead crewmates behind her and then the head of the board says, 'Look at this from our perspective', and suddenly the camera retreats into a long shot of Ripley and the photographs down the entire length of a table full of unfriendly faces. As the discussion goes on, the perspective shifts so that it runs along the length of the table, entirely excluding Ripley from the shot until she explodes with frustration and insolence – 'Did IQs suddenly drop while I was away?'

She is disgraced by the board of inquiry, which strips her of her rank – we know that they are accusing her of delusions over what we know to be the truth; she is Cassandra, the visionary whose truths are unpalatable and therefore ignored. She tells them these in a challenging way that ensures they will not hear her. They in turn tell her something she does not know – that the nameless planetoid now has inhabitants. It is the casual expression 'fifty or sixty families' that brings her up short against the real horror of the situation – she reacts instantly to the word families. 'Families? Jesus!' she mutters.

One of the reasons why the extended director's cut of the film is, on the whole, preferable in spite of its more leisurely pace is that it is important that we first meet Newt as a child who is part of a real family. We are taken to the colony world and shown busy managers coping with the simultaneous demands of a suit back on earth and the prospector they have sent out to check a map reference. We follow the manager as he transports his beaker of bad coffee around a vast open-plan office area – as always with Cameron, this serves a dual function, giving us a sense of how busy the colony is and also acquainting us with some of the geography of its administrative building. The presence of children – lots of them – is signalled by his subordinate's shooing of several of them, and their large-wheeled toy bike, away from the work area.

His talk of the prospector is the first implication that the company have actually paid attention to what Ripley told them – the fact that the managers regard checking the grid reference as an irrational mission and that Newt's father sees it as an opportunity to make some extra money gives us our first of many bad moments. The fact that the planetoid now has an atmosphere just means that the people who live there are not wearing breathing masks, just goggles against dust, and are so much more vulnerable. This is neither routine, nor chance; it is the same nightmare starting all over again.

This is all the more the case because for Newt's family, this is little more than an outing – she and her brother lark around in the back of the family vehicle while their mother tries to control them and to dampen her husband's enthusiasm. Her scolding reference to 'playing in the air ducts' is a typical example of Cameron's economic placing of markers for things that will be important later. We know that these are innocents who are going to their deaths and we do not know that Newt is going to survive. And of course the inevitable happens – they find the ship and they go inside, and the children comment that they have been delayed. The next thing we know, Newt's mother is back and the children are learning that something is horribly wrong. Newt looks through the door and down at her father and starts to scream.

Cameron is not in general a director who uses visual puns, but the cut from the long grasping arms of the face-hugger on the face of Newt's father via a shot of cigarette smoke pluming to a close-up of Ripley's long elegant figures clutching a cigarette and dangling from the arm of a chair is an interesting exception. There is a connection – neither we nor she yet knows what it is – between the Newtons being sent out to the alien ship and her awakening; she has a connection with the monsters, and part of it is simply that she is uncanny.

The concept of the uncanny is an interesting one, with the word's implication that it is possible to be strange simply because you know things that other people do not. In Anglo-Saxon, a kenning is a pregnant riddle that tells us more than is obvious; in early modern Britain, a cunning man or woman was a healer whose family passed down secret recipes for cures – all of these words are etymologically linked. The equivalent German term is *unheimlich* (un-home-like) and Ripley is that too, having lost her place in the world, her home.

We do not see Ripley smoking on a regular basis – Cameron's economy of approach ensures that this shot establishes the matter of her smoking for later, when he will make further use of it. The shot travels up her arm and to her face in gloomy repose; the pun is book-ended by the screaming child and the gloomy adult, making clear the linkage between them. In his book *The Alien Quartet* (1999) David Thomson, who is not interested in these aspects of the film, nonetheless picks up on this shot as something extraordinary.

Ripley is visited in her isolation by Burke – who has clearly neglected her since her disgrace – and the unimpressive Gorman, and asked to join the Marine rescue mission. Cameron has said in interview that one of the most difficult things to plot in the film was the reason why Ripley would place herself back in jeopardy and he lays out all the reasons why it is a bad idea. Ripley is terrified – she cannot sleep for nightmares – and they are asking her to go back.

Burke cajoles her and makes her promises: she will be reinstated if she goes; it is worth noticing that the mere fact that she has been vindicated does not automatically reinstate her – truth and falsehood are not the issue, only utility. He proves all the more untrustworthy for the fact that some of what he says is valid and true – Ripley does need to confront her fears and needs her true work. He sees the labouring job she has taken, running the loaders that will be important later, as degrading – at the same time, he assumes that her true work is doing what the company says, not being the protector of humanity.

He also introduces her to Gorman, saying that she will be safe, that she will be protected, that the Marines are 'tough hombres'; Burke is always at his most untrustworthy and inauthentic on the few occasions when he slips into his version of street talk, which usually involves his using Spanish words. The fact that Gorman, commander of these tough hombres, has come apologetically as Burke's sidekick on this diplomatic mission, does not augur well for his decisiveness – Gorman does not impress on our and Ripley's first viewing of him. His use of the word 'protect' is part of a discourse that runs through much of the film; some of the characters know what it means and others, like Gorman, use it unconvincingly.

When Ripley tells him, 'You don't need me, I'm not a soldier', Cameron is stacking up dramatic ironies for future use – Ripley is not a soldier, but she demonstrates when it proves necessary that she is something else, a warrior. Gorman is a soldier but, almost until the end, he shows no sign of knowing what that means – it is a career for him, not a set of responsibilities.

Cameron has acknowledged that *Aliens* is, in part, a film about Vietnam; the character of Gorman is an important part of that – he is a man inadequate to the command of the good troops he leads, partly because he is constantly looking over his shoulder at the company's man for approval of his actions. At the same time, he is so little acquainted with the men of his new command that he confuses Hudson, the loudmouth, with Hicks, the quietly competent corporal.

What fascinates Cameron about the Vietnam war is not that it was wrong so much as that it was a war in which a high-powered technological nation was beaten by poor peasants – it is a film about the question 'Why are we losing?' There are a lot of answers to that question in this film, but it is hard to describe it as an anti-war film; it is a film that admires soldiers too much for that.

Ripley refuses to join Gorman and his men on their mission – and then, later, wakes from a nightmare. We don't see the nightmare, this time, just her awakening, but the way that she feels her chest and abdomen to check that they are whole tells us all that we need to know about its content. It is easy to praise Weaver for her heroics and her vehemence, but the context in which those showy virtues operate is made up of many quieter subtler moments like this. It is her portrayal of the constantly renewed stress of her dreams that makes us believe that Ripley will put herself back in danger, partly because of the colonists, but mostly because she needs to escape the dreams.

She extorts from Burke a promise that the creatures will be destroyed, not studied. Cameron has carefully constructed our sense of Burke as plausible but a liar to the point where, at this moment, we think no worse of Ripley for trusting him and automatically assume that he is lying to her. Yet, at the same time, she does know better at some level; when her suspicions come to the surface at the colony itself, she knows where to look for the evidence.

The first film had shown, as one of Ripley's few attractive personal characteristics, her concern for the ship's cat and the early sequences here show her relationship with it continue – Burke persuades her that he is likeable by bringing Jones to her and it is to Jones that she whispers that they have made it home. When she makes her decision to go to the colony world with the mission, she explicitly and rather touchingly says farewell to Jones: 'And you, you little shithead, you're staying here.' Ripley mocks her feelings for the cat – leaving it behind rather than take it into danger is the right thing, but painful. There are many points at which Cameron pays deliberate homage to Scott's version; this is one of the few moments at which he says 'no more' to it.

We move straight from that farewell to the depths of space and to an almost fetishistic shot of the Sulaco – Cameron is one of the few directors of SF who can make us feel what Larry Niven called 'the romance of great machines'. The Sulaco is like a great shark, or like a Swiss Army Knife – it is an image of brutal strength and ingenious efficiency. Horner's score, as we watch the ship move through space, is at the same time military and mournful, horn and trombone calls and drumbeats – there is a tremendous dignity here, but also a sense of foreboding.

The interior tracking shots that follow are an explicit reference to the similar scenes in *Alien*: they establish some of the ship's internal geography

– our eyes travel across what we later learn to be the loaders and the shuttle so quickly that we hardly register them. The tracking shots also remind us, through establishing shots of later versions of similar technology, that we have moved sixty years forward between the films – it helps that both sets of ship's fittings were largely designed by the same man, Ron Cobb. The hypersleep caskets in particular are more mechanical, less organic looking – their lids are hydraulically raised and they are a row rather than a cluster. The random movements of the Nostromo's breakfast room mobiles and drinking plastic birds have been replaced by a complicated executive toy, steel balls moving in pre-arranged patterns.

The scene of awakening is crystal clear in its sound and dialogue in a deliberate contrast to Ridley Scott's *Alien*, which deliberately kept us from hearing what the characters were saying – no civilian sloppiness here, the Marines wake up and start within seconds the character-establishing banter that is their common characteristic. Cameron has waited until now to introduce most of the ensemble who will be with us for the rest of the film and the teasing and gymnastics and kvetching that ensue are a useful shorthand for their characters and for a fair number of their interactions.

We learn, for example, almost immediately, that Hudson is a licensed clown and not nearly as brave as he would have us believe; that Apone, the sergeant, rules by example as much as by mockery – and that a cigar is in his mouth within seconds of his awakening. We learn that Vasquez can effortlessly bat away Hudson's attempted put-downs and that the blond angular Drake is her particular friend – not in any sexual way, but purely because, as the people who walk point, and who carry their squad's Really Big Guns, they are special and separate.

There are some concessions to realism in this film's portrayal of soldiers – the actors who were playing the Marines spent a fortnight with the British SAS – but they are also Cameron's tribute to soldiers in film and in books. The internal dynamics are ones we have seen in a hundred war films – slightly different, but only slightly, because of the fact that these are sexually integrated troops, portrayed casually and with far less prurience than the soldiers in Verhoeven's *Starship Troopers*. There is a sense in which *Aliens* is far truer to some of the spirit of Heinlein's book than the weaker and derivative film which is overtly an adaptation; Cameron made his cast read the book as part of their preparation for their roles.

However, as against that view, it might also be argued that the Colonial Marines of *Aliens* are all of them obsessed with soldierliness as a performance, that one of the ways in which they cope is to be 'on' and in a sense on stage all the time. The fact that video and audio links monitor their every move means that, in a very real sense, they are especially 'on' in combat Apone, with his big cigar and his routines: 'A day in the corps is like a day on the farm – every meal a banquet, every formation a parade'. He is a glorious ham and Hicks, the competent soldier who grabs catnaps whenever he can, a lazy-eyed Mitchumesque performance of quiet masculinity.

The two soldiers who don't quite cut it are the two whose performances are inadequate – Hudson overacts (most of the bits of soldier-speak we take away from the film, all the 'Yo' and 'Check it Out' are actually his) and moreover insists on doing it around people who are not interested, like Ripley. Gorman, when the crunch comes, is no actor at all – he misses his cues and dries on his lines; it is significant that all his previous combat experiences have been simulated. When Ripley takes command, she is less like a soldier and more like a director – she knocks Hudson into shape by critiquing his performance... For Cameron, clearly, soldierliness, good direction and masculinity are all parts of similar performances.

The establishment of these military personae continues during the first meal, along with the ordeal by knife that helps display Hudson's essential cowardice and establishes that the mild-mannered Bishop is other than human. The game, in which Bishop repeatedly and rapidly stabs the table with a knife between his and Hudson's splayed fingers tells us that one of the reasons why the android is valued by the other members of his squad is that he is good at things – the fact that they tolerate Hudson in spite of the fact that he is a loudmouth implies that he is good at something too.

One of the standard tropes of films in which there is going to be a high body count among the central group of characters is that we are introduced to people we are going to watch die, and have to be kept from having too ready a sense of the order in which this is going to happen. This is at the same time a film about soldiers and a horror film – we know the rules. Those characters whom we don't get to know especially well are most obviously cannon fodder – the woman shuttle pilot Ferro, for example – but Cameron makes a point of not making the order of his characters' deaths comply with any obvious expectations.

What he does is make all of these characters more or less likeable – perhaps rather too much so by comparison with Scott in *Alien*. What he does manage to convey is that this group of men and women have known each other for a long time: Ripley, Gorman and Burke are outsiders who eat at the far end of the table. Both films use the meal to establish divisions within their crews, divisions that have to do with class.

In all of these early sequences on the Sulaco, Ripley is being watched by the Marines, who want to know if she is their sort of person or a suit like Burke, by whom they are not taken in for a second, or an inadequate like their com-

mander, Gorman – whose lack of experience they pick out in seconds. Ripley
is, as far as they are concerned, a combat virgin 'Snow White' and someone
who 'saw an alien once'; they are sceptical about the value of the mission
– which they see as rescuing colonists' daughters from their virginity or as 'a
bug hunt'. It is a bug hunt, but one in which the bugs will do the hunting.

Ripley's outburst against Bishop does not impress them – they know and
trust him and they do not know her. Her tongue-lashing of Vasquez, on the
other hand, for refusing to take the mission seriously, impresses them, both
because she refuses to let Gorman speak for her and because of the sheer
vehemence of which she is capable. It is significant that Hudson contents
himself with remarks that question Gorman's authority; Vasquez already has a
sense of Ripley as someone whom it is appropriate to challenge.

What really makes Ripley acceptable to the soldiers is her preparedness to
do physical labour; the skills that were seen as part of her disgrace on Gateway
– her ability to run one of the exoskeleton-like loaders – are seen as something
that separates her from Gorman and Burke. In the first film, Ripley was one
of the officers and in a combative relationship with the crew – here she wins
the approval of Apone and his corporal Hicks by not having any side. She asks
'Is there anything I can do?' and Apone asks her right back 'I don't know – is
there anything you can do?' She gets into one of the loader exoskeletons and
proves her point – the two NCOs grin at each other and at her. She is not an
officer any more, and this is a good thing – the skills that Burke considered a
degradation build a trust that will become very important.

The sequence that follows is deliberately epic in its feel – the soldiers arm
themselves and take their places in the tank-like armoured personnel carrier
which is then driven up into the shuttle. We realize that part of the job of the
commanding officer Gorman is to stay behind and monitor the transmissions
of each soldier's headset – sound and vision and also vital signs. This is a far
more sophisticated version of a technology we saw in *Alien*, where Dallas had
improvised links and they availed him not at all. Over a pounding drumbeat
– not part of Horner's score, this one – our expectations are at the same time
hyped up by the aspect of this that is like a war game in which everything
is supposed to go smoothly, and our sense that we are in the world of the
dynamic contingent, where things do not go as they are planned to.

The trip down to the planet is made worse for the anxious Ripley by
Hudson, who chooses this moment for a heavy-handed rant about himself
and his colleagues:

> I am ready, man. Ready to get it on. Check-it-out. I am the ultimate
> badass... state of the badass art. You do not want to fuck with me.

Hey, Ripley, don't worry. Me and my squad of ultimate badasses will
protect you. Check-it-out... Independently targeting particle-beam
phalanx. VWAP! Fry half a city with this puppy. We got tactical smart-
missiles, phased-plasma pulse-rifles, RPG's. We got sonic electronic
allbreakers, we got nukes, we got knives... sharp sticks –

His heavy-handed sexual innuendo is useful to the film as a whole because
it acknowledges and therefore defuses the film's sexualization of weaponry.
The rant also ironically foreshadows what the troops will gradually be reduced
to – not perhaps knives and sharp sticks, but not their high-tech gear in the
end. It also imparts some information that the audience needs – we actually
need to be told what these future weapons are and what they do.

The first sweep through the colony by the two squads is a perfect and entirely
pointless demonstration of what they are good at and how things are supposed
to work; it is a by-the-numbers exploration of strategic space which at first finds
nothing except bad memories. One of the first things they find is a false alarm
– the motion sensors pick up a group of mice in a maze, not the worst metaphor
for their own position, did they but know it. They find no sign of the colonists
and only gradually do they find signs of the aliens – and the signs they find are
also an absence, the gaping holes gouged in the structure of the building by their
acid blood. It is at this point clear to everyone that everything Ripley has told
them is true – it is another benchmark in their acceptance of her.

In one of Cameron's drafts, Ripley stays behind in the APC when Gorman
and Burke go into the colony building and then realizes that her place is
with the others. Cameron cut this as demonstrating a degree of alienation and
loneliness which is not even true of Ripley by this point. She is still the outside
adviser at this point, but not so obviously asking for special treatment that she
cannot, when things come to a crunch, step effortlessly into a leadership role
in a group which suddenly needs her to do more than warn of doom.

One of the things that makes this plausible is that the further she goes
into jeopardy, the more lithe and less defensively hunched Sigourney Weaver's
performance becomes; she becomes almost physically taller the further the
film proceeds. She enters the building last of the group and she is standing
very tall – significantly, Hicks' body language at the door already welcomes
her in a way that he does not welcome his commander or Burke. We also see
the more explicit attitude of the ordinary troops to Gorman – even Hudson
feels entitled to be rude about him and Vasquez dismisses him bilingually
– 'Pendejo jerkoff'.

The party moves through territory we have encountered either in their
first sweep or in the original shot of the colony when it was full of working

people – and they find the medical lab with its complement of face-huggers in great storage jars. The fact that one of them proves to be alive, and to react to Burke when he goes too close, is a neat foreshadowing of later events; it is also a superb piece of misdirection so that, when another motion sensor goes off, one of the soldiers fires off rounds and it is only Hicks' quick reaction that prevents the killing of the colony's one survivor, Newt, the mute feral child that we hardly recognize as the child we last saw screaming.

Earlier, the soldiers joke about rescuing the colonists' daughters from their virginity. What they find is a child too young to be the subject of sexual humour and who does not want to be rescued: when he tries to grab her, she bites Hicks – who just saved her from his trigger-happy point man – hard. She retreats into the air ducts where she has lived in isolation; Ripley follows her and forces her out into the company of other humans. Newt experiences, in a sense, a second birth into social being; among the junk Newt has accumulated in her nest, Ripley finds a photograph of her, a trophy for citizenship, with her name Rebecca on it.

Gorman of course insists on treating the child as a resource and the medical technician Dietrich as a merely medical problem. Ripley, in a scene that strikes dangerously sentimental false notes, bonds with the child by feeding her hot chocolate, and cleans her face, trying to find a way past her truculent silence by reminding her of femininity. It is only when she tries the magic of knowing the girl's name that she gets a response; she calls her Rebecca and is told that her name is Newt, only her brother called her Rebecca. Rebecca is a name that she is called by the dead – Newt on the other hand is a name that at one and the same time implies her brilliance and her capacity to wriggle and escape – it is a self-chosen name for an identity that has kept her alive.

A significant part of the film has gone by without all that much happening – we have established character. This is one of the ways in which Cameron has deliberately imitated Scott, a slow pace with occasional shocks and no major trauma that is not instantly taken back by revealing it to be a dream. Hudson's discovery that the colonists' locator chips place them in the atmosphere plant sets off a sequence in which this is made up for in bravura fashion.

The fool's errand of the sweep through the colony fills the Marines and their commander with an inappropriate confidence – Ripley has already explained to Gorman that their sweep through the colony does not mean that they are secure there, and she has been ignored. One of the first things that indicates potential disaster is the way that the interior of parts of the atmosphere plant have been remodelled with resin – Ripley has to admit that this is something she has not seen before and of course this is true, because the scene in which she saw the resin, and the cocooned Dallas, was cut from *Alien*, even though it is clearly Cameron's model for this and some of the subsequence scenes.

Ripley fulfils her role as the bearer of unwanted news when she points out, backed up by Burke, that the Marines are taking high-explosive rounds into an area filled with the coolant pipes of a fusion reactor. It is typical of Gorman's inadequacy that he issues orders that the Marines are not to use their guns, only their flame-throwers, without deigning to tell them why and in the incorrect expectation that they will pay him any attention at all:

Wierzbowski   Is he fucking crazy?

Hudson   What're we supposed to use, man?
                   Harsh language?

On Apone's orders, they hand over their magazines; once his back is tactfully turned, they reload with spares Vasquez has by her for such occasions. Hicks meanwhile displays the shotgun he keeps for emergencies – a shotgun whose crucial firing a few minutes later may almost be a joke about the appropriateness to Cameron's methods of the Chekhov line about foreshadowing quoted earlier.

The room where the colonists are is a charnel house, full of dead people with their chests burst open, and withered empty eggs, and the dried out corpses of the face-huggers. The Marines witness the death of one last colonist – she begs them to kill her and they try to assure her that they are there to rescue her and within seconds she is dead. All their glib comments about rescue turn to ashes – they incinerate her corpse and the creature that has been born from it.

And within moments, half of them are dead too – the motion sensors go wild and creatures uncoil from their resting places tucked into the resin. This is a memorably creepy image – as with the alien quietly ambushing Ripley in her own shuttle in the first film, for a moment we do not realize what we are seeing. The Marine's firepower works against them – Dietrich is pulled up screaming into the ceiling and burns Frost with her flame-thrower as she dies. Gorman sits at his microphone complaining irrelevantly that they are firing against his orders, trying to understand what is happening amid the confusion and the electronic interference – he dries and is worse than useless as Wierzbowski dies and Crowe dies and Apone dies and their monitors fail one by one. His paralysis is a powerful image of technological warfare gone wrong.

Ripley screams at him to act, and then acts herself, belting Newt in and seizing the wheel of the APC. There is no smoothness or measure or ordered routine to Ripley's approach to combat – she is so very much not a soldier;

she simply drives the armoured vehicle through doors and down ramps and finds her way to the surviving Marines by brute force without finesse. The useless and redundant Gorman is thrown around as he shrieks at her to obey his orders; Burke, who has always deferred to him while he was useful, ignores him. Only Hudson and Hicks and Bishop and Vasquez make it through the doors. In a bitter irony, Vasquez's attempt to save Drake from one of the creatures kills him when her shot smashes it like a bug and its acid blood burns his face and chest off. An alien tries to get through the door and Hicks fires his gun straight into its mouth – sometimes Cameron sets things up for a payoff a long time ahead but here Hicks' possession of the shotgun pays off within minutes.

We have waited a long time for this explosion of ultra-violent action and it is genuinely thrilling when it comes. Cameron's cutting is deliberately staccato so that our sense of what happens is confused in detail and overwhelming in its sense of humiliating defeat. We lose six of the cast in seconds, including two that we had come to think of as important members. The speed of the cutting, and the darkness illuminated by sudden flashes and fires, obscures the fact that there are, in fact, only six aliens; as in later scenes they just keep coming from different angles.

Cameron is also good at directing his actors so that their physicality in violent action is as much part of their characterization as their dialogue. Jeanette Goldstein in particular is impressive in this sequence – we have thought of Vasquez as personally formidable in her aggression and we now get to see how deadly she is, and are touched by her emotional agony at having killed her friend. Michael Biehn as Hicks translates his lazy easy body language into an equally minimal and utterly effective quiet efficiency – he has real authority when, after an equally fearsome hell-ride out of the plant, he tells Ripley to stop driving: 'Ease up. Sounds like a blown transaxle. You're just grinding metal.'

One of the major differences between the screenplay of *Alien*, which passed through many hands before being stripped down and refined by Scott, and Cameron's screenplay is Cameron's perpetual quest for the money shot line or exchange. There are almost no memorable lines in *Alien*, whereas *Aliens* is full of confrontations with snappy Hollywood dialogue. The scene in which the up-to-this-moment unspoken alliance of Ripley and Hicks takes command of the survivors is one such – I remember seeing a preview of the film with a crowd of science fiction professionals who cheered to the echo exchanges like:

> Ripley   I say we take off and nuke the entire site from orbit. It's the only way to be sure…

Hudson   Fucking-A.

Burke   Hold on one second. This installation has a substantial
         dollar value attached to it.

Ripley   They can bill me.

Burke   OK, look. This is an emotional moment for all of us,
         OK, I know that, but let's not make snap judgements.
         This is clearly an important species we're dealing with
         and I don't think you or I or anybody has the right to
         arbitrarily exterminate them –

Ripley   Wrong.

Vasquez   Yeah. Watch us.

Hudson   Maybe you haven't been keeping up on current events,
         but we just got our asses kicked, pal!

Burke   Look, I'm not blind to what's going on, but I cannot
         authorize that kind of action, I'm sorry.

Ripley   I believe Corporal Hicks has authority here.

Burke   Corporal Hicks!?

Ripley   This operation is under military jurisdiction and Hicks
         is next in chain of command. Am I right, Corporal?

Hicks   Yeah. Yeah, that's right. Yeah.

Burke   Look, Ripley, this is a multimillion-dollar installation.
         He can't make that kind of decision. He's just a grunt!
         (*glances at Hicks*) No offence.

Hicks   (*coolly*) None taken. (*into mike*) Ferro, you copying?
Ferro   (*voiceover; static*) Standing by.

Hicks   Prep for dust-off. We're gonna need an immediate evac.

> (*to Burke*) I think we'll take off and nuke the site from
> orbit. It's the only way to be sure.

What the mere words of the script, subtly modified and cut in performance –
Burke has more to say originally, for example – cannot convey is the way that
the body language of the five main actors here adds to its crackling tension. As
Burke speaks, Vasquez prowls around behind him waiting for her anger to reach
boiling point. Ripley considers her every word both as part of a conversation
with Burke in which he is treating her as if she were potentially his ally, and a
declaration to the Marines that she is not. And Hicks watches her and slowly
considers his position. This is the scene in which the groundwork Ripley has
laid comes to fruition and Burke finds that with Gorman unconscious he has
no allies and, for the moment, no ability to impose his views.

The survivors pick their way through nameless technological shapes to a
potential landing field; again, soldierliness is very much a performance as the
wary Vasquez poses with her pistol and Hicks throws a flare. What follows
is economical short cuts – Ferro and Spunkmeyer are picked off by an alien
which has somehow managed to get on board the shuttle and the shuttle
crashes, spreading debris everywhere. Ripley is the first to realize something
is wrong and she and Hicks again hold things together. Hudson throws a
wobbly and Burke is no more use with his sarcastic talk of lighting a fire
and singing songs – these two are relegated to the background while in the
foreground Ripley and Newt talk realistically about the situation, posed with
the small child raised on a hillock so that they talk as equals:

Newt	I guess we're not leaving, right?
Ripley	I'm sorry, Newt.
Newt	You don't have to be sorry. It wasn't your fault… We should get back, 'cause it'll be dark soon. They come mostly at night. Mostly.

They are posed not just as mother and daughter, but as the mother and
daughter of official, possibly Soviet, art, with the sunset in their faces; not
only each of them individually, but their relationship, is constructed as heroic
and exemplary.

The first time we see the various rooms of the colony building, they are
an inhabited space; the second time, they are a haunted palace or funhouse
which the soldiers explore and where things loom, or jump out, at them. The

third time, they are a killing field through which they will retreat and where they will learn some of the worst and best things about their own humanity. The colony is still essentially a human space into which the aliens intrude; the point of the overlong sequence in which the robot guns exhaust their ammunition firing at an inexhaustible supply of aliens is that this intrusion is ultimately inevitable. One of the most terrible things about Burke's attempted betrayal of Ripley and Newt is that he takes a temporarily safe space and makes it unsafe. He also betrays sleep – sleep which in the film is coded as the safe place where the monsters cannot get you.

Except that, of course, they can. Ripley encourages Newt to sleep and rests herself and this is very nearly the last thing that either of them ever do. The ensuing sequence is one of profound wrongness – Ripley tries to get the people in other rooms to hear her and Newt's screams but the room proves to be soundproof and the sound link to the observation monitors turned off. She has to save herself and Newt. Burke has betrayed the fundamental contract of humane interactions and Ripley, at a point where she has relaxed into thinking of herself as not merely an isolate – in, for example, the scene in which Hicks teaches her to use a gun – finds herself dependent on her own resources, having to hold the two face-huggers off with her own strength of arm and will.

I have already commented on the efficiency with which Cameron sets Ripley up as an occasional smoker earlier in the film – in a brilliant piece of lateral thinking, she uses her lighter to trigger the room's fire alarm and sprinkler system, alerting the others to her plight in spite of Burke's sabotage. The brief scene in which she explains his scheme to them is a stock moment from detective fiction – she demonstrates to them that the logic of Burke's actions is a plan to murder all of them. He meanwhile argues that her reading of what has happened is a paranoid delusion. After a scene in which Ripley uses rational ingenuity to escape the brute face-huggers, we have a scene in which both she and Burke are using rhetoric and logic to recruit allies – she has Vasquez and Hicks entirely on her side and Burke is still relying on Gorman.

This very brief interlude of human conflict is interrupted by what is really important and renders Burke's little schemes irrelevant. Another of the ways in which *Aliens* imitates the first film while also increasing the stakes comes with the use of a proximity indicator. Hudson reads it off and at first the bad news is something we are prepared for – the creatures are at the sealed door, through it, through barricades, outside the room that the squad has retreated into. And then things get worse and Hudson's panic grows ever more intense the more incomprehensible the results are; suddenly the aliens are in the room, though not visible and not yet attacking.

When the power goes down and the lights go out, Hudson has already panicked – he does not want to believe that the creatures are more than animals, that they can plan as well as kill. His terror – and Bill Paxton has made the character, in spite of all his flaws, someone who speaks for the audience in this – is all the more intense because the creatures have thought of something which has eluded Ripley and the others. They are, of course, in the ceiling, as Hicks finds out when he sticks his head up and finds them there.

The shot of creatures advancing inside the false ceiling is one of the most terrifying in the film simply because it is so unclear. In fact, there are only six actors in that ceiling, because Cameron had to make the entire film with only six alien suits for reasons of cost and he makes it look like more by having them advance in a variety of ways, some of them on wires so that they can crawl at a different angle. It is a shot that is almost more scary because it makes no sense – the creatures are advancing more slowly than they need to for efficiency's sake because Cameron needs them to be terrifying visually.

Things happen fast – the business with the proximity indicator has been one of those points at which Cameron makes the timescale of the action improbably slow and now he speeds it up again. Hudson is seized from under the floor and goes to his death with less obvious fuss than we would have expected; Burke finds one of the doors in his escape route unlocked and his death on the other side of it.

In the screenplay, Ripley finds him still alive but cocooned during her return to the atmosphere plant and gives him a sort of mercy – a grenade with the pin pulled. Cameron presumably cut this for the excellent reason that it duplicated and therefore weakened the deaths of Vasquez and Gorman, one of the most moving moments in the whole film. Vasquez mounts a last stand in the tunnel to which they have retreated as Newt leads the others into a narrower duct she tells them leads to the outside – her flame-thrower runs out of fuel, her large gun runs out of ammunition, her pistol used effectively kills an alien at the price of burning her terribly with its blood and trapping her under its dead bulk.

Goldstein is magnificent here partly because she is not playing a superhero – she is playing a soldier bravely doing her job to the last moment. One of the reasons why this is an interesting and complex film is that Cameron respects values for which people are prepared to die. Gorman has been an inexperienced and incompetent officer, too concerned with the views of the company man for whose approval he is constantly looking – he does the right thing, knowing he will die for it. He comes back and tries to get Vasquez to safety and they are rapidly surrounded on all sides. There is no hope for them.

She utters one of those insults – 'You always were an asshole Gorman' – which is an admission to her world as an equal and the two of them clasp hands on a grenade and go out in glory together. There is an odd tenderness to the moment as well as a lot of testosterone – the very butch non-white woman and the officer-class white man die expressing human solidarity. Earlier, Ripley condemned Burke by pointing out that the creatures do not betray each other for a percentage; we need to have this counter-image of human beings giving up their lives so that someone they do not even like does not die alone.

Bishop is off calling down the shuttle and so the survivors are now down to the basic nuclear family unit of man, woman and child. We know because of genre expectation that there will be more reversals yet, and the next reversal that comes is the loss of the girl Newt – she gets caught up in one of those bits of inexplicable hardware that always crop up in the ducts in SF films and thrillers and plunged into an unsafe space where the aliens get her, leaving behind, floating in the pool of water where Ripley penetrates too late to save her, only the doll's head she always carried as a reminder of her lost childhood.

The gadgetry in which she becomes entangled is designed in such a way that it reminds us of the Wheel of Fortune, the Tarot card of destruction and mutability, the wheel of martyrdom. The underworld in which Newt is trapped and from which she is dragged off to an even worse place is a dark version of Alice's Wonderland – the underwater room where she is caught and where Ripley finds the doll's head is a Pool of Tears.

There follows a prolonged sequence which is one of the most mythic moments in SF film. Where in *Alien* Ripley stripped down to her undervest because she thought she was safe, and was not, here she strips down to it because she is going to war and descending into hell. She wears a minimum of clothing because she is armoured in righteousness. The scene fetishizes her as warrior woman; it also eroticizes her preparation of gun and flame-thrower taped together, her gathering up of cartridges and grenades.

In one of his scene-setting notes earlier in the screenplay, Cameron describes the atmospheric processing plant:

> VISIBLE across a half kilometer of barren heath, b.g., is the massive complex of the nearest ATMOSPHERE PROCESSOR, looking like a power plant bred with an active volcano. Its fiery glow pulses in the low cloud cover like a steel mill.

When Ripley makes Bishop fly the shuttle in through the broken opening into the plant, the shot we see – which is not described in his screenplay, where they are first seen already inside – is one of an entrance like a maw or a hearth blazing amid the darkness; it is no exaggeration to say that it has become the Gate of Hell. Cameron later on, again in a direction, makes the allusion to

Dante explicit – Ripley is doing what she knows she must rather than with any hope of success and it is at the moment of her deepest despair. She looks down, horrified to see Newt's tracer bracelet lying on the floor of the tunnel. All hope recedes, disintegrating into mindless chaos. Then she hears Newt scream.

Ripley finds Newt – her 'child' – in a chamber full of eggs – the Queen's children. She also finds herself unexpectedly confronted by the Queen herself, the great Satan at the heart of this Inferno. This is one of the film's great money shots – all the more so because we have not previously put it together that the aliens have this one thing in common with hive insects, and because Ripley instantly takes it in her stride. She experiences the Queen as an opportunity rather than as a threat – her sense of herself as a mother robbed of her child means that she has a sense of the Queen as a mother who can be threatened and tricked with the same loss.

What follows is a near-tragic piece of overreaching by Ripley – once the Queen has gestured to her guardian warriors that they should stand down, and Ripley and Newt have safely exited the chamber, Ripley cannot resist going back on her implied word. Since she knows that the Queen and her hive are already doomed – the atomic pile will blow in what is by now a very few minutes – her decision to flame the eggs is a self-indulgence. This is, I would argue, one of the moments at which Cameron is making a populist gesture about the ruthlessness needed to win wars, a moment all the more false in that he is himself a Canadian.

Cameron makes less of the countdown element of this point in the film than does Ridley Scott – we know that the pile is going to blow and we know that, even now she has retrieved Newt, Ripley is unlikely to make it out in time. Some of the means he uses to up the tension are predictable – and no less effective for that – like the fact that the shuttle with Bishop and Hicks is not at the rendezvous and only just gets back to it in time, after making a necessary diversion. Some of them are less so – the Queen, once she has torn off her ovipositor in a rage at the eggs' destruction, proves capable of following Ripley in the other lift it never occurred to her to sabotage. The sound of the second lift coming up the shaft is genuinely chilling, not least because it tells us that the Queen at least is capable of planning and using machinery.

The fact that Bishop arrives in the nick of time is a genre trope – and is followed by the inevitable scene of the shuttle's escape from a titanic explosion. What follows is a cliché of 1980s film, and one which makes comparatively little literal sense. We are supposed to believe that the Queen hitched a ride on the exterior of the shuttle without being noticed and survived high-speed escape from an explosion, and a sudden transition to the vacuum of high orbit. We are even supposed to believe that a warship equipped for 'bug hunts' lacks automatic detectors for extraneous material entering its bays. And of course this does not matter, because we know what to expect and nightmare has its own logic; the Queen has to have survived for one last go around, because this is an *Alien* film and that rematch is a part of the series' own rules.

Suddenly the Queen is on the Sulaco, and Bishop has been reduced to foam-spraying plastic fragments; the blinded Hicks is already out of action. For a moment Ripley seems to be running away and abandoning Newt. In fact, however, she has a plan and assumes correctly that Newt has the skill and dexterity needed to evade the Queen for a while as it plucks up squares of floor grid and jabs its stinger through, as well as the guts to keep on hiding and not despair.

The final death duel between Ripley as mother and the self-sterilized Queen that is trying to take revenge for the death of its children by killing Newt has, to have its full emotional and mythic resonance, to take place on something approximating equal terms. To stress yet again the obsessive economy of Cameron's plotting – the scene where Ripley bonds with Hicks and Apone by showing a preparedness to do scutwork is also a scene which establishes just what powerful machines the quasi-exoskeletal loaders are. When the doors slide open and Ripley is revealed in her transcended glory, with the light behind her, and utters the line 'Get away from her, you bitch', the sheer blissful power of the moment has been worked hard for much of the film.

Cameron has established the Queen as a figure even more menacing than her cohorts and suddenly this vast creature that amalgamates spider, ant and scorpion finds itself being bitch-slapped with huge metal claws. Ripley is still in huge danger, of course, and knows it – the stinger and the inner jaws come awfully close to her at various moments in the fight – but she has a simple objective, dumping the Queen into the airlock, whereas the Queen has lost the initiative. There is a sense in which all of this is a terribly corny Hollywood moment – all that has gone before gets resolved by a brawl – but the femaleness of both participants is only one of the things that stops it being a John Wayne moment.

Some of what follows is by-the-numbers suspense – of course the Queen drags Ripley and the exoskeleton into the airlock/pit with her and of course, when Ripley gets free of the exoskeleton, the Queen momentarily snags her foot until Ripley loses a sneaker, and of course the opening of the airlock nearly sucks Ripley and Newt and Bishop out after the Queen. There are other resonances here though – unlike the Queen, who is the prisoner of her own highly evolved savagery and built-in armament, Ripley can take off the exoskeleton almost as easily as she put it on, and abandon it as a dead weight to pin the Queen to the bottom of the pit.

The Queen dies, and Ripley and Newt survive – this too is one of the rules of the series, as is the film's closure. It begins as it ended with sleep, but this is not the doom-laden sleep disturbed by fragmentary menace in the score of the opening, and it is not the sleep of the earlier moment of Ripley's caring for her new child – a moment of illusory safety snatched in a monster-haunted room. It is a consoling sleep, guaranteed by soft strings and lighting. The film ends with a promise that the two remaining sequels were to dedicate themselves to subverting.

Alien³

'We set out to make a release date and not to make a movie.' – Jon Landau

As shot, the third *Alien* film starts as it means to go on, spending its first few minutes erasing Newt and Hicks during the titles and demonstrating unequivocally that there was another alien on the Sulaco at the end of *Aliens*, in spite of all indications to the contrary and the near impossibility of retrofitting the plot of *Aliens* so that this is even remotely plausible. Ripley failed to save her replacement daughter; she failed to stop an alien surviving; she failed the man who looked up to her as his commander.

She manages, later in the film, to reawaken the wrecked android Bishop, only to be told that he would rather be non-existent than imperfect: 'I can be re-worked but I'll never be top of the line again. I'd rather be nothing.' She too will make the decision to die because it is the only humanly decent option left to her. One of the strengths of this deeply flawed film is that it has so entirely the courage of this negativity; one of its major weaknesses is that its revisionist vision is oppositional to the previous film rather than, like that predecessor, growing organically out of themes in the first.

Alien³ undercuts its predecessor in a number of other respects. *Aliens* was a film whose iconography is all about escalatingly big personal hand-weapons – guns so big that they have to be worn; the prison location of the third film means that there are no weapons of any kind in it. When Ripley asks if the new set of prospective victims have anything with which to defend themselves,

Brian Glover's prison administrator, Andrews, looks at her pityingly, as if she has not understood anything. She spent the previous film learning to fit in to a particular world – the world of the Marines – and nothing she learned in that film proves relevant in this one.

Cameron's version of Ripley was a liminal being who had survived Scott's film to become superhuman. The Fincher version is cut down to size – she has to make alliances and has to be protected. The scene in which she is overpowered and nearly raped by a selection of the convicts makes this very clear – she is a sacrificial victim and her pose, held over their heads with hers hanging down, prefigures her eventual redemptive sacrifice when she swan-dives backwards into the furnace. She is still a heroic figure, and at times a commanding one, but it is a far more passive and a far more human heroism that we see here.

One of the crucial features of Cameron's film was that Ripley is, as part of her core identity, a mother – the only time that this is mentioned in *Alien³* is when the company man, the original Bishop from whom the android was modelled, offers the chance of motherhood as an example of the normal life Ripley might yet have if she surrenders to him. The only motherhood she is actually going to have – and this is very much stressed by the long sequence in which she is examined with ultrasound in the infirmary – is the emergence of a new alien queen from her body.

In the theatrical release, this is stressed at the expense of plausibility – when the miniature alien queen emerges from her chest, halfway through her dive into molten lead, she is explicitly shown as caressing its head. (The recently released special edition omits this shot.) Where Kane's death was one of stomach-turning violence and violation, there is something almost gentle about this birth, which is to be followed in seconds by absolute eradication of both her and the infant. It is only by dying herself, and quite literally taking the alien with her, that she can be finally sure. 'It's the only way to be sure,' Cameron's Ripley memorably said about blowing up the atmosphere plant, and she was wrong.

It is typical of the way the studio meddled with this film that there was serious discussion of changing this ending for fear that it would be too like that of Cameron's *Terminator 2: Judgment Day*, which had not yet been made, but whose script was a known quantity.

Both Ridley Scott's *Alien* and Cameron's *Aliens* make considerable play with the internal geography of the sites which are to be the creatures' killing ground for their human victims – this is easier for Scott to manage with the limited and claustrophobic locations of the Nostromo and its shuttle, rather harder for Cameron who has to teach us the way round the Sulaco, the main base and the atmosphere plant, but nonetheless manages to do so, with remarkable efficiency.

The heavily cut theatrical version of *Alien³* fails to do this with any great skill – even the section of the Sulaco which brings Ripley to the penal colony has a shape that does not clearly correspond with the ship we saw in the previous film, nor was any capacity of that ship to detach sections of itself ever mentioned. The penal colony is a maze of rooms and industrial plant the internal arrangements of which only become clear in the longer special edition.

Where the first two films contrasted the places that had been touched by the aliens and the entropy they bring with them with the efficient cleanliness of, say, the Nostromo's kitchen and the Sulaco's loading bay, *Alien³* is set in a place which is falling apart. The penal colony is already quasi-derelict before the arrival of what will kill everyone who lives there – there is a rancid dinginess even to the supposedly hygienic surgery and rust wherever there is naked metal. This is a great look, well-lit, but it makes far less sense than the backgrounds of the earlier films – the hand of Ron Cobb is very much missed. The lead foundry is shown, on its first appearance, in a sultry red light, with portentous chords on the sound track that make it eminently predictable that someone or something is going to end up smelted.

The decision to make some of the film take place from the alien's point of view is a radical departure and not an especially useful one – the radical disjunction of viewpoint makes the geography even less clear. This is particularly disruptive at the film's climax, where the suspense of what we are being shown depends on rapid movement through locations of which we have no especially clear sense – compare, for example, the final capture of the main base in *Aliens*, where our quite precise knowledge of the terrain over which the characters are retreating makes what we are seeing considerably more upsetting. When, in *Alien³*, the creature jumps out from crawl spaces whose existence we have not suspected, the effect is arbitrary; when, in *Aliens*, the creatures prove to have been advancing through crawl spaces we have observed but not noticed, it is considerably less so.

Obviously, as David Thomson points out in his study, the authorship of *Alien³* is a far more complex question than that of any of the other films in the franchise. There were many abortive scripts, including one by William Gibson, the creator of the cyberpunk sub-genre of SF. Gibson's script, to a story by Walter Hill, is one from which Ripley is almost entirely absent save as a coma victim whom others have to protect – it is the story of how Hicks and the android Bishop escape from one of two politically opposed research stations. (Away from Earth, the cold war is going strong.)

The principal point of intellectual and cinematic interest here is that the aliens prove capable of yet another mode of reproduction – they can dissolve into nano-machines that convert humans and other beings into more aliens from the inside. About the only thing that made it from Gibson's script – which is better than its reputation – to the final *Alien³* is the nape-of-the-neck barcodes; the basic storyline – researchers meddling with things they are not competent to deal with – is of course a significant element in *Alien Resurrection*. (A further indication that Joss Whedon, author of the fourth film's script, was acquainted with Gibson's script is that Gibson's climax – a converted human rips off their skin to reveal the alien within – is echoed in 'Go Fish', an episode of Whedon's *Buffy the Vampire Slayer* television series.)

At one point, Remmy Harlin was considered as director, but his idea for the film was that it should either deal with a trip to the aliens' home planet or that it should deal with an invasion of Earth by them. These ideas, which are still occasionally touted as the possible subject for a renewal of the franchise, were regarded by the production team and the studio as likely to involve too much expense; CGI was not so advanced in the late 1980s that such projects were viable. The idea of a prison ship as locale was put to Harlin and he rejected it on the grounds that the franchise had already dealt in 'lots of corridor and bulkheads'. The prison concept was one to which the producers kept coming back and they eventually got their way.

The screenplay by John Fasano from a story by Fasano and Vincent Ward (director of *The Navigator*, another study in neo-mediaevalism) has considerably more to do with the final *Alien³* than has sometimes been thought – many critics have been put off by the concept of a wooden spaceship and have not considered it further. In fact, the ship has wooden cladding over metal and wooden interiors – and the whole point of this is that it is not meant to be a viable long-term residence for the monks who inhabit it. It is supposed, in fact, to be a death-trap for them and the literary, anti-technological culture they represent, one of several ways in which their beliefs are destructive.

Though the monks are male and celibate, their dislike of Ripley is almost entirely fuelled by her status as a representative of the technological world; misogyny is to an almost surprising degree absent. Their refusal to listen to her is one of several examples of their untenable and self-destructive passion – they have brought their precious books into a place that is essentially designed to be a fire hazard and in due course burns down to the hull. They refuse to listen to her because she is talking about aliens rather than demons, and they all die as a result, with their world flaming about them.

One of the nicer touches to the Fasano script is that Ripley has no way of knowing for sure when she is – she believes that she has only been asleep on the Sulaco for a short period, but the Abbot's talk of a new Dark Age and the destruction of Earth is plausible too. The Abbot is a barn-storming role, rather too much of one, and the android monk/spy Anthony too morally compromised to be especially clearly characterized; there are reasons why this script was never made and among those reasons are that some of the part-writing is unrewarding.

Perhaps the strongest element is John, the young monk-librarian who forms an alliance with Ripley in spite of his dislike of technology because of his desire to save her from the sin of despair. She is also a surrogate for the mother he never had, as he becomes a replacement for the daughter she left behind and for Newt, who in this version too has been killed by an alien which found its way onto the Sulaco, sabotaged the hypersleep chambers and impregnated Ripley. In one draft, he chooses to die in Ripley's place – forcing the alien out of her chest and into his own open mouth and walks into the flames of the Abbey – this death is not her failure as a parent, but the result of her sentimental education of the young man to the point where he can die as part of an informed ethical choice. In the draft Sigourney Weaver preferred – she was keen to be done with the franchise – Ripley walks sacrificially into the heart of a blazing wheat field.

In interviews, Vincent Ward has expressed considerable bitterness at his treatment by the studio executives who signed off on the Fasano script and the design work that had been done and only later changed their minds, at a point when the sets for the Abbey had started to be built. Ward claims that he was extensively spied upon and was eventually presented with a list of demanded changes that he declined to expedite, preferring to be fired. At this point, David Fincher was hired and found himself working on a film that had no definitive script.

My considerable reservations about Fincher's film – reservations which have more to do with the theatrically released version than with the more impressive extended cut – have to take on board the considerable achievement Fincher accomplished in difficult circumstances. There was no script; he was overseen by studio executives who were uncertain that they had done the right thing in hiring a first-time director and his first choice for cinematographer – Jordan Cronenweth – was diagnosed with Parkinson's disease in the first weeks of shooting. If the film ends up being about Ripley's displaying grace under extreme pressure, it is in some measure a film about its own making.

In both the Fasano/Ward version and the final Hill/Fincher version, the death of Newt is felt by Ripley as a failure – in Cameron's film she is represented as a successful good mother, and this is retrofitted so that this was an illusion and she was not. In fact, the reason for the absence of Newt in the third film was a practical decision and not an aesthetic choice – Carrie Henn, ten years old during the shooting of *Aliens* was sixteen by the time *Alien³* was eventually made and therefore not so much unavailable as unrecognizable.

(Michael Biehn had been under the impression that he and Carrie Henn were guaranteed parts in any third film – so strong had been his sense that this was being set up by Cameron's portrayal of Ripley, Hicks and Newt as a family unit. He was sufficiently embittered by the decision to kill his character that he refused permission to the new film's creature designers to construct a corpse in his image, and ended up charging a fee for the use of a single photograph of him that amounted to almost as much as his fee for appearing in *Aliens*.)

What is interesting about all of this is that, in both cases, Newt's death becomes a starting point for a process of withdrawing from the goddess-like Ripley of the Cameron film, a way of making the character feel guilty. The Fincher film takes this a shade further with an emotionally gruelling sequence in which Ripley has the doctor Clemens conduct an autopsy on the dead girl and watches as her surrogate child is dissected. The cuts to surgical instruments and to blood draining away can be seen as echoing the cuts in the opening sequence between the various actions of the alien aboard the Sulaco. Ripley goes through the obscene ritual of having Newt dissected because of earlier failure. This scene was originally even more graphic and gruelling – one of the points at which the intervention of the studio was probably a good thing.

Some quite trivial matters from the Fasano version of the script find their way into the final film – the friendly dog that replaces the cat of *Alien* and the idea that the alien can use animals as hosts – here it is from one of the Abbey's sheep rather than from the dog that the alien emerges. In the theatrical release, the alien emerges from a guard dog and in the special edition from one of the oxen used to haul the Sulaco's escape vehicle from the water into which it has crashed. (Paradoxically, in order to complete and insert this sequence, it was necessary to use an unsatisfactory shot of a scampering small alien which is in fact a whippet in a rubber suit.)

More complicatedly, one of the least satisfactory details of the Fincher film is a half-memory of an element in the Fasano script, where the alien's abilities include taking on some aspects of his environment, so that parts of it come to imitate wood and wheat in the pastoral setting of the Abbey. At the climax, it is coated in molten glass – the Abbey, though made of wood, has large furnaces in it – and then cold water is dropped on it; it has taken on some characteristics of the glass and shatters.

At the climax of the final version of *Alien³*, hot lead and then cold water is poured over the alien which likewise shatters – this of course makes no sense at all, whereas the Fasano version at least made some sort of poetic sense in its own terms. It does not seem to have occurred to Walter Hill or to David Fincher that lead melts at a far lower temperature than glass and that the consequence of pouring cold water on molten lead is that the lead cools and solidifies.

The current version is credited to three writers and to Vincent Ward for the storyline. Of the three credited writers, Walter Hill is perhaps the most distinguished and the relationship between Ripley and Dillon has some of his trademark buddies-made-by-adversity snappiness. Nonetheless, especially in the undercutting of every aspect of the Cameron film, it seems probable that David Fincher needs to be regarded as *Alien³*'s auteur. His own film projects – this was early in his career and very much work for hire – have always dealt with the vanity of human wishes and aspirations and with the demonstration to his protagonists that they are not in control of their own destinies. If this makes him a perverse choice for *Alien³*, well, his obsessions were less obvious at the time and the result is certainly interesting.

The two detectives in *Se7en* (1995) discover that they are as much manipulated into serving as moral exempla as the serial killer's previous victims when the younger one discovers that his wife has been killed and he murders the killer in the rage that is the last of the seven deadly sins to be enacted. The hero of *The Game* (1997) discovers that his life can be unravelled around him; Meg Altman in *The Panic Room* (2002) learns that courage and moral integrity are far better defences than steel sheeting and deadbolts.

Part of what drew Fincher to Chuck Palahniuk's novel *Fight Club* for his 1999 film was this sense of control being an illusion; Fincher must also have loved the chance to play vicious tricks on the audience's belief in its own godlike omniscience. To pick one example, the scene in which Jack and Tyler Durden are having one conversation and Jack and Marla another is a tour de force of misdirection in that it appears to provide, but does not, objective evidence of Tyler's actual existence.

Cameron and Fincher both have obsessions with shadow doubles and secret sharers, but their use of these tropes is radically distinct, so much so as almost to account for the sheer aggression of Fincher's deconstruction of the end of *Aliens*. For Cameron, shadow selves are one of the hallmarks of liminality, a way of being beyond humanity by being more identities than just one; for Fincher, anything of the kind is a snare and a delusion and a sickness. This is true in *Se7en* where the insane murderer is a step ahead of the detectives at all points; it is particularly true in *Fight Club*, where Jack's secret sharer Tyler is explicitly both shadow self and hallucination. There is a real polemic edge to his approach to what is left over of Cameron's material – so much so that the two films are a particularly telling example of dialectical metonymy, echoing another text in order to pick a fight with it, one of the few full-blown examples in filmed SF.

For Fincher, what is interesting about the Ripley of Scott's movie is that she is ordinary and human and responds to circumstances with a grace and efficiency that are admirable precisely because she is not superhuman. He wants Ripley to be a hero who is ordinary, not someone well on the way to evolving into a goddess – he would see his approach as bringing her down to earth, not as cutting her down to size. Nonetheless, the way that Ripley is subjected to indignities in this film – the near-rape, the demand that she shave off all of her hair both to prevent lice and to remove temptation from the convicts – and the way in which these indignities are fetishized would be quite surprising in a film on which Sigourney Weaver was credited as co-producer were it not that she is on record as saying that one of the things which interested her in David Fincher when he was suggested was that in a preliminary conversation she asked him how he saw Ripley in the new film and he answered, tersely, 'Bald'.

It would be crude and unsubtle to accuse David Fincher of downright misogyny – but there is a worrying tendency in all of his films to undervalue the autonomy of his female characters. All of the victims in *Se7en* are subjected to horrific abuse – the woman who is fucked to death with a sharp implement not more so than the male glutton force-fed to death – but one is disfigured on the assumption that she will kill herself rather than live with the mutilation, an interesting take on female self-perception. Gwyneth Paltrow as the younger detective's wife is murdered not for anything she has done but purely as an instrument that will tempt him to the sin of anger. Again, in *The Game*, Christine is at once the object of Nicholas' desire and compassion and entirely untrustworthy; her identity is as fluid as everything else in the unreliable world of conspiracy in which he finds himself.

There is an extent to which, in *Fight Club*, Marla is something more than the female character necessary to draw the fangs of the implicit homoeroticism of Jack's apparent relationship with Tyler Durden. Much of this, though, has to do with Helena Bonham Carter's charismatic performance – Fincher allowed her free rein to make the character more than she was in Palahniuk's book, but chose the project in the first place. Palahniuk's Marla is a comic monster of neurosis; Bonham Carter makes her so thoroughly herself that the monstrosity is transcended.

The Panic Room ought to be, and to some extent is, about Jodie Foster's Meg and her daughter outwitting the criminals who have trapped them in their home; it ought to be about her empowerment. In fact, though, it is at least as much about how her resistance turns Forest Whitaker's character around – she is the means of his redemption from earlier bad choices.

There is a distinctly negative side to this aspect of his later films which perhaps helps point to a problem with *Alien³* – where Cameron is obsessed with a particular model of female empowerment that is arguably romanticized to the point of fetishism, Fincher is determined to be 'realistic' to an extent that means that there is a remarkable amount of freely expressed misogyny in this film. The two earlier films have been criticized for the way in which body fluids and quasi-genital shapes are seen as monstrous – the eggs that unfold, the inner mouths that project – but in *Alien³* sexuality itself is seen as aberrant, except in one or two entertainingly perverse jokes like 'I've taken a vow of celibacy – and that includes women.'

The ultimate plan to kill the alien involves some elaborate quasi-sexual metaphor. The convicts set themselves as bait for it, shutting doors on it when it pursues them in order to drive it into a chamber where a giant piston will shove it into a mould into which molten lead can be poured. There is a constant emphasis on the fact that the piston can only be used once – it takes a while to get it ready for use again. Where in other films the alien is seen as a vast walking sexual metaphor, alternately penile and vaginal, here it is to be shoved by a vast penis into a slot-trap that will subsequently filled with hot liquid.

Of all four *Alien* films, *Alien³* is the only one in which the alien itself is hardly sexualized, with only one real moment of exception. It is clear that Ripley has sexual intercourse with Clemens – the only time she definitely has sex in all four films – but we never actually see this happen. She seduces him in order to avoid having to tell him the story of what happened in the previous two films, again, and in order to persuade him to be frank about his own history – she already knows he has one, though it is only after their sexual encounter that she realizes he is an ex-convict.

Tellingly, the only penetration that takes place between them on screen is his injection of her with his cocktail of drugs, an injection he is about to repeat when he is killed. Given that the crime for which he was sentenced was medical malpractice that led to eleven deaths, deaths caused by drugs that he prescribed in an addicted haze, there is an interesting complex of argument between the sex, the drugs and his sudden violent death – just as Ripley is perhaps finally and belatedly about to tell him the story so far.

Ripley scrabbles across the floor to avoid the creature which has just killed her lover. It looms after her as she forces herself into a smaller space, and it extrudes one of its supplementary mouths and drools on her. It is marking her as its sexual territory after killing her lover. In Fincher's version, the alien is very definitely male – at one point Ripley says that this one is not like any she has seen previously and it is simply a killer.

The people it kills are bloodily killed and there is no attempt to cocoon or implant them. One of the several ways in which *Alien³* is far more a sequel to *Alien* than to *Aliens* is that this version of the creature's life cycle is simple and ignores the deleted sequence from the first film in which it is clear that any single alien can start the process of reproduction all over again by cocooning its victims and implanting embryos in them in some way not specified.

The purposelessness of its killings renders it the moral equivalent of the convicts, who under their surface of religiosity are stone bad killers and rapists – as much designed to be that way as the alien is. Much is made of the chromosomal status of the convicts – with the exception of Clemens, perhaps, they are all XYY. (This is an aspect of the film which has already dated badly – the theory that criminal psychopaths could be detected by a chromosomal test is already so intellectually discredited as to be almost forgotten.)

If its killings are meant to dispose of potential threats to Ripley, or more precisely to the embryo implanted in her, then it fails. The killing of Clemens can be seen in this light, but surely hardly any of the others. One of the incoherencies of the plotting is that no one on the project seems to have sat down and thought about just how intelligent this particular incarnation of the alien is supposed to be. Where Cameron is clearly something of an SF fan, and Scott's record as director of SF material (*Alien*, *Blade Runner*, even the *Metropolis*-like 1984 Apple Mac commercial) is exemplary, there is no sense here that either Hill or Fincher has any feel for SF logic.

In the opening sequences, for example, the alien has managed to kill Hicks in a way that looks like a complicated accident and drown Newt in her hyper-sleep container in spite of fail-safes. It has managed to impregnate Ripley with an alien queen without leaving any obvious marks on her and to do so without showing up on any of the Sulaco's internal systems. Yet, at the same time, it has been sufficiently sloppy as to leave a mark on Newt's cryochamber that alerts Ripley to the possibility that these deaths were in fact more than accidents. Moreover, it has seemingly done so in the larval face-hugger stage – the first time in the series that the larvae have shown any sign of mental processes beyond a tropism to the living and warm.

This is the first time that any alien save the queen has shown any ability whatever to negotiate human technology – an ability which deserts the alien at the climax of the film where it is being driven to its death by the constant locking of doors against it and its response is to break through doors and windows rather than to attempt to open them. (It would appear that the face-hugger which managed all of this was supposed to be a specialized queen face-hugger, but that material which made this clear was never actually made or necessarily scripted – certainly a queen face-hugger was built.)

The killings of the Sulaco survivors show an instinct for manipulating humans and their expectations which is entirely absent from its later dealings with humans. The killing of Andrews, for example, makes little sense if the alien is a mere beast gratifying its appetite for slaughter – it snatches him out of a room full of people through a convenient hole in the ceiling, behaviour a little too dramatic to be predator instinct. If, on the other hand, it is meant to be thinking its actions through, then clearly it is incompetent – Andrews' death creates a power vacuum which the alliance of Dillon and Ripley fills, an alliance far more of a threat to the alien than Andrews ever was.

In fact, of course, the death of Andrews is a mere plot device to create that power vacuum. It is emotionally satisfying, a 'yes' moment, because Andrews as played by Glover has been so consistently annoying a carper at everything that Ripley says. The casting of Glover is not so much inter-textual as short-hand; while the actor is a great deal more – see his portrayal of God on stage in the Coventry Mystery Plays – his persona here draws on roles such as the gym teacher in *Kes* (1969), jacks-in-office with a nasty streak of bullying and a campness that is less about sexuality than social pretension.

Where Scott and Cameron both get great individual performances and ensemble playing from their actors, Fincher is far less successful in this respect. There is something deeply stagy about much of what we see, even in Charles Dance's mellow portrayal of the disgraced doctor. The extreme fondness of him expressed in interview by all his cast perhaps indicates an excessive tolerance for their self-indulgences. Fincher appears to have adopted Glover as a father figure for the duration of the shoot. His directorial style in this film involved controlling everything from a monitor – at the time, his cast talked of marvelling at the control he could exercise in this way, though interestingly Weaver contrasted 'people who just look at a monitor' unfavourably with the physically close involvement of Jeunet on the next film.

These come to a head in the scene of the attempted rape; the actors mop and mow as if they were performing in the Marat/Sade and in the over-acting of Paul McGann as Golic, who in the extended special edition frees the alien after it has been trapped, in an attempt to act as its Renfield. McGann has pointed out in interview one of the more unfortunate consequences of the film's punishingly fast shooting schedule – there was never a chance to repair some significant inconsistencies in Golic's accent.

Weaver is as authoritative as ever, where the script allows her to be as is Charles S. Dutton as Dillon. There is, however, a fundamental incoherency to Dillon's character – he is supposed to be a sexual psychopath who kills women, and who has been 'cured' by his religious conversion. When Ripley explains to him that it may be necessary for him to kill her to save her from giving birth to the alien inside her, he accedes with a promise that her death will not hurt and expresses his notional moral struggle by hitting the bars of a cage with a crowbar. His passionate piety when he speaks at the funeral of Newt and Hicks is less impressive if the killer in him is still there – the solid brilliance of each of his scenes at a time fails to add up. The actor is let down by the theatrical cut – the extended version has longer scenes between him and Ripley, and longer scenes in which he preaches to his flock, which enable his character's full complexity to emerge better.

The actor best served by the script is probably Lance Hendriksen, who plays both the android version of Bishop and the real Bishop from whom the android was modelled, and who turns out to be a Company functionary sent precisely because of the android's resemblance to abuse Ripley's trust. Where in Cameron this kind of doubling would have metaphysical resonance, for Fincher and Hill it is a piece of fraud and trickery.

This is a bleak film about disappointment in which everything goes wrong for everybody except for those who belatedly realize that what they want is death – which is, as it happens, most of the characters. Bishop and the other representatives of the Company fail either to corrupt Ripley's adamantine will or to get the creature they want to use as a weapon. Dillon does not get to kill that tantalizing last morsel – a woman who actually wants to die. Clemens dies so suddenly he does not get to contemplate the redemption he seeks; Andrews discovers in a sudden agonizing second just how illusory is his control of the situation. Ripley fails at everything except, in the last analysis, putting herself through the most agonizing of deaths to save humanity – and, in a Fincher film, there is no metaphysical resonance to this whatever even when Ripley stretches out her arms in a crucifixion pose as she plunges to her death. It is not clear that most viewers experience this film with either the terror or the delight that are stock reactions to the earlier films in the franchise.

Alien³ has always had its admirers; those who find *Aliens* too gung-ho and implicitly militarist and filled with a mythic religiosity were always going to be attracted by a contrasting film which plays with nihilism and despair. When they defend this least-loved of the franchise, they argue that it is bracing or gritty.

I remain unconvinced – much of the despair is arrived at by cheating, and too many scenes consist of people running around screaming to no especial purpose. The alien itself becomes boring – the case that is often made against *Aliens* that whole hordes of the things are less deadly than the original ignores the fact that, by the end, we are less interested in the standard model of the creature than in its terrifying, because intelligent, Queen. Here we are back with a straight killer, and not a very interesting one.

Though the longer, even moodier special edition is a far better film, many of the same cavils still apply. The longer film has wonderful sequences: the scene by the sea – or is it a lake? – where the Byronic Clemens finds a half-drowned Ripley and the wreck of her escape vehicle and runs back to the infirmary with her naked body in his arms, is visually stunning, as is the succeeding one in which convicts in quasi-monastic cloaks haul the ship ashore with oxen. The intercutting of Dillon's funeral speech with the hatching of the new alien from the ox is an obvious gambit, but works nonetheless; the sequence of the trapping of the alien is as effective an action sequence as the finale. And the omission of a squirming puppet lends Ripley's last moments some dignity.

If the franchise was to be kept alive, the third film had to build from the first two. Part of the problem was just this – the studio had become dependent on the film and so gave everyone who worked on the third film far less freedom than had been the case the first and second times around. The obsessively micro-managing behaviour of Twentieth Century Fox and of the producers included stopping filming so that a cut could be assembled and notes given on anything further that they thought needed to be added to the mix. All of the *Alien* films have suffered from studio meddling, but this one more than most – the significant inferiority of the theatrical release to the version that appeared years later on the film's second DVD appearance demonstrates this.

There were also problems with the concept of the film. The idea that, this time, Ripley herself is infected is an adequate, but depressing, spin on the material; it was probably a mistake to combine this adequate idea with a poorly imagined penal colony. With the heroine dead at the end of the film, it looked as if the franchise had been left with nowhere else to go – which is a logical way for Fincher's nihilism to take the franchise.

Alien Resurrection

'At least there's part of you that's human.'

The fourth *Alien* film, *Alien Resurrection*, has at its core a gallant but doomed attempt to provide a sequel to *Aliens* that does not pretend that *Alien* never happened. It plays fair by the sharp turn that Fincher and Hill had brought to the series' storyline, while working with the symbolic and metaphysical material that Cameron had brought to things – once again, Ripley is something of a goddess, something of a mother, but in ways skewed out of shape by her self-sacrificing death. Specifically, the film explores even more comprehensively the theme of liminality, of threshold states and double natures, that is so crucial to *Aliens*. If *Alien Resurrection* is a failure, and in some respects it is if compared to the first two films, it is never less than a failure with good intentions.

Part of the problem was a good idea which did not entirely work out – the idea of teaming up two particularly hot talents to work on it. Joss Whedon had yet to become the superstar of television series writing that he was shortly to become, but he already had a growing reputation as a screenwriter, while Jeunet's two previous films *Delicatessen* and *City of Lost Children* had demonstrated a personal style of real originality and creative integrity. What follows tries to do justice to both contributions, which inevitably means looking at their work separately.[1]

1. Accordingly, a synopsis: The military under General Perez have taken charge of cell samples taken from Ripley in the prison colony, samples in which her DNA has been contaminated by alien material, and army scientists – Gediman and Wren – cloned her. The resulting clone has an alien Queen gestating inside her; she retains Ripley's sense of identity in spite of having alien attributes – strength, acid blood. Pirates bring sleeping colonists to act as hosts for more aliens – predictably, the aliens escape and kill the soldiers. The pirates form an uneasy alliance with Ripley, Wren and a surviving but impregnated colonist Purvis and trek back to their ship – many die on the way. Call, who travels with the pirates, proves to be an android trying to save humanity from the aliens. The alien Queen gives birth to a male monster, which kills her and escapes on the pirate ship with Ripley, Call and other survivors; Ripley kills it.

Another part of the problem seems to have been meddling by the studio, which disliked, for example, the script's original ending and demanded an alternative which, in the event, makes little sense.

More importantly, though, the combination of these two talents did not entirely gel. Whedon has made, or arranged for, many sour jokes about the collaboration. In an episode of *Angel*, for example, Fred's mother talks about her husband's taste in movies:

> I mean, Rog's always had a thing for those disgusting *Alien* movies, all the slime and teeth. He just can't get enough of 'em. (*thinking about it*) Except for that last one they made. I think he dozed off.

Whedon's script was part of what brought Sigourney Weaver back to a franchise she felt she had done with – indeed she was sufficiently impressed that she asked Whedon to make the character edgier, even more ferally sexual. Jeunet liked the script and the project became something more than work for hire, or a chance to do his Hollywood picture – but there is no sense that he developed a close working relationship with Whedon at any stage and Whedon was not asked, for example, to participate in the commentary to the DVD release.

Part of the trouble with the film, however, has to do with Whedon's shortcomings. He is a brilliant fantasist, but one of his real strengths works against his entire plausibility as a writer of science fiction. He has, and displays at various crucial moments in the television series *Buffy*, a real knack for plot moments that make poetic rather than literal sense; at the climax of Season Five, for example, Buffy decides that she can die in the place of her magic-generated younger sister because their blood is mystically the same. Emotionally, this works, even though it makes no literal sense, and when you are dealing in magic, what works emotionally and poetically is what works.

The same cannot be said if you are dealing in science fiction terms. Specifically, the premise of *Alien Resurrection* is not merely that Ripley has been recreated as a clone from cell samples taken in the previous film, but that the alien implanted in her had contaminated her DNA so that she is reborn as a hybrid, with another alien implanted inside her. She is the eighth in a line of such hybrids, variously deformed or more contaminated with alien-ness, and, we assume, lacking the implanted alien which the researchers wish to harvest. (There is an unresolved ambiguity here – the seventh and most human clone, a mass of distorted tissue, has a scar adjacent to its one fully formed breast similar to the one on Ripley's chest. We are never told specifically that the fragments of alien tissue in small jars adjacent to it are what was pulled from the clone.)

This makes poetic sense in a beautifully wrong way – Ripley's sacrifice is not only taken back but made the source of entirely new evil – but none whatsoever in terms of the scientific concepts with which it is playing. To give but one example, Ripley's body appears to be made of standard human tissue, albeit with greater muscular strength, yet the blood in her veins is, as is crucial at a couple of points in the plot, the strongly corrosive acid of an alien; how can the one contain the other? There are other scientific illiteracies in the film that make narrative sense – the eventual death of the newborn alien sucked piecemeal into near-vacuum through a small hole in the Betty's porthole is a satisfactory climax, but a piece of entire nonsense.

I have suggested the possibility that Whedon knew the aborted William Gibson screenplay for *Alien³*; I would suggest further that the idea that Ripley's DNA has been rewritten by the presence of the alien within her is an elision from Gibson's idea that at a molecular level the aliens are made up of nano-technological robots capable of rebuilding humans from within. The male alien to which Ripley's offspring gives birth is another sort of hybrid – again, this seems to be an elision of the idea in the unused Ward screenplay that the aliens can adopt genetic structures from their hosts, so that an alien which grows inside a dog is four-legged, one from a sheep woolly. If we compare Gibson's quite detailed setting up of the nano-technology concept with the way *Alien Resurrection* fudges the issue of how the Ripley clone has detailed personal memories of her earlier life and personality, we can see Whedon's weakness in this area.

The idea that the aliens, and thus Ripley, have genetically transmitted memory is dealt with in a deliciously cavalier fashion – the scientists Gediman and Wren discuss the improbability of this being the case, accept it is so, and move on. And it is clear that her memories are fuzzy – we are never told precisely which bits of, say, the previous films she remembers – except that she knows she was impregnated with an alien and died. She also remembers and recalls a fragment of dialogue with Newt, in *Aliens*, which is quoted in a voiceover; in the special release edition of 2003, she talks about Newt to Call, but cannot remember the girl's name. She remembers precisely enough that the character is recognizably Ripley, played by Sigourney Weaver, which is close enough for Hollywood, if not for strict logic.

On the other hand, this tendency to the mythic for the sake of which logic is fudged is one of the things that Whedon has in common with James Cameron. Both men are obsessed with the liminal to an extent which makes it one of the most important concepts in their *Alien* films and in Whedon's *Buffy the Vampire Slayer* television series. Ripley in this new incarnation is both promise and threat, the woman who saved humanity from the aliens and the woman through whom they have entered the world again; she is both human and beast – 'quite the predator' as Wren remarks. Her liminality extends to her identity – she both is and is not Ripley. Like Buffy, in that show's last two seasons, it is possible that she came back wrong.

Where earlier versions of Ripley were sexless to the point of androgyny, this Ripley's sexual predation is striking. She has real chemistry with the brutish pirate Johner whom she humiliates on the basketball court. The attempt by Call to kill her or persuade her that she wants to die becomes a bizarre flirtation (somewhat hampered by Winona Ryder's whiny low-key performance – though there is chemistry in the scene, much of it comes from Weaver). When she is captured by the aliens, she writhes among them in what is clearly sexual ecstasy – the studio appears to have disliked this scene quite a lot and Jeunet had to fight to keep it in. The special edition makes this point even more clearly – the flirtatious component in the relationship with Call is even more obvious as is the extent to which Ripley effectively seduces the Newborn in order to distract it from Call before she kills it.

This sexualization is one aspect of a profound opportunism which links her to the aliens – she will always do or offer to do the thing that most serves her interests and says to the pirates, 'Who do I have to fuck to get off this ship?' A few moments earlier, she has used the corpse of the pirate leader Elgyn as a hide from which to shoot an alien that was menacing the dead man's crew. Only Call is appalled by this – a part-alien Ripley is killing her own, so how can she be trusted? Part of the point of the film is that there is some essence of Ripley that can – but the question has to be posed and who better than the equally liminal Call to pose it?

Nor is she the only liminal being on offer – this film's version of the alien Queen is as affected by the human as Ripley by the alien, giving birth through parturition as well as egg-laying and producing an even more hybrid creature with a humanoid skull-exoskeleton from which panicky mad eyes stare. The aliens here are far more obviously rational beings than in any previous film – presumably because they have been as changed by Ripley as she by them. They think tactically – two of them kill a third in order to burn their way out of confinement with their dead broodmate's blood while Gediman is distracted by a security monitor showing the fight between pirates and soldiers.

Like the new Ripley, they are opportunistic and ruthless. In *Aliens*, Ripley remarks that the aliens, unlike humans, do not betray each other: 'I don't know which species is worse. You don't see them screwing each other over for a fucking percentage.' Clearly, once contaminated with the human, this is no longer true and the alien Queen's humanoid child kills its mother. This is the bleakest of the series because the encounter of human and alien has corrupted both – the armed forces that were once merely the corruptible but fundamentally honest arm of the companies have now replaced them as the focus of power and corruption.

The seven failed clones of Ripley are imperfect threshold beings in whom the blend has produced the grotesque and pathological. They provide a set of variations which manifest physically the admixture of corruption, combination and co-optation that is crucial to the plot – some are almost entirely alien, and some almost human, but they are all Ripley and they are all monstrous. And they have all been preserved as numbered objects of utility by the company scientists, the dead ones in specimen jars and the living one in agony on a bed among them.

The pirates, who betray ordinary humanity as represented by the colonists, and yet are loyal to their own, are both criminal and the sort of outlaws whose lives outside the law makes them strangely honest. The relationship between Elgyn and Hillard is shown as touchingly sensual – a scene which appears to be of intercourse is revealed in an effective double-take to be one of his giving her a foot massage. Both are competent leaders, who die as a result – Elgyn because he is on point and Hillard because she has acted as rearguard.

The gun-man Christie is superbly competent in combat, shooting down armed soldiers who menace him before they can react; he is also a loyal friend, who carries Vriess when the latter has to abandon his chair and who sacrifices himself to save Vriess when he has been burned by an alien and is entangled with its dead weight. In one of the scenes restored in the 2003 special edition, he and the soldier DiStephano bond rather sweetly with a geeky discussion of Christie's specialized disposable guns.

The two pirates who survive – Johner and Vriess – are by far the most double-natured, something that is established on their first appearance with Call, in a cargo bay where she and Vriess are working on the harvester machines which in an earlier version of the script they use to kill the final alien. Johner appears in shadow on a high platform making monkey noises and gestures; he throws a knife at his friend's leg and this reveals that Vriess's legs are dead or artificial. Johner is morally ambiguous – he talks of leaving Vriess behind as expendable and of killing Call – and yet is as effective in combat as Christie. (Interestingly, the two characters are both echoed in Jayne, the mercenary gunman in Whedon's later TV series *Firefly*, the central characters of which can be seen as echoing various of the Betty crew.) Vriess is an effective engineer, perhaps because when he is riding his mechanized chair he is more than half-machine. Johner's double nature is also demonstrated by his weapon – a gun hidden inside a flask of rotgut. They are, of course, also characters written to be played by Ron Perlman and Dominique Pinon, actors who often work with Jeunet.

The basketball scene is effective because it is at the same time sexual and violent; the crew of the Betty find Ripley playing basketball by herself and Johner decides to have some fun. (Later he defines both his character and his purpose in the crew as 'Mostly I just hurt people.') He accosts her in language that elides the violent and the sexual: 'How about a little one on one?' She effortlessly humiliates him, passing the ball around him and tossing it from hand to hand behind his head with her arms on either side of his neck. When he asks her to give him the ball, she does so, bouncing it hard into his genitals and then knocking him flying; hit in the face by his friend Christie, she does the same to him. She demonstrates to all of them that she could choose to hurt them more than she does, and then leaves, throwing the ball over her head and into the basket as she does so.

(Interestingly, this shot is not a special effect. Jeunet devoted some real thought to how to achieve it, but Weaver was sure she could manage it, and did so. Accounts differ as to whether it was on the first take or the fifth. In an era of digitized magic, sometimes the miraculous is achieved live on camera.)

We have been told that Ripley is no longer quite human, but this scene demonstrates the fact far more eloquently. The fact that the blood from a minor cut on her face sizzles as it hits the floor is almost less telling than her physical prowess. 'What are you?' Christie says and the question is one which much of the film will be spent answering. There is also something intensely animalistic about her response to Johner – the struggle for dominance between them is a mating dance in which he fails to impress her. Yet Wren still has a non-sexual dominance over her because he has real power – the power of physical force – and can whistle her to heel like a dog, something he does later with an arrogant gesture to the implanted colonist Purvis whom he also regards as his property.

The scene is particularly effective because of its positioning immediately after the slow horrid scene of the delivery by the pirates of the colonists to their fate, and the colonists' delivery to the aliens. We cut from one of the colonists, who has just woken from cryo, screaming at the sight of the face-hugger which is about to leap out of an egg to a long-shot of Ripley playing basketball by herself; she is not a solitary – she is part of the same process, the same life cycle.

Almost as liminal as Ripley herself, there is Call, the robot so ethical in her obsession with defending humanity that she has become a terrorist and an accomplice of murderous pirates who kidnap sleeping colonists and sell them to the military; she will sacrifice individuals for the sake of humanity which makes her morality suspect, however integral to her perception of herself. The deferring of the revelation of her android status is as effective as the equivalent delay in identifying Ash as a robot – in a piece of misdirection, she tells Ripley that the older woman is not who she thinks she is: 'You're a thing, a construct. They grew you in a fucking lab.'

Call is the culmination of the series of androids in the films – quite literally, given that the first was called Ash and the second Bishop and her initial completes the alphabetical series. Where Ash had an amorality which made him the perfect company man and Bishop was ultimately ineffectual, she is sinister in her moral fanaticism. She also shares with Ash a quasi-sexual relationship with Ripley, but where his is based on the antagonism of difference, hers is based on a repulsion that comes from identification.

When Call enters Ripley's cell and pulls a huge knife from her boot, her intention is clearly murderous, but almost at once things become more ambiguous. She uses the knife to push aside Ripley's laced top and reveal the scar down her cleavage. Ripley reveals that she is awake with a remark as sexual as the ones to Johner in the basketball scene: 'Are you going to kill me, or what?' As she gradually turns the tables on the younger woman, offering to kill her in the terms Call had used to her earlier, and talks about the extent to which a sense of herself as the alien lurks behind her eyes, she caresses Call's face before seizing her by the throat; sex is threat is death here.

At the same time, Call shares with Ripley (and Whedon's Buffy) a capacity to die and be reborn and save people; her apparent death involves arms outstretched as in a crucifixion. She reappears to rescue people and, rather against her will, helps the survivors by interfacing with the USM Auriga's control AI, 'Father'; this is not the last of Whedon's teasing references to Christian mythology. Her very name, Call, implies that she is a woman with a mission long before the meddling that demonstrates what it is. Both Ripley and the Newborn place their fingers in her wounded side – this is at once highly sexual and an expression of scepticism associated with St Thomas the Doubter's reaction to the resurrected Christ.

Call offers Ripley death as a freedom from the anomaly of her condition: 'I can make it stop. The pain… this nightmare. That's all I can offer you.' Later she makes it clear that she cannot understand why Ripley will not accept the death she offers: 'Why do you go on living? How can you stand it? How can you stand… yourself?' Specifically, this is a matter of identifying Ripley's dual nature with her own; Ripley is at least partly human whereas Call is entirely a simulacrum of humanity.

This exchange occurs in the context of a conversation subsequent to the revelation of Call's nature in which Ripley is browbeating her into exploring her non-human nature still further by interfacing with, and taking over, the computer that controls the Auriga. Call does this from the ship's chapel, where she, unlike the humans, genuflects and crosses herself – she has a sense of the sacred to which Ripley responds with an incredulous 'Are you programmed for that?' Since the Auriga's computer is called Father – as the Nostromo's was Mother – her accessing it, from a church, has resonances of gender ambiguity; given Call's messianic name, it is also the sort of complex game with Christian mythology that both Whedon and Jeunet enjoy.

Ripley tells her that the answer to her anguish is pragmatism – 'Not much choice' – and forces Call to admit that, like Ripley, she dreams. It is this capacity for dreaming that renders them both ultimately human – dreaming is a liminal state, but a universal one. In the context of the series as a whole, it is associated both with the moment in *Aliens* where Ripley realizes that she is still in jeopardy and with the closure of the first two films when Ripley encourages her daughter substitutes Jones and Newt to feel secure. Here, her view of dreaming is considerably more double-edged – 'No matter how bad the dreams get, when I wake up it's worse.'

Call both is, and is not, a replacement daughter figure – the hint of sexual attraction to the relationship is there partly to distinguish this relationship from Ripley's earlier relationship with Newt. Significantly, these are the only characters in the film represented as having an inner life or as motivated by something much beyond themselves – the paradox of the film is that the two characters whose humanity is called most into question are the most humane. 'I should have known it,' Ripley says on discovering Call's true nature, 'no human being is that humane.' When she asks Call why she cares what humanity does to itself, Call replies in anguish, 'Because I'm programmed to.'

They are complements because Call's double nature has forced the ethical perception on her that Ripley's double nature has robbed her of. Yet Call's influence is good for Ripley; she says of her revealed nature, 'I suppose you think that's pretty funny,' and Ripley responds with 'I've been finding a lot of things funny lately... But that doesn't mean they are.' Call cannot choose and Ripley can – in the end, though, both are better and more ethical that any of the people around them.

It is significant that it is Call who helps Ripley by handing her a flame-thrower in the scene where she discovers the other versions of herself, the earlier distorted clones. The living clone is human enough, in spite of its appearance, to ask for death. There is, of course, a profound ambiguity here – Ripley is at the same time giving merciful death and destroying the outward sign of her own inner monstrosity. Call, for reasons of which we are as yet unaware, identifies with Ripley's repulsion and self-hatred; this is one of several moments at which the two women are twinned. Confrontation with these other selves is the one point at which Ripley loses her cool and is on the brink of hysterical weeping or of killing Wren; Call punches Wren for her and then, in a long-shot, consoles her with a pat on the shoulder.

Significantly, the Betty crew, the scientist Wren and the soldier DiStephano regard Ripley's interest in the clones as a waste of time, their destruction as a waste of ammunition. The two non-humans understand what is an appropriate human reaction; Johner responds, in a classic Whedon moment, with a puzzled shrug and the remark 'Must be a chick thing', making his incomprehension of their actions a gender divide. Similarly, the reactions of the humans to the revelation of Call's nature from the ribald – Johner's 'To think I almost fucked it' answered by Vriess's 'Like that'd be the first time you fucked a robot' – to the geekily enthusiastic – Vriess and DiStephano's expository discussion of her brand history – to the dismissive – Purvis' 'Fine, she's a toaster oven.'

The weaknesses in the script start to outweigh its considerable strengths as the film wears on. Part of the problem is that it becomes formulaic – we know by now that there will be a climax in which the humans are trying to escape from the aliens against a ticking clock, and there is a limit to how many variations on this can be worked in a series. Adding a sequence in which the human party has to swim to supposed safety pursued by aliens who suddenly demonstrate perfect adaptation to underwater sports is not radical enough a departure, and too much of the time they are simply running down corridors. 'Corridors and bulkheads' was Remmy Harlin's dismissive comment about the projects on offer to him for the third film and neither Whedon nor Jeunet was able to reinvent the franchise without them.

We know, because it has become part of the formula, that the Auriga will be set for self-destruction, that the Betty will be delayed in getting off it, that Ripley will only just make it onto the Betty in time after a diversionary encounter with aliens, that one of the aliens will get on board and kill at least one more character, that it will be ejected into space. *Alien* avoided some of this – the objective having changed to killing all aliens before the company can nab them and used hot metal rather than vacuum – but there was still a lot of running around; one might have hoped that the fourth film would come up with something a little more radical.

And, indeed, what appears to be an early version of the script available online does so to some extent, deferring the confrontation with the newborn semi-human alien until after the landing on Earth and having Call and Ripley eviscerate it with harvester machines from the Betty's cargo. In this version, the machines' existence is set up in an early shot – it is turning them on, rather than a thrown knife, which establishes the violent teasing relationship of Johner and Vriess. Machines of unspecified purpose which fit the description are still in shot in scenes set in the Betty's hold, which would indicate that the decision was made at a latish stage, as other accounts seem to indicate it was. In the end, though, the studio wanted a cheaper alternative.

Certainly the final solution – Ripley makes up to the alien sexually, deliberately grazes her hand on its fangs, uses the blood to burn a hole in a window, the alien is sucked out piecemeal by vacuum and slipstream as the Betty crash-lands – is unsatisfactorily close to the deaths of the aliens in the first two films. The decision to have the creature utter half-articulate sounds, which may indicate that it is referring to Ripley as its mother, sits uneasily, even though it was established earlier by the talking head of the cocooned Gediman. It is no more Ripley's child than was the embryonic queen she took with her into the vat of molten lead – Whedon has allowed his vision to be contaminated by Fincher and Hill's sour take on Cameron's over-idealized picture of Ripley as mother/saviour.

There is another possible take on the Newborn, which is hardly more satisfactory. Its semi-articulacy, and the trapped humanoid eyes behind its skull-like face make it the downside of double-naturedness. It is a double parricide, killing both its monstrous birth-mother and one of its creators; it is a liminal creature to begin with and it makes itself more so by this act of self-orphaning. If it regards Ripley as its mother, there is something profoundly ambiguous about their embraces. Its double nature is a contamination that makes it a threat, where the double natures of Ripley and Call make them saviours of humanity – the over-rapid pacing of the sequences involving this version of the creature mean that none of this gets properly developed or complexly imagined.

If the newborn creature is in any sense Ripley's offspring, it is because what was done to her – the cloning – has produced a self-fertilizing queen with a human womb as well as its egg depositor. However, as experienced on screen, the birth of the Newborn follows on from – and is therefore experienced as caused by – Ripley's unnatural congress with the alien hive. This linkage is further made by the way that the Newborn works its way free from a membrane to be born, echoing the sequence in which the newly created Ripley slowly uncovers herself from a membrane-like piece of nylon sheeting.

The Newborn is linked directly to other moments in which Ripley associates sex and death. She kills the alien which has just slaughtered Elgyn by firing from beneath and inside his mutilated body, and then, in a mocking parody of courtship, tears out its tongue-head and offers it to Call, who has been arguing against taking her with the other survivors. When Johner threatens Call, after the younger woman has been revealed as a robot, Ripley seizes him by the tongue and offers to rip it out. When the newborn alien approaches Ripley, it opens its mouth and there protrudes, not the expected set of nested heads with fanged jaws, but a colossal version of a human tongue which licks her. It is as double-natured as the two women and as complexly eroticized.

Its death can be seen as a ritual of unbirth in which Ripley uses her blood to take back the thing which she helped to create – the creature is sucked out a piece at a time into a vacuum into which its skull-like face is the last thing to disappear. Ripley and Call help secure each other against the sucking, just as in the cockpit Vriess and Johner, hitherto always at odds, have to cooperate to pilot the ship down safely in the absence of the two more competent women. The women merely hold each other for safety, whereas Johner congratulates Vriess for the successful landing with a smacking kiss – it is the women's hug that is represented erotically.

The last moments of the film are ones of reconciliation: Ripley's 'I'm a stranger here myself' is another identification of herself with Call, and, to a lesser extent, the two surviving men. Interestingly, the special edition takes them out of the Betty and into sunlight – they are standing in a sparsely vegetated landscape which is revealed as the camera pulls back over Ripley's line to be the hills overlooking a devastated Paris identifiable by the stub of the Eiffel Tower. The special edition also restores dialogue at this point that indicates Ripley and Call now regard themselves as partners in crime, who will have to go on the run together.

Jeunet's personal vision was at first sight at odds with the visual grammar established by the earlier *Alien* films. *Delicatessen* and *City of Lost Children* are both in love with gadgets as decor, gadgets that have the air of plumbers' bodging, technology which was semi-improvised and has to be coaxed constantly into working. In *Alien* and *Aliens*, most of the technology we see is shiny and new and works, and, more importantly, looks as if it works because Ron Cobb's designs gave it a fine gloss finish. The Giger designs for the creatures and the spaces of their own which they create either by co-option or construction create a clear dichotomy of place between the safe and the unsafe, the home-like and the uncanny.

In Ridley Scott's *Alien*, there is an exception to this: the workshop areas where Parker and Brett make use of the half-repaired and non-functional to create a site of class resistance, an area too messy and dirty for the officers and the tunnels and storage spaces which are the first to fall under the alien's domain. In a reversal of this, in *Aliens*, we have the space in which Newt has stored up comforting junk as a refuge once the aliens have definitively taken the whole glossy human space of the colony as their hunting ground. The decayed institutional look of the *Alien³* interiors and the lack of any construction on the part of the third film's alien are one of the areas in which the visual grammar of that film makes a break with the past – the restoration of the cocoon scene in the 2003 director's cut of *Alien* exacerbates this point.

Jeunet's film suffers from similar problems. The technological human spaces of *Alien Resurrection* are too often ribbed and curved to create the necessary distinction between the friendly-because-human-constructed and the organic and of inhuman origin. The interior lighting of the Auriga, the military ship, is too often not only dim, but also green or blue, which are shades of lighting we have grown to associate with the aliens.

This applies even in the scene in the operating theatre where the alien embryo is removed from Ripley's chest – one can see why these black ops scientists need to be coded as living in darkness, but it makes little sense to conduct a difficult and crucial surgical procedure in dim light. This dimness produces strong shadows – Jeunet gets great close-ups from it and the scenes in which, say, J.E. Freeman as Wren gets to be a talking head are effective as a result.

Jeunet's cinematographer Darius Khonjy is in love with making darkness visible. Some of the most impressive shots he achieves are a matter of achieving real texture with black against black against black in a dark background. Never before have the models of spaceships looked so good or so real – and some of the scenes with aliens, notably Ripley writhing among them in their nest, have a real sensuousness that derives from the almost entire absence of obvious sources of light. At times, though, this obsession with darkness becomes a mannerism.

One of the few well-lit areas we ever encounter is the basketball court – but that is a site of transactions between humans; it is as if Jeunet decided to code the crew of the Auriga, if not the piratical crew of the Betty, as inhuman even before they start to be changed or eaten. The other is the cafeteria where Wren and Gediman brief Ripley on how she was cloned and she tells them, unblinkingly, that they are doomed.

For reasons that have everything to do with decor and nothing to do with common sense, Ripley comes to awareness in a bare circular cell with a transparent ceiling several storeys up. She has been taken from the operating theatre and wrapped in a thin translucent membranous sheet which she gradually tears her way out of in a scene that is a compendium of mime and dance representations of birth. John Frizell scored this scene's soundtrack first and his swooping erotically charged music uses this as its thematic cell.

Ripley is voyeuristically presented as neither naked nor clothed at this point – which probably has less to do with the theme of liminality than with Sigourney Weaver's lithely attractive body. Oddly, she appears to have been born with nails perfectly manicured and painted – if these are meant to be claw-like and to indicate her partly bestial nature, the point is not made effectively. On the other hand, the presence on her arm of a number eight is a nice teaser for a later pay-off, though the slow reveal on it is a little too much of a pointer.

Some of Jeunet's alterations to Whedon's script are solidly positive ideas. Whedon at the start of the film announces his return to honouring Cameron's take of the franchise with a specific verbal echo. In a voiceover, the dreaming Ripley muses, 'My mom always said there were no monsters – no real ones – but there are', echoing her dialogue with Newt in *Aliens* in which Newt uses the same words and all Ripley can do is assent. In Whedon's script, however, it is a younger Ripley that utters them, in a dream pastoral landscape gradually corrupted by chittering eating insects.

Jeunet drops the dream sequence and the child or adolescent Ripley; the voiceover in the final film accompanies a shot of the un-decanted sleeping Ripley in her tank surrounded by the grotesque heads of Gediman, Wren and other unnamed science officers. There is not, I think, an explicit iconographic reference by Jeunet to Bosch's dreaming Christ on his way to crucifixion, accompanied by the grotesque heads of his persecutors, but the analogy between the shot and the picture is nonetheless striking once it occurs to one. The alteration appears to have been decided upon at a late stage, since an actress is credited as playing the young Ripley in the end credits.

The insect idea sparked an idea of Jeunet's own. The special edition reinstates an opening that the studio had rejected as too jokey and disorienting and which Jeunet had replaced with the morphing body parts title sequence we know. A face all eyes and teeth and menace fills the screen and we pull back from it revealing it to be a small bug which a space pilot squashes against his windscreen, then flustering around trying to clean the mess without ramming his vessel into the slowly revealed bulk of the Auriga. There are two takes possible on this – the studio's and one which welcomes it as establishing Jeunet's attempt to take this material and assimilate it to his own vision.

The vat scene is echoed later in the scene in which Gediman, Wren and Perez, again coded as grotesques, stare in at the alien Queen which has been born from Ripley as Perez remarks that, as far as he is concerned, Ripley, Number Eight, is a meat by-product to be terminated if she so much as looks at him funny. Certainly one of the weaknesses of the film is that Jeunet is better with grotesques than he is with three-dimensional characters and that this has an unfortunate synergy with Whedon's occasional tendency to write in a shorthand that refers lovingly to cliché and to the bad habits of some of the cast.

Jeunet had brought two of his favourite actors with him – Dominique Pinon (Vriess) and the American Ron Perlman (Johner) – and both do fine work for him here as elsewhere, work which includes the grotesque but is never swamped by it. However, Perez is directed as a buffoon, written as a brute and acted, by Dan Hedaya, as a reprise of various earlier performances as lycanthropic street person and Richard Milhouse Nixon. Even his scenes with Elgyn show him at too much of a disadvantage. Beside the charismatic, dapper (possibly Gauloise-smoking) Elgyn, Perez is a boob, unworthy of command, whereas Elgyn is so decisive, such a good leader, that we know he will be one of the first to die.

The script at least allows Perez a moment of authority in which he attempts to lead his men to safety, where the final film shows him saluting the dead, slammed in the back of the head by an alien's tail, reaching around and pulling away what appears to be a fragment of his own brain and left dead with a cartoony moronic expression. The only moment allowed him of inner life is a rather touching one – he blacks his own boots in the best military manner, heating the polish so as to get a fine shine.

Jeunet also makes Brad Dourif's Gediman into a grotesque, though it has to be said that Dourif makes something of a habit of this sort of performance. He adds an area of sexual perversity not hinted at in the script to his portrayal of the younger and marginally less unpleasant of the film's two named scientists. There is a dream-sequence scene in the script where Ripley seduces and then kills him, metamorphosing into a part-alien to do so; this finds an even more perverse echo in the final movie in the sequence where Gediman taunts one of the aliens born from the dead colonists by kissing the thick glass between its mouths and his, and squirting it with liquid nitrogen when it responds. His reappearance as – literally – a talking head, cocooned by the Queen and killed by the Newborn, has him mutter deliriously and lecherously that the newborn creature is a 'pretty little butterfly', a largely unsayable line to which Dourif adds little.

Wren, on the other hand, is an effective creation partly because he gets good lines – he is the only character in the film who gets the better of Ripley conversationally; when she tells him that they can't hope to succeed in teaching the alien tricks, he responds, 'Why not? We're teaching you.' He has the arrogance and certainty that come from his position in a hierarchy – he is by definition the opposite of a liminal being, one in whom there is no ambiguity at any time. He is a perfect model of ruthless will – J.E. Freeman's performance is finely judged and perhaps the best thing he has done.

Khonjy's love of strong shadows that make faces into maps of light and shadow is at its best here – Freeman mugs away like anything as he threatens the pirates with collective execution for Call's acts, betrays Call when she is trying to help him escape with the other survivors and finally tries yet another double-cross for which he dies. He is a splendid melodramatic villain who transcends the merely grotesque.

His eventual fate is one of the best things in the film, both as scripted and as shot, because it is emotionally satisfying and neat. Wren combines all of the worst things that Ripley can find to say about human beings and he is killed by a man she mocks and underrates, Purvis, the lone survivor of the frozen colonists. Originally, Purvis is nothing more than a mildly deranged victim whose best hope is a mercy-killing, or perhaps to be frozen until such time as the creature within him can be cut out.

He awakes to be surrounded by monsters – literal ones in the shapes of the alien face-huggers he has seen on his friends and his own face, and the larger deadly creatures he has thus far avoided. The humans he finds himself escaping with are little better: the scientist who has experimented on him, the pirates who sold him, one of the soldiers who were part of it. And Ripley, who explains to him teasingly, 'I'm the monster's mother.'

Jeunet's camera treats Purvis with equivalent mockery – he is another grotesque, whose bespectacled face is a visual echo of such other victims as Eisenstein's governess on the Odessa Steps. His victimhood is a failure of perception on his part which has perpetually to be explained to him – we first see him with his spectacles frosted over. For most of the journey through the Auriga he is a supernumerary with no skills or fighting ability.

Yet when Call is taken hostage by Wren, who wants her to reverse the countdown and prevent the Auriga from crashing, so that he can preserve his deadly research project, it is Purvis who turns the tables when Johner and DiStephano have had to put down their weapons. (Ripley is at this point off on her erotic adventure with the aliens.) Knowing that he is about to die from a chest-burster, Purvis rushes at Wren, taking bullets in his hysterical fury and enabling Call to break free. He smashes Wren's face against a grating repeatedly and then pulls the back of the scientist's head against his chest so that the alien emerges straight from it into Wren.

This feels like justice and is a point at which both script and shooting are perfectly combined. The dim lighting of the scene does not prevent us seeing clearly what happens. The blocking of the characters never feels forced or unnatural and their movements are easy to talk through in retrospect. Everyone is in character and yet each moment of the scene is an effective surprise. And it reminds us that, in the first film, before she became a goddess, a victim or a monster, Ripley was an ordinary human being like Purvis who acted with great heroism. Purvis chooses to take revenge on the man who is ultimately responsible for his death and to do so in a way that saves Wren's various human instruments as well as Call, who always spoke up for him.

The final moments of the theatrical release, in which Call and Ripley look out from the Betty into a heavily overgrown landscape with dawn breaking above them is a nicely judged ending to a series that seemed at that point to be over. The creatures are apparently gone for good, and the aspect of them which Ripley still holds encoded inside her DNA is one which, by killing the Newborn, she has effectively renounced. Earlier she and Call found common ground in dreams; now they find it in wonder at the world they have never seen. It is a touching picture and far from a banal one – in some ways, it is to be preferred to the special edition's reveal shot of a ruined Paris, which slingshots a moment of peace into unease and which is too obvious an echo of the original Charlton Heston *Planet of the Apes*.

However, there is still talk of renewing the franchise – both Cameron and Ridley Scott have expressed interest in making the film that would explain where the aliens came from, and what created them. (It is clear that Scott, at least, favours the idea that they are in some sense artefactual.) Even more likely is a film of 'Alien vs Predator' which would combine these two franchises as they have for years been combined in the spin-off comic books that pit these two incomprehensible monsters against each other. It remains to be seen what new variations screenwriters and directors will find to add to the subject matter and look created by the original movie.

Index of Films

Index